Tall Dark Stranger

About the Author

Corrine Kenner specializes in bringing metaphysical subjects down to earth. Her work on the Tarot is widely published and her Tarot classes and workshops are perennial favorites among students in the Midwest.

Corrine is a certified Tarot master; she has studied Tarot under the auspices of the Tarot School of New York, the Wanless Tarot Institute, and Builders of the Adytum. She also holds a bachelor's degree in philosophy from California State University, Long Beach.

Corrine has lived in Brazil, Los Angeles, and the Twin Cities of Minnesota. She now lives in rural North Dakota with her husband, Dan Horon, and her daughters Katherine, Emily, and Julia. In her everyday life, she is the vice president and communications director of CADgraphics Incorporated, a company that specializes in developing software for fire alarm and security systems.

Corrine is the author of *The Epicurean Tarot*, published by U.S. Games Systems, Inc., and the creator of Llewellyn's *Tarot Calendar*. A former newspaper reporter and magazine editor, Corrine was also the editor of Llewellyn's popular *Astrological Calendar*, *Daily Planetary Guide*, and *Sun Sign Book*, as well as an anthology of supernatural accounts called *Strange But True*. She is also the author of two forthcoming books: *Tarot Journaling* and *Crystals for Beginners*, both from Llewellyn.

To Write to the Author

If you wish to contact the author or would like more information about this book, please write to the author in care of Llewellyn Worldwide and we will forward your request. Both the author and publisher appreciate hearing from you and learning of your enjoyment of this book and how it has helped you. Llewellyn Worldwide cannot guarantee that every letter written to the author can be answered, but all will be forwarded. Please write to:

Corrine Kenner
℅ Llewellyn Worldwide
P.O. Box 64383, Dept. 0-7387-0548-9
St. Paul, MN 55164-0383, U.S.A.
Please enclose a self-addressed stamped envelope for reply,
or $1.00 to cover costs. If outside U.S.A., enclose
international postal reply coupon.

Many of Llewellyn's authors have websites with additional information and resources. For more information, please visit our website at http://www.llewellyn.com

Tall Dark Stranger

Tarot for Love and Romance

Corrine Kenner

Llewellyn Publications
St. Paul, Minnesota

First Edition
First Printing, 2005

Cover and title page illustration from The Lovers card from *Tarot Art Nouveau* © 2001 Antonelle Castelli and reprinted with permission from Lo Scarabeo
Cover design by Gavin Dayton Duffy
Interior cards from the *Universal Tarot* © Roberto De Angelis and reprinted with permission from Lo Scarabeo
Interior illustrations by the Llewellyn Art Department

Llewellyn is a registered trademark of Llewellyn Worldwide, Ltd.

Library of Congress Cataloging-in-Publication Data (pending)
ISBN 0-7387-0548-9

Llewellyn Publications
A Division of Llewellyn Worldwide, Ltd.
P.O. Box 64383, Dept. 0-7387-0548-9
St. Paul, MN 55164-0383, U.S.A.
www.llewellyn.com

Printed in the United States of America

Epigraph

"I can't wait to tell you—Margie read me in cards today, three times, because she said she never saw anything like it. Three times! I saw the cards come up myself."
"Oh! Lord!"
"You won't be so suspicious when you hear. You always poke fun about tall dark strangers. You can't guess what it was about? Well—you want to guess?"
He said, "Mary, I want to warn you."
"Warn me? Why, you don't even know. My fortune is *you*."

—John Steinbeck, *The Winter of Our Discontent*
(New York: Viking Press, Inc., 1961)

Contents

Contents

Contents

Contents

Contents

Contents

Acknowledgments

A number of teachers and writers have helped me crystallize my thoughts, especially Wald and Ruth Ann Amberstone, founders of the Tarot School of New York City; Nancy Antenucci, founder of St. Paul's Tarot Circle; Janet Berres, president of the International Tarot Society; Norma Cowie, author of *Tarot for Successful Living*; John Gilbert, founder of the American Tarot Association; Mary K. Greer, author of *Tarot for Yourself*; Marcia Masino, author of the *Easy Tarot Guide*; Rachel Pollack, author of *Seventy-Eight Degrees of Wisdom*; and Bellezza Squillace, my first Tarot teacher at the Stonehenge shop in St. Paul, Minnesota.

The chapter on Tarot's romantic history was synthesized largely from the research and work of a wide range of experts: the Internet's Tarot-L group, as well as Michael Dummett, Mary K. Greer, Bob O'Neill, Christine Payne-Towler, Tom Tadfor Little, and Brian Williams. The works I referenced in writing the chapter are all cited in the "Recommended Resources" section in the back of this book.

While there are any number of customs associated with the Tarot, the traditional interpretations I refer to in this book are based mostly on the standards developed by the Hermetic Order of the Golden Dawn. The Golden Dawn did most of its work at the end of the nineteenth century; I have relied on David Allen Hulse's book *The Key of It All* for a structured, systematic overview of their thought.

I also would like to thank: Claudine Gervais, a newspaper editor in Manitoba, and Cari Kenner, an English professor in Texas. Both helped edit my manuscript—and I like to think they would have reviewed it willingly, even if they weren't my sisters. My parents, Wayne and Carolyn Kenner, also helped. They all remind me of the extended family depicted in the Ten of Pentacles; they helped make it possible for me to write this book.

Preface

When I first met my husband, I did what most Tarot readers do: I consulted the cards. I wanted to know what a future with him might hold.

I drew the Ace of Wands, the Lovers, and the Knight of Pentacles.

If you already know something about the Tarot, you'll probably recognize that that was an encouraging three-card spread. Simply put, the Ace of Wands generally symbolizes fiery new beginnings with a powerful dose of spiritual attraction. The Lovers, of course, represents romance and partnership. And the Knight of Pentacles is the archetypal knight in shining armor, with a grounded, steadying effect that can help a long-term relationship take root and grow.

Encouraged by those three cards, I agreed to go out with him.

Of course, even without the cards I knew there was a spark between us—just as the Ace of Wands had indicated. Before long, we were not only spending all of our free time together (like the Lovers) but we were also working together in true Knight of Pentacles style.

Actually, it was the Knight of Pentacles that encouraged me the most. Maybe it was my own bias, but I didn't want to rush into a commitment, like I suspected we might have if I had drawn the love-struck Knight of Cups. Likewise, I didn't want to fall into a pattern of breaking up and getting back together, like we might have if I had drawn the fiery Knight of Wands. And, most importantly, I didn't want to get into a relationship with a man who would soon move on to other conquests, like I might have if I had drawn the quick-moving Knight of Swords.

If you're new to the Tarot, and that all sounds like a strange secret language, keep reading. By the time you reach the end of this book, you'll be able to see for yourself if love is in the cards—for yourself or for your family members and friends. More importantly, you'll be able to use Tarot cards as a tool to help you find romance and keep love alive.

I know that Tarot cards can be a useful tool for those who want to find romance and improve their relationships. And I know this system works, because I used Tarot cards to help find my own Knight of Pentacles. Right now, he's in the living room with our one-year-old Page of Cups asleep on his chest.

I saw her arrival in the cards, too … but that's another story.

Corrine Kenner
Summer 2003

Introduction

For centuries, the lovestruck, the lovesick, and the lovelorn have consulted Tarot cards with questions about romance. Each one brings a wide range of emotions to the card reader's table: joy and sadness, hopes and fears, passion and pain. And in each and every case, the Tarot responds with a corresponding measure of reflection and advice.

Ultimately, that is the Tarot's greatest strength. Whether you read for yourself or someone else, the Tarot is a remarkable tool for people who want to build better relationships.

When you use the Tarot, you can literally see yourself in the cards—openly, honestly, and objectively. You can also see other people and explore your relationships with them. You can spot current trends, explore your options, and make changes in direction. You can even use the Tarot to prepare for future partnerships.

And, regardless of what you may have heard, you can read Tarot for yourself.

Historically, some Tarot experts have warned against the practice. It's difficult to stay objective, of course. You might see only what you want to see. You might even want to shuffle and redo a reading. But at the same time, you can find astounding new revelations in the cards—insights and observations that you might not spot without their help.

So go ahead: shuffle the deck. Your future is in the cards, and this book will show you how to find it.

Part I

History and Mystery

Chapter One

Tarot's Romantic History

For centuries, the Tarot has been used to answer questions about love and romance. From teenage girls in Renaissance Italy to contemporary cartomancers, the cards have been shuffled and spread in search of tall, dark strangers.

Love at First Sight

Picture yourself in Italy, in the year 1440. You are living during a momentous time in history. The Renaissance has begun, and culture is literally being reborn. For the next two hundred years, society and culture will undergo a dramatic transformation, as Europeans leave the dark ages of medieval times behind and give birth to the modern world.

The leading thinkers and artists of the day are inspired by the golden age of Greece. Age-old myths are told and retold, and the ancient gods and goddesses are everywhere—in art, in song, in poetry, and in drama. Young people are even memorizing the classic philosophical works of Plato and Aristotle.

In the winter of 1440, a teenage girl named Bianca Maria Visconti found herself immersed in the heart of Renaissance art and culture when she was sent to visit the royal court of d'Este in Ferrara, Italy, a regional center of Renaissance art and culture.

Bianca was the daughter of a duke, so she was a member of high society. In those days, young nobles would travel from palace to palace to study and spend time together. Their pursuit was high-minded: the young aristocrats were preparing to assume the rulership of their country. So by day, Bianca and her friends would read, ponder, and debate the great works of science, history, and literature.

But at night, they played cards.

Bianca was especially fond of a new card game called *tarocchi*. It was a complicated pastime, because it involved a whole host of literary and mythological figures, all of whom embodied the virtues and ideals of the ancient Greeks and Romans. There were twenty-two cards that depicted allegorical figures like Justice, the Wheel of Fortune, and the Moon. There were also four suits in each deck, numbered one through ten, as well as four sets of court cards—a page, a knight, a queen, and a king.

Bianca was so captivated by the game that when it was time for her to go home in January 1441, one of her friends gave her a set of fourteen hand-painted cards to take with her. And later that year, when Bianca was engaged to marry a young man named Francesco Sforza, her father Filippo actually commissioned a deck of his own to commemorate the wedding.

Bianca's *tarocchi* deck, of course, was the forerunner of today's Tarot. And Bianca's wedding deck, the *Visconti-Sforza* Tarot, is one of the oldest Tarot decks still in existence. To this date, it also rates as one of the most romantic decks of all time. In fact, the Lovers card may even be a portrait of the newlyweds Bianca and Francesco, dressed in their wedding best. Many of the surviving cards are housed at the Pierpont Morgan Library in New York City, and you can find replicas of the deck practically anywhere Tarot cards are sold.

At first, *tarocchi* was a game reserved exclusively for royalty and upper-class socialites like Bianca. Typically, adventurous noblemen would discover card games on their travels, and then bring them home to entertain the ladies at court. From there, the pastime spread—to the cooks in the kitchen, the maids throughout the palace, the gardeners. Before long, the game moved off of the palace grounds and out into the rest of society.

Initially, Bianca may have been attracted to the game because the cards themselves were breathtaking. Every card was a miniature masterpiece, hand-painted with expensive pigments that had been ground from semiprecious stones and gilded with real gold.

Later, the designs were simplified a bit, as wood-block printing made it relatively easy and inexpensive to produce card decks for the masses. Playing cards soared in popularity. Parents even bought specially designed decks for their children to use—in part, to keep them entertained, but also in the hope that their children would pick up a few moral lessons from the game.

The Game of Life

Ultimately, a core set of ethical values and beliefs were at the heart of *tarocchi*. While most people treated the cards as a game, it was a game with meaning—because those who played it, like Bianca and her friends, were well versed in the allegorical symbolism of the cards.

Renaissance people were trained to see beyond the literal and the obvious. They spoke the secret language of symbols that was firmly woven throughout their culture and their studies. That language was the foundation of their worldview.

Bianca and her friends had been taught that the world was a place of symmetry and order. They believed that four elements—earth, water, air, and fire—combined to form the physical world. They believed that mankind was the measure of all things and that humanity's place was squarely at the center of the universe.

They also studied the metaphoric language of astrology, in which the movement of the planets measured and reflected the forces that shaped human existence. They knew that the sun was more than a mass of incandescent gas: it represented enlightenment and the illumination of God's will.

Bianca and her friends were well versed in the corresponding symbolism of mythology, too. They knew that Apollo was the Roman god of the sun, Venus was the goddess of love, and Mars was the god of war. When mythological figures appeared on the first Tarot cards, Bianca wasn't confused: she knew that the Magician was closely allied with Mercury, the trickster and messenger of the gods, and she understood that Cupid would naturally make an appearance on the Lovers card.

Other ancient gods and goddesses from the cards were also present in daily life, personified and clothed in the guise of the Christian virtues of faith, hope, and charity, as well as the Greco-Roman virtues of justice, fortitude, temperance, and prudence. In fact, images of Christian life abound in the Tarot. During the fifteenth century, Pope Pius II and Cardinals Bessarion and Cusa even used *tarocchi* cards with allegorical images to enhance their discussions during a church council in Mantua.

The Language of Love

Tarot cards were first developed in Italy and then spread to France. Given the fact that those are two of the most romantic cultures in history, it's probably not surprising that the Tarot's first language is the language of love. In fact, some of the Tarot's design might even be based on the starry-eyed poetry of a hapless Italian romantic named Francesco Petrarch.

In 1327, when Francesco was twenty-three, he met a nineteen-year-old blonde named Laura—at church, no less. Unfortunately, Laura was married, so Francesco was consigned to love her from afar. When Laura died of the plague shortly after their first encounter—heartbreakingly young and still beautiful—Francesco wrote a poem called "To Laura in Death," in which he pined, "To be able to say how much you love is to love but little."

Throughout Francesco's life, he continued to dedicate his musings to poor, dead Laura. His poetic masterpiece, the *Trionfi*, describes six allegorical figures: Love, Chastity, Death, Fame, Time, and Divinity. The poem is important to Tarot historians, because each one of those figures is remarkably similar to the images depicted on the early *tarocchi* cards.

In the poem, Love conquers ordinary men—like Francesco himself.

But then Chastity comes along and conquers Love, just as the chaste young Laura declined Francesco's advances.

Death defeats Chastity in the same way that the plague had stolen Laura away.

But then Fame defeats Death. To illustrate, Francesco describes how Laura's memory lived on even though she was gone.

Time has the upper hand, however. It trumps even Fame, because those who once knew Laura also pass away, and Laura's memory is slowly erased from the face of the earth.

Finally, Eternity triumphs over Time, as Francesco looks forward to rejoining his beloved, forever, in the afterlife.

The Dawn of Divination

The symbolism and depth of the early Tarot images naturally inspired at least one form of divination: some players used the cards to improvise clever sonnets about other people, which they called *tarocchi appropriati*.

Over time, the structure and the symbolism of the cards also lent themselves to use as a more traditional fortune-telling device—similar, in many ways, to other systems of divination that were already in use, like dice. Eventually, some experts believe, wandering bands of Gypsies picked up and spread the practice of telling fortunes with Tarot cards, and they've been associated with the art ever since.

The Gypsies had migrated away from their native home in northern India during the mid-ninth century, and they moved west through Afghanistan and Persia. In smaller groups they crossed Egypt, Spain, Turkey, and Greece. In 1417, Gypsies were first reported in Germany. By 1430, they were also in England.

In Europe, many people mistakenly believed that Gypsies were the descendants of ancient Egyptians—hence their name. In some places, Gypsies were also known as "Bohemians," because their route into Europe brought them through Bohemia.

Wherever they went, Gypsies earned money as acrobats, animal trainers, musicians, dancers, and singers. For a price, the Gypsies would also read palms, tea leaves, and crystals. Ultimately, the Gypsies became legendary for their skill at divination with playing cards. Eventually, they helped romanticize the use of Tarot cards for fortune telling.

In Russia, a teenage peasant girl named Zaira seems to have learned the Gypsies' art of card reading. In 1765, when she became the traveling love slave of the notorious Giacomo Casanova, she took her cards with her.

In his memoirs, Casanova gushed about her physical beauty, but he also reported that her dependence on the cards was a serious character flaw.

"Her skin was as white as snow," he wrote, "and her ebony tresses covered the whole of her body, save in a few places where the dazzling whiteness of her skin shone through. Her eyebrows were perfectly shaped, and her eyes, though they might have been larger, could not have been more brilliant or more expressive. . . . If it had not been for her furious jealousy, and her blind confidence in fortune telling by cards, which she consulted every day, Zaira would have been a paragon among women, and I should never have left her."

Casanova recounted the episode that nearly forced him to abandon his young lover: One morning, after a wild night on the town without her, Casanova returned to find Zaira enraged. She had "seen" his exploits in her cards. His description of a fortune-teller's spread she used is actually the first such description we have on record.

"I got home, and, fortunately for myself, escaped the bottle which Zaira flung at my head, and which would infallibly have killed me if it had hit me. She threw herself on to the ground, and began to strike it with her forehead. I thought she had gone mad, and wondered whether I had better call for assistance; but she became quiet enough to call me assassin and traitor, with all the other abusive epithets that she could remember. To convict me of my crime she showed me twenty-five cards, placed in order, and on them she displayed the various enormities of which I had been guilty."

Macho man that he was, Casanova simply threw Zaira's "damned grimoire" into the fire and threatened to leave. She apologized profusely and reportedly never touched another card.

The Magic and Mysticism of the Cards

Before long, Tarot aficionados all across Europe were using Tarot cards for divination and related pursuits. Most of them used a deck that is still available today—the *French Marseille* Tarot. One of the mystic scholars was Antoine Court de Gebelin, a Swiss pastor. He was the first person known to seriously pursue the use of Tarot cards for "esoteric" or secret studies.

In 1781 Gebelin announced that the Tarot was actually a secret book of ancient wisdom passed down from the ancient Egyptians. Unfortunately, he made up the theory out of thin air. Eighteen years later, in 1799, archeologists discovered the Rosetta Stone, which made it possible for scholars to translate hieroglyphics for the first time. Since then, despite many rumors to the contrary, no one has ever found a link between the Tarot and ancient Egypt.

Gebelin's book, *Le Monde Primitive* (or *The Primitive World*), was notable for one thing: it included the first two essays we have on record about esoteric Tarot. Gebelin found a fan and a follower in Jean-Baptiste Alliette, a wig maker who reversed the spelling of his name and used the pen name Etteilla. He was the first to develop correspondences between Tarot, astrology, and the four ancient elements of earth, air, fire, and water.

Etteilla also wrote two books about divination with cards: the first, in 1770, focused on regular playing cards; the second, in 1785, was dedicated to Tarot cards. In about 1788, he published the first Tarot deck specifically designed for divination.

The trend continued with Alphonse Louis Constant, who used the pen name Eliphas Levi. He wrote a book based on the twenty-two trump cards—the first to link the Tarot with the twenty-two letters of the Hebrew alphabet. It was a milestone for Tarot interpretation.

Dr. Gerard Encausse took the process a step further by issuing cards based upon Levi's ideas; they were signed by a man named Oswald Wirth. Encausse's book *The Tarot of the Bohemians* claimed that the cards had originated in Egypt and traveled with the Gypsies.

Meanwhile, mysticism was growing in popularity all across Europe.

In Paris, a fortune teller named Marie-Anne Adelaide Lenormand was renowned for her card-reading skills. Although her deck wasn't a Tarot deck, her technique set the tone for generations of seers to follow. In fact, variations of her thirty-six-card deck still exist. It's known as the *Petit Lenormand* or the *Gypsy Witch* deck, and it's still popular with cartomancers—people who tell fortunes with cards.

Marie Lenormand was born in Alencon, France, in 1772. When she was fourteen, she started studying astrology, mythology, Tarot, and numerology. During the French Revolution at the end of that century, members of the upper class visited her salon in Paris's *Rue de Tournan* to get their fortunes told. Unfortunately, some of them didn't have much of a future, and Lenormand occasionally had to tell them they were doomed.

Marie even read cards for the Emperor Napoleon and his wife Josephine. Marie reportedly met them at a swanky, high-society party. Napoleon reportedly laughed out loud when she predicted that he would ascend to the throne of France. But later, when her prophecy came true and Marie followed up by predicting Napoleon's eventual divorce from Josephine, the emperor had Marie imprisoned until the split was final. And later, when Marie predicted the fall of his empire, Napoleon banished her from Paris.

Modern Love

Modern Tarot was born in 1909, when a scholar named Arthur Edward Waite designed a new Tarot deck and asked an artist named Pamela Coleman Smith to execute his designs.

By trade, Smith was a stage designer and set decorator. She used her theater background to add drama to the Tarot deck by painting a scenic illustration on every single card. Until then, the only cards that featured people and places were the Major Arcana cards. Minor Arcana cards generally consisted of a repeated motif, such as six cups in a row, or seven swords. Smith's illustrations worked as a prompt for each card's meaning, and the concept revolutionized the Tarot.

Both Waite and Smith also found inspiration from their membership in a turn-of-the-century secret society called the Order of the Golden Dawn. Both Waite and Smith were active members of the group, which was similar in many ways to other secret societies, such as the Masons. The Golden Dawn borrowed liberally from other esoteric studies, and the *Rider-Waite-Smith* deck, as a result, incorporates many elements from astrology and kabbalah.

While you don't need to know anything about the Golden Dawn, Masonry, astrology, or kabbalah to use Tarot cards, you'll undoubtedly notice symbols and signs that are derived from their work. The more obvious examples are described in this book and examined in a little more detail in the chapters on astrology and kabbalah.

Most beginner's books and classes are based on Rider-Waite-style imagery, and most Tarot readers are well versed with the images on each card. Many Tarot readers consider it the standard by which all other Tarot decks are compared, if not judged. In fact, most of the meanings and correspondences listed in this book as "traditional" are derived from Waite's descriptions of each card.

Chapter Two

Stacking the Deck

The structure and symmetry of the Tarot deck reflects the basic framework of human experience. The Tarot's elegant design makes it easy to apply what you learn in a reading to life in the real world.

Size Matters

Open up a new box of Tarot cards, and two things will probably strike you: first, there are a lot of cards in a Tarot deck—seventy-eight. Second, those Tarot cards are probably bigger than playing cards you're used to handling.

There are two reasons for the bulk. The larger size of the cards makes it easier to spot details and symbols within each image. Also, the sheer number of cards makes it possible to incorporate an entire cosmology, or model of the universe, within a single deck.

A standard Tarot deck is divided into two sections: the *Major Arcana*, which is Latin for "Greater Secrets," and the *Minor Arcana*, which is Latin for "Lesser Secrets."

The Major Arcana cards depict dramatic, life-changing forces in life—events like falling in love, getting married, or moving to a new home. The Minor Arcana cards show us how we experience those events on an everyday basis.

Neither Arcana is more important than the other. For that matter, neither Arcana is more powerful than the other. In fact, the two parts of the deck work hand in hand to describe the full range of life experiences and events.

While the Major Arcana cards show us important developments, like falling in love, the Minor Arcana cards show us how those occurrences unfold. You may draw the Lovers card from the Major Arcana, but that doesn't mean you're going to rush out into the street, meet a perfect stranger, and end the day married with children and a house in the suburbs. A more detailed Tarot reading, however, complete with a full complement of Minor Arcana cards, could show you that you're headed toward marriage. Minor Arcana cards typically reflect the day-to-day development of a romance, as a couple starts to date, and then proceeds through a thousand routine interactions: cooking, eating, shopping, cleaning, and growing both as a couple and as separate individuals.

While the Major Arcana cards can summarize the process of transformation with bold, dramatic images, the Minor Arcana cards show us images of our progress along the way. While we might think of our lives in Major Arcana terms, we live our lives in the real world of the Minor Arcana. When we think of a wedding, for example, we generally think of it as one special day. In the real world, however, the blushing bride has spent more than a year planning the ceremony and dieting into her dress.

Like formal portraits, Major Arcana cards depict the big events: the engagements, the weddings, and the anniversaries. On the other hand, Minor Arcana cards are the casual snapshots we take during the course of ordinary events: the couple on the couch, the kids in the yard, and Dad with his new car.

In other words, the Major Arcana cards show us the roles we play in life. The Minor Arcana cards show us how we play those roles on a daily basis. Together, the cards depict the gradual process of development, during which we spend our days living out the Minor Arcana—with a pause, every so often, when we pose for a professional portrait.

The Archetypes of the Major Arcana

The twenty-two cards of the Major Arcana depict the "Greater Secrets"—the big mysteries of life. You'll probably recognize many of the images in the Major Arcana. The Death card makes perennial appearances in horror movies and murder mysteries, but you're probably also familiar with the image of Justice holding her scales and the perpetually spinning Wheel of Fortune.

That's because all of the Major Arcana cards reflect the *archetypes* that serve as a framework for our understanding of the world.

Carl Jung, a psychotherapist and a colleague of Sigmund Freud, was the first person to theorize that we are all born with an ability to understand archetypes. In fact, he said, that ability is built into our psychological makeup; it comes as standard equipment on most models. We are preprogrammed to look for archetypes in our everyday lives, and when we find them, we can make sense of complicated relationships.

Carl Jung's descriptions of commonly recognized archetypes include the *hero*, the *maiden*, and the *wise old man*. Other archetypes include the *anima*, the feminine aspect of a man's personality; the *animus*, the masculine aspect of a woman's personality; the *mother*, which typifies a nurturing, emotional parent; the *father*, a physical, protective parent; the *trickster*, or rebel; and the *shadow*, the hidden, antisocial dark side of human nature.

Throughout history, artists and writers have used archetypes to explain how people fit into the universe. In classic myths and legends, archetypal heroes like Odysseus encountered archetypal villains like the one-eyed Cyclops. Even today, archetypal characters—like Frankenstein's monster or Star War's Luke Skywalker—are the mainstay of popular books, movies, and television shows.

Technically speaking, an archetype is a model that serves as a pattern for other, similar things. An archetype is an example that represents the essence of any idea, and archetypes are frequently expressed as symbols and images.

You might think of an archetype as a cosmic stereotype. Archetypes instantly communicate a whole set of shared understandings and beliefs. Archetypes transcend language barriers, as well as the limitations of time and place. Throughout history, all around the world, people from a wide range of cultures and civilizations have shared similar archetypal concepts—like the wandering fool, the powerful magician, and the mysterious, wise woman. It's no coincidence that those are the first three figures pictured on the first three cards of the Major Arcana.

In many Tarot decks, the twenty-one numbered cards of the Major Arcana are labeled with Roman numerals: I, II, III, and so on. The Major Arcana cards are:

0. The Fool

I. The Magician

II. The High Priestess

III. The Empress

IV. The Emperor

V. The Hierophant

VI. The Lovers

VII. The Chariot

VIII. Strength (in some decks, Strength is switched with Justice)

IX. The Hermit

X. The Wheel of Fortune

XI. Justice (or, in some decks, Strength)

XII. The Hanged Man

XIII. Death

XIV. Temperance

XV. The Devil

XVI. The Tower

XVII. The Star

XVIII. The Moon

XIX. The Sun

XX. Judgment

XXI. The World

Obviously, the archetypes of the Major Arcana cards are powerful. But the drama and energy of those archetypes is expressed, on a real, practical level, in the everyday cards of the Minor Arcana.

The Minor Arcana

Even if you have never seen a Tarot card deck before, the Minor Arcana will seem familiar to you—assuming, of course, that you have played card games like rummy or poker at some point in your life.

The Minor Arcana is structured exactly like a deck of playing cards. Just as a deck of playing cards is divided into the four suits of Clubs, Hearts, Spades, and Diamonds, the Minor Arcana is divided into the four suits of Wands, Cups, Swords, and Pentacles. Sometimes, depending on the deck, the names of the suits can vary. Wands may be called Rods, Batons, or Staffs. Cups may be called Chalices, and Pentacles may be called

Coins or Discs. Usually, those subtle variations don't make much of a difference in the essential structure of the deck or how the cards are read.

In fact, the similarities between playing cards and Tarot decks have led some experts to suggest that playing cards were actually the forerunners of the Minor Arcana. Most Tarot historians, however, tend to believe that the two types of decks developed independently of each other.

Each of the Tarot's four suits is further subdivided into numbered cards, which run from Ace through Ten, and the court cards: the Page, the Knight, the Queen, and the King. Occasionally, court cards carry other titles, such as Knave, Prince, and Princess.

Some people call the Minor Arcana "pip" cards, because pips are the marks that indicate the suit or numerical value of a playing card—the nine diamonds, for example, or six clubs. In Tarot, some Minor Arcana cards are similarly illustrated with a numbered pattern of Wands, Cups, Swords, or Pentacles, especially in historical decks, such as the *Marseille* Tarot. For the most part, however, modern decks portray individual images of people going about their everyday lives, doing normal things like working, shopping, drinking, dancing, and sleeping.

The ancient Greeks had a saying: "The unexamined life is not worth living." The four suits of the Minor Arcana make it easy to examine one's life—in detail. Each one of the Tarot's four suits represents a separate area of existence: spiritual, emotional, intellectual, and physical. Combined, the four realms provide a complete, holistic system for analyzing and contemplating your life.

In fact, if you memorize the significance of each suit, it will be much easier for you to learn the meanings of all seventy-eight cards. The suits alone can serve as the basis for your interpretations. Just remember:

- Wands cards depict spiritual life.
- Cups cards portray emotional affairs.
- Swords cards illustrate intellectual concepts.
- Pentacles cards show physical and material concerns.

Elements of Attraction

Each one of the Tarot's four suits also corresponds to one of the four ancient elements: fire, water, air, and earth.

Alchemists and philosophers believed that the four elements were the building blocks of the natural world and that the elements could be combined and recombined in any number of ways. Just as the four elements were once believed to constitute the material universe, many believed that the human body was made up of four elements, as well. Some people, for example, have always been considered "fiery."

While modern science eliminated that concept centuries ago, it still holds as a valid psychological model.

- Wands, the cards of spirit, correspond to the element of fire.

- Cups, the cards of emotion, correspond to the element of water.

- Swords, the cards of the intellect, correspond to the element of air.

- Pentacles, the cards of physical existence, correspond to the element of earth.

The imagery on each card makes it easy to remember the correct associations. Here are some hints to get you started.

The Suit of Wands

Wands cards depict spiritual life, energy, and drive, and correspond to the element of fire.

In most Tarot decks, Wands look like freshly cut branches from leafy trees. That is your cue that wands can be set on fire and burned. You might want to picture each wand as a flaming torch that can be used for light and heat— in other words, enlightenment and inspiration. Our spiritual lives can catch fire. Our spiritual development can be ignited by our ideals and fueled by our passions, our hopes, our fears, and our desires. We can be enlightened.

Don't be afraid to grab onto fire analogies when you encounter Wands cards. In a romance reading, the presence of Wands cards may indicate that sparks are about to fly, that passions may be inflamed, and that an affair will get hot. Wands cards may tell you that someone is carrying a torch, or burning with desire. Wands cards might even suggest that an old romance will be rekindled or that someone is playing with fire.

Wands also have an obvious connection to magic. After all, what magician would be caught without a magic wand? Magicians use their wands to direct their spirits—their energy, will, and desire—into the physical world. The rest of us also use wands that serve equally "magical" purposes in the real world. As infants and children, we use our fingers to point, to question, and to direct the world around us. As adults, we use wand-shaped pens, pencils, and paintbrushes to express ourselves. We even use wand-shaped devices to curl our hair and change channels on the television.

The Suit of Cups

Cups cards portray emotional affairs and correspond to the element of water. When most people think of romance cards in the Tarot deck, they picture the suit of Cups.

Cups can hold water—the essence of life—or, for that matter, any liquid that holds sentimental significance, such as wine or champagne. The connection to emotion is clear: we use cups to toast each other in celebration, to commune with others during religious ceremonies, and sometimes, we use cups to drown our sorrows.

Because Cups represent emotions, Cups cards often relate to issues of needs and desires. Cups cards are especially suited to describing relationship issues.

Because Cups cards correspond to water, they serve as a reminder that the well of human emotion runs deep. Just as the human body is seventy-five percent water, the human psyche is driven by an overwhelmingly emotional combination of wants, needs, drives, and desires.

In a romance reading, water analogies can be especially useful. The presence of Cups cards may indicate that emotions are welling up under the surface or that still waters run deep. Someone may have ice water running in her veins, for example, while another person's heart may seem to be frozen. A situation may be fluid or on the rocks.

The Suit of Swords

Swords cards illustrate intellectual concepts and correspond to the element of air. Swords cards also describe the way we think and communicate our ideas to others.

Historically, swords have been weapons of war. It's important to remember, however, that swords have served other, equally important purposes. During the High Middle Ages, swords were an emblem of power, because they were the exclusive purvey of a skilled, highly educated upper class. Medieval knights began their training when they were seven or eight years old, and they continued to hone their skills throughout their lives. Swordplay, jousting, and tournaments were all time-honored ways to bring young men into a social and cultural group.

Swords also connote a long romantic tradition. Sword-bearing knights were sworn to protect and defend the helpless, and they subscribed to a strict moral code of chivalry.

Because Swords represent the intellect, Swords cards often relay issues of thoughts, ideas, and related issues of communication—especially when the ideas we try to communicate come into conflict with others or seem especially cutting. In a romance reading, the presence of Swords cards may indicate that a person or a situation is especially sharp, pointed, or cutting-edge. Someone may have a rapier wit.

Swords are in their element when they move through the air. It's no coincidence that radio and television broadcasters use airwaves to transmit their messages and that people frequently say, "The pen is mightier than the sword."

All sorts of air analogies apply to Swords cards. It may be that someone with many Swords in a reading is feeling especially heady. They might even have their head in the clouds or act like an airhead.

The Suit of Pentacles

Because Pentacles correspond to the element of earth, Pentacles cards often represent material and physical matters.

In most Tarot decks, Pentacles look like coins with star-shaped designs. That pattern is symbolic of our physical nature: When you stand with your arms extended and your feet apart, someone could trace the shape of a star around your body. The five points on the star would be the top of your head, your two outstretched hands, and your two feet, widespread but firmly planted on the ground.

Pentacles, like the coins they resemble, symbolize the tangible realities of physical life. They represent the things we can touch, the things we can feel. They can represent money or property. They can also symbolize spiritual and emotional treasures—the values we hold dear, the memories that are close to our hearts, the people and things we love most and carry with us always.

In a romance reading, the presence of Pentacles cards may indicate that a person or situation is well grounded or that an attraction may be physical. You can use any number of analogies when you read Pentacles cards: a relationship may be heavy, or rocky, or down to earth. Some people might be earthy . . . or just plain dirty.

Courting Favors

There are four court cards in each of the Tarot's four suits: Pages, Knights, Queens, and Kings. Occasionally, court cards carry other titles, such as Knave, Prince, and Princess. In most Tarot decks, however, the four figures constitute a complete royal family.

Court cards have a wide range of functions. They can represent other people, or they can reflect aspects of our own personality. Sometimes they can even illustrate what we think of ourselves by depicting qualities that we like and dislike in others.

Pages are young and enthusiastic. During the Renaissance, pages were the youngest members of the royal court. Pages would frequently serve as messengers; it was their job to take news from one person to another. And because they were young, pages were students, learning their future roles through apprenticeships. Nowadays, when Pages show up in a Tarot reading, they frequently represent young people, students, or messages.

Historically, Knights were usually on a sacred quest—for success, for honor, and for the ever-elusive gifts of the spirit. Sworn to the pursuit of justice, it was a Knight's duty to defend and rescue the helpless. Knights frequently embarked on long-term adventures. When Knights show up in a Tarot reading, they may indicate that a new quest or adventure is about to begin or that rescue is on the way.

Queens, of course, are rulers—but classically, their rules were based on the feminine principles of safeguarding and nurturing their realms. When Queens show up in a Tarot reading, they may imply that an issue or a person is being safeguarded and nurtured.

Kings are mature, worldly men. Most have successfully completed the quests they began as knights, and they have moved on to accept the corresponding responsibility of their achievements. Kings are active rulers, unafraid to aggressively wage war and grow their kingdoms through conquest. When Kings show up in a Tarot reading, they may suggest that similar action is imminent.

Tarot card readers need to be cautious and open to possibility when they interpret court cards. They frequently represent other people in a situation—but just as often, court cards represent aspects of one's own personality. The two options are not mutually exclusive, however. A psychological concept called "projection" is often the key to understanding what the court cards mean. Simply put, we tend to view and judge other people based on our own attitudes, likes, and dislikes. We "project" our own beliefs onto other people—usually without realizing that we're doing so. Similarly, we draw others to ourselves because they reflect aspects of our own personality, both good and bad.

Opposites Attract: The Duality of the Tarot Deck

Throughout the Tarot deck, you will find that the world of the Tarot is a world divided by two. Aristotle said, "Most human things go in pairs." People, concepts, and themes are consistently depicted in pairs: male and female, light and dark, day and night, summer and winter, hot and cold, birth and death, yin and yang.

Even the structure of the Tarot deck itself is divided by two. Obviously, the deck is split between the "big secrets" of the Major Arcana and the "little secrets" of the Minor Arcana. Likewise, the four suits of the Minor Arcana are divided into two groups. For ease of reference, Wands and Swords are considered "masculine" suits, while Cups and Pentacles are "feminine." Wands and Swords are "active" and Cups and Pentacles are "reactive." Even the court cards reflect a division between male and female, and a corresponding role—either active or passive. That language isn't intended to be sexist. It simply reflects how most of us perceive the world and how we think. We see the world in terms of pairs. We learn by comparing and contrasting opposites and extremes. Along the way, we define ourselves not only by what we are (male or female, tall or short, blonde or brunette), but also by what we are not (happy or sad, young or old, quiet or loud).

Most of us spend our lives searching for the perfect balance between two extremes. Should we work or should we play? Should we speak or stay silent? Should we pursue our own interests, or should we collaborate with someone else? The twofold nature of the Tarot helps us see both sides clearly, so that we can find a comfortable balance in our own lives.

Chapter Three

The Secret Language of Symbols

Symbolism permeates our world, from the timeless classics of art and literature to popular music, television shows, movies, and ads. The Tarot speaks the secret language of symbols—a language that is spoken all around us, every day. In this chapter, you will learn how you can become well-versed in the Tarot's language of symbols, so you can speak it fluently and interpret it for others. Admittedly, some of the information in this section is highly technical. It's kind of like a crash course in esoteric thinking. However, it might seem a little intimidating—especially if you're just starting to read Tarot cards. Don't panic. You don't need to memorize this material, and there's not going to be a quiz at the end of the chapter. You simply need to know that there is a rhyme and reason for all the symbols you'll find in the Tarot deck. If you feel overwhelmed, simply skim through the text, stop when you find a passage that interests you, and know that the rest will be waiting here until you're ready to use it in your own work with the cards.

Symbols and Stories

Symbols are everywhere. We are so used to seeing symbols that most of us hardly give them a second thought during the course of an average day. For many of us, symbols are no different than the ordinary signs that mark a street corner or an off-ramp.

Symbols, however, represent a wealth of information that can only be experienced by understanding the history and tradition that underlies their surface meaning. Christians, for example, use the symbol of the cross to refer to the entire life, death, and resurrection of Christ. Patriots point to the flag as a symbol of our nation, a symbol that embodies the full range of its history. When wedding guests throw rice at a new bride and groom, they are symbolically showering them with their hopes and best wishes for a long and productive life together.

The stories behind our symbols are important. Those stories make it possible to read Tarot cards for yourself and for others.

At first, it might seem difficult to translate the symbols into words. Symbols speak to us on a spiritual and emotional level. In order to discuss them—in order to find the words to express them—we need to draw each symbol, dripping wet, up from the well of our unconscious. Then we need to filter it and wring it through our intellect.

The problem is compounded by the fact that the same symbol may represent an entirely different concept to each individual. Although most symbols do connote certain standard meanings, they also are open to interpretation. The significance of many Tarot symbols will vary from person to person and even from reading to reading. Your own experience—in everyday life as well as in your study of the cards—will affect how you perceive and interpret the symbols on the cards.

The best way to begin studying symbols is by noticing them. Pay attention to the way that symbols are used in the Tarot, as well as how they're used in everyday life—in movies, on television, and in books.

The glossary at the back of this book offers a number of interpretations for symbols found in many Tarot decks. You might also wish to consult a symbol dictionary for a guide to traditional meanings. You might even want to start keeping notes about your own interpretations, which will probably grow and change over time.

The Objects of Your Desire: Basic Symbolism

Typically, symbols are ordinary objects that are used to represent invisible concepts, like love, honor, truth, and justice. An apple, for example, may represent health—or the temptation of forbidden fruit. A wild beast may symbolize our untamed animal nature. A hat, which covers the head, may refer to one's intellectual ability.

There is no right or wrong way to interpret the objects depicted on most Tarot cards, but there are traditional meanings for most symbols in a standard Tarot deck. Check the symbol dictionary in the back of this book for a guide to specific symbols that frequently appear in Tarot card imagery.

A Great Hue and Cry: The Symbolism of Color

Tarot card artists use color symbolism to add layers of meaning to their illustrations. Most color symbolism is obvious.

Black, like the color of night, symbolizes darkness and obscurity. Black may also represent the absolute darkness of midnight, which symbolizes death.

Blue, the color of sky and sea, frequently symbolizes depth and calm. The clear blue color of heaven might also represent spirituality and clarity of vision and thought.

Brown, the color of bare earth, may represent untapped or undeveloped potential.

Gold, like the precious metal, may symbolize richness, wealth, and royal majesty. Gold can also represent the sun.

Gray, like a cloudy, overcast day, usually represents depression, neutrality, and indifference.

Green, the color of nature and vegetation, represents fertility and growth.

Orange, the color of fire, can represent heat, passion, and burning desire.

Pink, a mix of passionate red and pure white, can represent a more innocent, romantic form of love.

Purple, the traditional color of royalty, symbolizes leadership and divinity.

Red, the color of blood and wine, symbolizes passion and will. Red is also the color of danger, alarm, ambition, and anger.

Silver, the traditional color of the moon, symbolizes the passive lunar energy of reflection and intuition.

Violet, the color of spirituality and religion, is used to express God's power and dominion.

White, the color of bleached cotton and driven snow, symbolizes spirituality and purity.

Yellow, the color of the sun, represents fiery heat and radiant energy.

Figuratively Speaking: The Symbolism of Numbers

The sequence of the numbered cards also carries weight in a Tarot reading. The system is as simple as one, two, and three.

- In general, the first few cards in a series represent the early stages of development. Aces, Twos, and Threes generally depict beginnings of a cycle or an issue.
- The middle cards—Fours, Fives, and Sixes—typically represent the growth and development of a subject or a concern.
- The final cards of each suit—Sevens, Eights, and Nines—tend to reflect conclusions, while Tens represent finality and preparation for a new cycle.
- Likewise, cards One through Seven in the Major Arcana may represent beginning phases, Eight through Fourteen the middle, and Fifteen through Twenty-one the culmination and conclusion of a series of events.

Each number also connotes a specific set of symbolic meanings:

Zero

Zero precedes all of the other numbers. It symbolizes the period before existence, or the state of nonbeing. Because it has a circular shape, zero also represents the "cosmic egg" of the universe, the wheel of the year, and the cycle of life. Like a ring, it has no beginning and no end.

One

One is the first number, so it represents the source of all existence. As a starting point, one represents a beginning, a thesis, or an original concept. It also symbolizes unity—the concept of oneness. When the number one is written with the Arabic numeral 1 or the Roman numeral I, it may be a phallic symbol. As a geometric figure, it is illustrated as a single point—a dot. Graphically, that point may represent either an egg or a sperm, symbolizing fertility.

Two

Two symbolizes duality, partnerships, choices, and combinations. As a response to the number one, two can also symbolize an antithesis, counterpoint, or conflict. Two can sometimes symbolize an echo or a reflection. To Christians, the number two symbolizes the two natures of Christ: human and divine. Written as the Roman numeral II, it may be a representation of a gateway, or of female genitalia. As a geometric figure, it is illustrated as a line that connects two points.

Three

Three often represents creativity. It is a triad, the logical product of the combination of one and two. It is the child that is born from a mother and a father. Three represents a synthesis, the result of a thesis and an antithesis. Sometimes, the number three symbolizes the combination of body, mind, and spirit. It frequently symbolizes past, present, and future, as well as the course of human existence: maiden, mother, and crone, and birth, life, and death. Three also carries a religious connotation: many beliefs describe a holy trinity, such as Father, Son, and Holy Spirit, or the triple goddess of the New, Full, and Old Moon. Plato described the three sister fates—Lacheses, Clotho, and Atropos— who controlled each person's destiny. During the Middle Ages, there were three god-desslike Graces: Splendor, Mirth, and Good Cheer, sometimes called Beauty, Gentleness, and Friendship. There are three theological virtues: faith, hope, and charity. Geometrically, three points constitute a plane. Many Tarot readers like to cut the deck three times before laying the cards out in a spread.

Four

Four is the number of wholeness and stability. That's because, geometrically speaking, four points combine to form a solid. There are four dimensions: width, length, height, and time. There are four cardinal directions: north, south, east, and west. There are four seasons, four winds, and four periods of the day: dawn, day, evening, and night. There are four phases of the moon: waxing, full, waning, and dark. There are four phases of life: infancy, youth, adulthood, and old age. There are four corners to a room or a house. Christians have four evangelists—Matthew, Mark, Luke, and John—with four corresponding gospels, as well as four horsemen of the Apocalypse, and four cardinal virtues: prudence, fortitude, temperance, and justice. There are four elements—fire, water, air, and earth—and four corresponding suits in the Minor Arcana.

Five

While the introduction of a fifth element upsets the stability of a perfect square, five often symbolizes the five senses, the five appendages (head, hands, and feet), five fingers, and five vowels. Some metaphysicians also consider five important because it symbolizes the "fifth element" or Spirit. The number five is frequently represented by a five-pointed star or pentacle.

Six

Six is generally considered to represent the human being, because God created man on the sixth day. Six also symbolizes the sixth sense—psychic ability—as well as the six directions of space: left, right, forward, backward, up, and down.

Seven

Seven is an exceptionally mystical number. Classically, there were seven days of creation. There are seven gifts of the Holy Spirit: wisdom, understanding, counsel, fortitude, knowledge, piety, and fear. There are seven deadly sins: envy, sloth, gluttony, wrath, pride, lust, and greed. There are seven virtues: faith, hope, charity, fortitude, justice, temperance, and prudence. During the Middle Ages, there were seven liberal arts: the trivium, consisting of grammar, rhetoric, and logic, as well as quadrivium, made up of arithmetic, music, geometry, and astronomy. Alchemists had seven metals: gold, silver, iron, mercury, tin, copper, and lead. There are seven visible planets: the Sun, the Moon, Mars, Mercury, Jupiter, Venus, and Saturn. There are seven musical notes, and seven chakras or energy centers of the body. To randomize your Tarot deck fully before a reading, shuffle it seven times.

Eight

Eight symbolizes infinity, because it resembles the lemniscate, the symbol of infinity. Eight is a symbol of baptism and spiritual rebirth; many baptisteries and baptismal fonts have eight sides. Eight also represents the eternal spiral of regeneration. There are eight musical notes in an octave.

Nine

Nine symbolizes conclusions. It hints at the nearness of the number ten, as well as the nine months of pregnancy.

Ten

Ten is the number of completion and perfection, probably because human beings have ten fingers and toes. There are ten spheres on the mystical Kabbalistic Tree of Life and ten numbered cards in each suit of the Minor Arcana.

Eleven

Eleven written with Arabic or Roman numerals, is a graphic representation of pillars or a gateway.

Twelve

Twelve represents the twelve signs of the Zodiac and the twelve months of the year. There were twelve gods on Mount Olympus: Jupiter, Neptune, Pluto, Vesta, Juno, Mars, Minerva, Vulcan, Apollo, Diana, Mercury, and Venus. There were also twelve tribes of Israel and twelve apostles.

Thirteen

Thirteen is usually thought to be an unlucky number, because there were thirteen diners at Jesus' last supper. In Tarot, the Death card is number thirteen.

It's Elementary: The Symbolism of Fire, Water, Air, and Earth

Alchemists and philosophers believed that the four ancient elements—fire, water, air, and earth—could be combined and recombined in any number of ways. In fact, for centuries those four ancient elements were presumed to be the building blocks of the natural world.

That tradition still lives on in the symbolism of the Tarot. The four suits of the Minor Arcana, for example, represent the four elements. So do the four types of court cards. Even the Major Arcana cards are assigned to the four elements, based on their astrological correspondences.

Some Tarot readers use the four elements to enhance the depth and breadth of their readings by referring to the "elemental dignities" in a spread. Simply put, the system simply refers to how well the cards, each in their own element, mix and match.

According to the ancient Greeks, the elements were primarily hot or cold, and secondarily, they were wet or dry. Under their system:

- Earth is cold and dry.
- Water is cold and wet.
- Fire is hot and dry.
- Air is hot and wet.

The Greeks believed that any pair of elements that shared a primary feature—for example, both cold or both hot—could mix easily. Elemental pairs that shared a secondary feature—both dry or both wet—could be mixed with care. However, elements that had nothing in common would destroy each other.

Using that system:

- Wands (fire) and Swords (air) mix well, because they are both hot.
- Pentacles (earth) and Cups (water) also mix well, because they are both cold.
- It's possible to mix Wands (fire) and Pentacles (earth), because they are both dry.
- You can also mix Cups (water) and Swords (air), because they are both wet.
- Wands (fire) and Cups (water) cannot be mixed, because they have nothing in common.
- Likewise, Pentacles (earth) and Swords (air) have nothing in common, so they are not compatible, either.

Branching Out: The Symbolism of the Tree of Life

A special type of symbolism runs through most Tarot decks: a correspondence with Kabbalah, a mystical philosophy first developed by the ancient Jews. In essence, Kabbalah is a philosophy that describes the creation of the universe, as well as man's place in the world.

The word Kabbalah itself is the origin of the English word "cabal," which means "secret." In fact, for centuries the study of the Hebrew Kabbalah was reserved for married Jewish men who were over the age of forty.

Some basic precepts of the Kabbalah include the following ideas:

- According to Kabbalistic thought, the universe was created in a single, lightning-like flash—a cosmic "Big Bang."
- At the moment of creation, the energy of pure thought was instantaneously transformed into physical matter.
- Although the creative process was practically instantaneous, there were ten separate stages in the creation of the universe. The energy followed a zigzag course—first right, then left, then right again—until finally, it came to rest in perfect balance in the physical world. A new stage of creation developed at each turning point.
- A diagram called the Tree of Life depicts the ten stages in the creation of the universe. On the Tree of Life, each stage is depicted as a sphere that dangles like fruit on the branches of the Tree of Life.

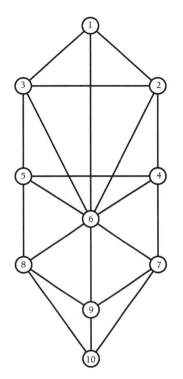

- Each of the ten spheres is imbued with its own mystical qualities, derived as the divine energy of creation flowed from point to point along the tree. The first sphere is pure energy. With each subsequent stopping point, that energy becomes less refined and more weighed down by the realities of physical existence.

- Human beings live in the tenth sphere, the world of matter. In one sense, the physical world is the least spiritual sphere of existence; in another sense, however, the physical world represents the culmination of God's creative efforts.

- The ten spheres are connected by twenty-two paths, by which humans can climb up the Tree of Life and rejoin their creator.

Ever since Tarot scholar Eliphas Levi linked the Tarot to the Kabbalah, Tarot scholars, artists, and designers have incorporated Kabbalah thought into their work with the cards. Kabbalistic themes run throughout the Tarot deck. For example:

- The lightning flash of creation is frequently depicted as the lightning flash on the Tower.

- The Tree of Life diagram is commonly depicted on the Fool's tunic, in the curtain behind the High Priestess, in the trees behind the Lovers, and on the Ten of Pentacles.

- The ten spheres on the Tree of Life—the ten stages of creation—correspond to the ten numbered cards of each suit. The significance of each number is reinforced by the meaning of each card: The Aces of each suit, for example, represent limitless energy. That energy is accessed and refined until it comes to the end of each cycle with the Tens of each suit.

- The ten spheres on the Tree of Life are linked by twenty-two paths that also correspond to the twenty-two letters of the Hebrew alphabet and the twenty-two cards of the Major Arcana.

- According to Kabbalistic thought, the Tree of Life is four-dimensional. In effect, it's actually four trees in one. The four worlds of the Kabbalah correspond to the four suits of the Minor Arcana. There is a world of archetypes, ideas, possibilities, and the urge to create (Wands); a world in which that urge can take shape, a world of fertility and creation (Cups); a subsequent world of thought, form, pattern, and design (Swords); and finally, the end result, a physical world of matter and activity (Pentacles).

- According to Jewish tradition, God's name is composed of four Hebrew letters: *Yod Heh Vau Heh*. In English, the letters are usually pronounced "Jehovah." Those four letters, also referred to as the *Tetragrammaton*, correspond to the four elements of the Tarot. *Yod* corresponds to fire, *Heh* corresponds to water, *Vau* corresponds to air, and *Heh* also corresponds to earth.

- The four letters in the name are reflected in the four suits of the Minor Arcana.

- The forty pip cards of the Minor Arcana—those that are left when the court cards are removed—also correspond to the four letters in the name of God.

- Those four letters are also reflected in the Minor Arcana's court cards, which consist of four families (Wands, Cups, Swords, and Pentacles) of four members each (Page, Knight, Queen, and King).

Chapter Four

Astrology and the Tarot

For more than a century, Tarot cards have been closely tied to astrology. Tarot and astrology are like an old married couple: to truly appreciate the subtleties and symbolism of the cards, you must look to the stars.

Signs from Above

Astrology isn't as old as the stars, but it is as old as humankind. Ever since the first humans gazed up into the night sky and pondered the changing face of the moon or gazed in amazement at the northern lights, astrology has shaped the way we think about the universe—and each other.

Astrology has had a major influence on the Tarot, too. Even though the cards were first designed as a game, they quickly became linked to the science of the stars.

The Major Arcana cards are each associated with either a sign or a planet. In the Minor Arcana, the four Aces and the court cards correspond to the four elements that play a crucial role in astrological interpretations. The remaining thirty-six Minor Arcana cards—the Twos through the Tens—all have a place on the 360-degree wheel of the Zodiac.

Sun Sign Correspondences

If you know your Sun sign, the corresponding Major Arcana card can offer insight into your personality. If you know the Sun sign of another person, you can compare your cards. At a glance, you can conduct an instant compatibility profile.

The technique is simple: just look at the cards. Pay special attention to pairs that seem to have a natural affinity for each other, such as the sun and the moon. Look for planetary rulerships, too. Cancer, for example, is associated with the Chariot card. Cancer is ruled by the Moon, which is assigned to the High Priestess card. When the Charioteer and the High Priestess show up in combination, you have a hit.

Most importantly, look for similarities and differences in the illustrations themselves. The figures in the cards might be facing each other or looking apart. They might share similar expressions, poses, clothing, or props, or they might have nothing in common. They might be shown in the same general setting with similar landscapes and backgrounds, or they might be situated worlds apart. Look for symbols and signs in the cards themselves, and trust your intuition.

Made for Each Other

Astrologically, the Major Arcana cards that correspond to each of the twelve astrological signs and their ruling planets are powerful pairs. They are:

- The Emperor (Aries) and the Tower (Mars)
- The Hierophant (Taurus) and the Empress (Venus)
- The Lovers (Gemini) and the Magician (Mercury)
- The Chariot (Cancer) and the High Priestess (the Moon)
- Strength (Leo) and the Sun (the Sun)
- The Hermit (Virgo) and the Magician (Mercury)
- Justice (Libra) and the Empress (Venus)
- Death (Scorpio) and Judgment (Pluto)
- Temperance (Sagittarius) and the Wheel of Fortune (Jupiter)
- The Devil (Capricorn) and the World (Saturn)
- The Star (Aquarius) and the Fool (Uranus)
- The Moon (Pisces) and the Hanged Man (Neptune)

Aries and the Emperor Card (March 21–April 20)

Because Aries is the first sign of the Zodiac, Aries people are natural-born leaders—just like the Emperor, the Aries card of the Tarot deck.

The Emperor typifies the Aries personality: courageous, bold, commanding, and self-confident. While Aries individuals can sometimes be hotheaded, headstrong, and unwilling to compromise, that same energy also makes them fiery and passionate in both love and war.

The ram is the symbol of Aries; you can often see images of rams incorporated in many versions of the Emperor card.

Aries is a fire sign. Just as in the Tarot, the astrological element of fire symbolizes spiritual energy.

Aries is ruled by the planet Mars, which is traditionally associated with the unbridled energy and passion of war, as well as aggression, self-defense, and action. In fact, Mars was the mythical god of war. In the Tarot, Mars is associated with the Tower card, which offers one illustration of the Emperor's warlike side.

While the Emperor is the card most people attribute to the sign, Aries is also associated with the Two, Three, and Four of Wands, as well as the Queen of Wands.

Taurus and the Hierophant Card (April 21–May 20)

People born under the sign of Taurus, the Bull, are generally earthy, grounded, practical, and conservative. So is the Hierophant, the Taurus card of the Tarot deck.

Taurus sensibilities also lean toward the sensuous. They like fine art, fine food, and fine furnishings. And, of course, Taureans—like the traditional church—all value loyalty, monogamy, and procreation.

The bull is the symbol of Taurus; you can often see images of the Taurus glyphs incorporated in many versions of the Hierophant card.

Taurus is an earth sign. In astrology, just as in Tarot, the element of earth symbolizes physical energy.

Taurus is ruled by Venus, the planet of love and romance. In the Tarot, Venus is assigned to the Empress card. Together, the Hierophant and the Empress are a formidable pair.

While Taurus is usually assigned to the Hierophant, it is also associated with the Five, Six, and Seven of Pentacles, as well as the King of Pentacles.

Gemini and the Lovers Card (May 21–June 20)

It is often said that people born under the sign of Gemini are the great communicators of the Zodiac. They are insatiably curious, talkative, flirtatious, and playful. One could say the same thing about the Lovers, the Gemini card of the Tarot.

The correspondence is a good fit, because both the Gemini twins and the two Lovers in the Tarot card represent the versatility and analytical skills that a team of approaches can bring to any situation.

Gemini is an air sign. In astrology, just as in Tarot, the element of air symbolizes intellectual energy.

Gemini is ruled by Mercury, the planet of speed and communication. Mercury was the messenger of the gods—and he was also known as the legendary Trickster of mythology. Fittingly, Mercury is associated with the Tarot's Magician card.

While Gemini is usually assigned to the Lovers, the sign is also associated with the Eight, Nine, and Ten of Swords, as well as the Knight of Swords.

Cancer and the Chariot Card (June 21–July 22)

The typical Cancer personality is a sentimental, nostalgic, nurturing caregiver who loves nothing more than a quiet dinner at home. So why is Cancer assigned to the Chariot?

Because even though they're homebodies, Cancerians don't need to stay home to feel at home. Just look at the crab, the emblem of the sign: he travels with his home on his back. In fact, Cancerians are perfectly willing to venture out into the world—as long as they can be assured that they will have all of the comforts of home, even when they're on the road.

The typical Cancer individual is far more like the Charioteer than you might expect. After all, he traveled in an early version of the mobile home. Both Cancer and the Charioteer are also remarkably resourceful, intuitive, and protective—all valuable resources for the warrior on the go.

Cancer is a water sign. In astrology, just as in Tarot, the element of water symbolizes emotional energy.

Cancer is ruled by the Moon, the planet of reflection, intuition, and inspiration. The Moon is assigned to the High Priestess card—a good fit, as she represents those same qualities.

While Cancer is usually assigned to the Chariot, the sign is also associated with the Two, Three, and Four of Cups, as well as the Queen of Cups.

Leo and the Strength Card (July 23–August 23)

Most Leos, the strong, self-confident showmen of the Zodiac, would have no qualms about stepping into the center ring of the circus—especially if it meant that they could demonstrate their courage and ability to a crowd of admirers. Like the brave young lion tamer in the Strength card, they take a certain pride in their ability to shine in the spotlight.

In fact, the ferocious beast in the Strength card is simply a reminder of Leo's signature animal, the lion. Leo people are generally as strong, brave, inspiring, and showy as the Strength card would suggest. They can also be vain, proud, and self-important—but, having tamed lion after lion, they probably have the right to show off a bit.

Leo is a fire sign. In astrology, just as in Tarot, the astrological element of fire symbolizes spiritual energy.

Leo is ruled by the Sun. The lion is an alchemical symbol for the sun, gold, and sulphur. In the Tarot, fittingly enough, the sun is represented by the Sun card. The combination of Strength and the Sun clearly illustrates the Leo personality's tendency to shine—and, occasionally, to feel as though they are the center of the universe.

While Leo is usually assigned to Strength, the sign is also associated with the Five, Six, and Seven of Wands, as well as the King of Wands.

Virgo and the Hermit Card (August 24–September 22)

When you need practical advice about your mental or physical health, look for a Virgo. You probably won't have to climb a remote mountaintop to find one—even though most Virgos share the same mind set as the Tarot's Hermit, the card assigned to the sign.

At their core, Virgos are somewhat isolated. It's their rational, practical, and analytical nature at work. In order to live up to their own high standards, Virgos often have to separate themselves from those who aren't as hardworking, resourceful, and well organized. They can be critical—although usually, they are most critical of themselves. They are also extremely helpful. Once you seek them out, they are more than willing to share the wisdom they have accumulated on their own journeys.

Virgo is the sign of the virgin, but they aren't always virginal in the usual sense of the word. In Latin, *Virgo* means "unmarried" or "self-possessed." Virgos give of themselves by choice, not out of a sense of duty. They have integrity.

Virgo is an earth sign. In astrology, just as in Tarot, the astrological element of earth symbolizes physical energy.

Virgo is ruled by Mercury, the planet of speed and communication. In the Tarot, Mercury corresponds to the Magician card. The combination of the wise old Hermit and the brash young Magician relates directly to Virgo's desire to teach and impress other people.

While Virgo is usually assigned to the Hermit, the sign is also associated with the Eight, Nine, and Ten of Pentacles, as well as the Knight of Pentacles.

Libra and the Justice Card (September 23–October 23)

Libra is usually represented by scales of balance, and no Tarot card depicts that concept better than the Justice card. Like living versions of the goddess on the card, most people born under the sign of Libra spend their lives trying to find a balance between extremes.

First and foremost, they need balance, beauty, and harmony in their lives—not conflict. They are skilled at solving problems, compromising, and arranging diplomatic solutions for any conflict. Occasionally, their need to see both sides of any issue makes them indecisive.

Their charm, however, makes up for it. Librans also have an innate need to balance themselves through relationships with others. They are typically friendly, gregarious, and charming. They are exceptionally social creatures. They are visionary, with high social and humanitarian ideals. They appreciate the beauty and harmony of art.

They are also born romantics who usually enter into relationships with marriage in mind.

Libra is an air sign. In astrology, just as in Tarot, the astrological element of air symbolizes intellectual energy.

Libra is ruled by Venus, the planet of love and beauty. In the Tarot, Venus is associated with the Empress card. The combination of Justice and the Empress reflects the Libran love of beauty and creativity.

While Libra is usually assigned to the Justice card, the sign is also associated with the Two, Three, and Four of Swords, as well as the Queen of Swords.

Scorpio and the Death Card (October 24–November 21)

There is no doubt about it: Scorpios can be intense. They are powerful and attractive. They are seductive. They are drawn to mystery. They are fascinated by the great secrets of life, even if those secrets seem dark and depressing to the rest of us. They are even willing to delve into mysteries the rest of us prefer to avoid—like Death, the Scorpio card of the Tarot.

Scorpios understand, perhaps better than any other sign, that Death does not always have the sting associated with its signature emblem, the scorpion.

Scorpio is a water sign. In astrology, just as in Tarot, the astrological element of water symbolizes emotional energy.

Scorpio is ruled by Pluto, the planet of death, regeneration, and unavoidable change. In the Tarot, Pluto is assigned to the Judgment card. The combination of the Death and Judgment cards reaffirms Scorpio's grasp of the deep mysteries of life, as well as its appreciation for the life to come.

While Scorpio is usually assigned to the Death card, the sign is also associated with the Five, Six, and Seven of Cups, as well as the King of Cups.

Sagittarius and the Temperance Card (November 22–December 21)

The archer of Sagittarius is a wily creature, a restless adventurer and ersatz philosopher. Half man, half horse, he is a happy-go-lucky explorer who travels the world in search of honest and visionary companions. He is enthusiastic, independent, footloose, and fancy-free.

Like their namesake, most Sagittarians are generous, good-natured, and honest to a fault. At first glance, however, they may not remind you much of the winged angel of Temperance, the Tarot card that corresponds to their sign.

Take a closer look. Temperance depicts the skillful blend of opposites and the bridge between two extremes. Likewise, the Sagittarian centaur is a seamless blend of man and beast. The archer's bow and arrow are a combination of motion and stillness: an arrow flies through the air, propelled by a stationary bow.

Sagittarius is a fire sign. In astrology, just as in Tarot, the astrological element of fire symbolizes spiritual energy.

Sagittarius is ruled by Jupiter, the planet of luck and expansion. In the Tarot, Jupiter is assigned to the Wheel of Fortune card. The combination of Temperance and the Wheel of Fortune depicts Sagittarius's balanced, optimistic nature.

While Sagittarius is usually assigned to the Temperance card, the sign is also associated with the Eight, Nine, and Ten of Wands, as well as the Knight of Wands.

Capricorn and the Devil Card (December 22–January 20)

People who are born when the Sun is in Capricorn are generally hard workers, high achievers, and responsible partners both at work and at home. They hardly ever have horns growing out of their foreheads—and yet, they have been assigned to the Devil card.

That's because the stereotypical Capricorn businessperson and the Devil share an important trait: both understand all too well the trials and temptations of the material world. If anyone could beat the Devil at a game of cards, it would be a Capricorn.

Most Capricorns are keenly aware of their social status. Like their symbol, the goat, they are constantly climbing and constantly seeking greener pastures. They are ambitious, driven, disciplined, and industrious. They are prudent, patient, stable, and enduring.

Capricorn is an earth sign. In astrology, just as in Tarot, the astrological element of earth symbolizes physical energy.

Capricorn is ruled by Saturn, the planet of boundaries and limitations. In the Tarot, Saturn is assigned to the World card. The combination is effective: the Devil is an earthly creature, firmly rooted in the material world, and closely associated with both the pleasures and pain of physical existence.

While Capricorn is usually assigned to the World card, it is also associated with the Two, Three, and Four of Pentacles, as well as the Queen of Pentacles.

Aquarius and the Star Card (January 21–February 18)

Aquarians are the forward-thinking, progressive people of the Zodiac. They are visionaries, revolutionaries, and pioneers. Their ability to dream of a brighter tomorrow links them closely with the Star card.

Aquarius, the Water Bearer, can be an unpredictable sign. Aquarians are usually unconventional, and they can sometimes be erratic. Despite their love of humanity, they occasionally spurn intimate, one-on-one relationships. They can even be aloof. Don't take it personally—most Aquarians are just a little farsighted.

Aquarius is an air sign. In astrology, just as in Tarot, the astrological element of air symbolizes intellectual energy.

While Aquarius is usually assigned to the Star, the sign is also associated with the Five, Six, and Seven of Swords, as well as the King of Swords.

Aquarius is ruled by Uranus, the planet of freedom and rebellion. In the Tarot, Uranus is assigned to the Fool. The combination of the Star and the Fool is a clear depiction of the dreamer who is not afraid to follow his heart.

Pisces and the Moon Card (February 19–March 20)

Pisces is often said to be the most mystical sign of the Zodiac. While most people live entirely on the dry land of observable reality, Pisces fish are usually most comfortable swimming through the deep waters of intuition and spiritual transformation. On land, Pisces individuals can be restless, changeable, and self-destructive. In water, they become adventurous, compassionate, intuitive, empathetic, sensitive, receptive, imaginative, and poetic.

Those otherworldly qualities are reflected in the Pisces Tarot card, the Moon.

Pisces is a water sign. In astrology, just as in Tarot, the astrological element of water symbolizes emotional energy.

Pisces is ruled by Neptune, the planet of mystery and illusion. In the Tarot, Neptune is assigned to the Hanged Man. The combination of the Moon and the Hanged Man reflects the mesmerizing appeal of alternate realities.

While Pisces is usually assigned to the Moon, it is also associated with the Eight, Nine, and Ten of Cups, as well as the Knight of Cups.

Planetary Correspondences

Some Major Arcana cards are also associated with the Sun, the Moon, and the planets. You can add depth to your Tarot readings by understanding the basic astrological symbolism associated with each of the heavenly bodies.

The Sun

The source of heat and light on earth, the Sun represents energy, enlightenment, radiance, and illumination. Because the sun is the center of our universe, it also symbolizes the center of every individual's world—the self or the ego. Naturally, the Sun card is assigned to the sun. The Sun rules the sign of Leo, which is associated with the Strength card.

The Moon

The Moon reflects the light of the sun, and symbolizes reflection and receptivity. The moon also represents the cyclical, changing nature of existence. The High Priestess card is assigned to the Moon. The Moon rules Cancer, which is associated with the Chariot card.

Mercury

The fastest-moving planet, Mercury symbolizes speed. Because Mercury was the messenger of the gods, Mercury also symbolizes communication. The Magician card is assigned to Mercury. Mercury rules Gemini, which is associated with the Lovers card.

Venus

The planet of love and beauty, Venus symbolizes attraction, romance, and fertility. The Empress card is assigned to Venus. Venus rules Taurus, which is associated with the Hierophant card.

Mars

The planet of energy and aggression, Mars symbolizes masculine force. Because Mars was the god of war, Mars also symbolizes self-defense and aggression. The Tower card is assigned to Mars. Mars rules Aries, which is associated with the Emperor card.

Jupiter

Jupiter is the planet of luck and expansion. The Wheel of Fortune card is assigned to Jupiter. Jupiter rules Sagittarius, which is associated with the Temperance card.

Saturn

The planet of boundaries and limitations, Saturn symbolizes discipline, limits, boundaries, and tradition. The World card is assigned to Saturn. Saturn rules Capricorn, which is associated with the Devil card.

Neptune

The planet of illusion, Neptune symbolizes glamour and sensitivity. The Hanged Man card is assigned to Neptune. Neptune rules Pisces, which is associated with the Moon card.

Uranus

The planet of freedom and rebellion, Uranus symbolizes independence. The Fool card is assigned to Uranus. Uranus rules Aquarius, which is associated with the Star card.

Pluto

The planet of death and regeneration, Pluto symbolizes unavoidable change. The Judgment card is assigned to Pluto. Pluto rules Scorpio, which is associated with the Death card.

Minor Arcana Correspondences

In the Minor Arcana, each of the four suits corresponds to fire, water, air, or earth signs.

- Aries, Leo, and Sagittarius are all fire signs. They correspond to Wands.
- Cancer, Scorpio, and Pisces are all water signs. They correspond to Cups.
- Gemini, Libra, and Aquarius are all air signs. They correspond to Swords.
- Taurus, Virgo, and Capricorn are all earth signs. They correspond to Pentacles.

Court Card Correspondences

In the Minor Arcana, the individual court cards also correspond to fire, water, air, and earth signs. You can find a complete list of those correspondences on the next page. For now, here is a brief explanation:

- The four Pages of the Tarot are all earthy, material individuals that combine the element of earth with the corresponding element of their own suit. In other words, each one personifies his element. The Page of Wands embodies the element of fire, the Page of Cups embodies the element of water, the Page of Swords embodies the element of air, and the Page of Pentacles embodies the element of earth.
- The four Knights of the Tarot are all fiery, spirited individuals. Each one combines the element of fire with the element of his suit. The Knight of Cups, for example, is a blend of the spirited nature of fire with the emotional nature of water.
- The four Queens of the Tarot are all watery, emotional women. Each one combines the element of water with the corresponding element of her suit. The Queen of Pentacles, for example, is a blend of the emotional nature of water with the physical nature of earth.
- The four Kings of the Tarot are all airy, intellectual men. Each one combines the element of air with the corresponding element of his suit. The King of Wands, for example, is a blend of the intellectual nature of air with the spiritual nature of fire.

There are sixteen court cards in all. Four of them represent the four elements in their purest form. That means twelve of the court cards, however, represent a blend of the elements. As luck would have it, there are twelve signs in the Zodiac—and they, too, represent a combination of traits.

Actually, it's not really a coincidence. By referring to the elements the suits and the signs have in common, it is relatively simple to associate each of the court cards to its place in the Zodiac.

	Wands	Cups	Swords	Pentacles
Page	Fire *In Physical Form*	Water *In Physical Form*	Air *In Physical Form*	Earth *In Physical Form*
Knight	Sagittarius *Spiritual*	Pisces *Spiritual and Emotional*	Gemini *Spiritual and Intellectual*	Virgo *Spiritual and Material*
Queen	Aries *Emotional and Spiritual*	Cancer *Emotional*	Libra *Emotional and Intellectual*	Capricorn *Emotional and Material*
King	Leo *Intellectual and Spiritual*	Scorpio *Intellectual and Emotional*	Aquarius *Intellectual*	Taurus *Intellectual and Material*

Moon Madness

Astrology is a complex science, but it's based on a few relatively simple concepts. Once you learn the first group of concepts, you can apply them to each subsequent group—because they keep reappearing, like variations on a theme. Learn the fundamentals of astrology and you can easily apply it to your Tarot readings.

Oddly enough, you don't even need to study too hard. The more you work with Tarot cards, the more you will learn about astrology, even without trying. All you need to do is keep one eye on your cards—and glance up, occasionally, at the changing face of the moon. You will probably find that it lights your path in more ways than one.

Chapter Five

How Does the Tarot Work?

Tarot cards often seem mysterious—even magical. Tarot cards seem to possess an amaz-
ing ability to reflect the many facets of one's body, mind, and spirit, as well as a wide
range of situations and circumstances. While the structure of the Tarot deck provides a
framework for exploring questions, every Tarot reader has his or her own theories about
the principles that make Tarot cards "work."

Art Imitates Life

Some Tarot readers avoid any magical, mystical, or even scientific explanations for their
success with the cards. The secret, they say, lies in the simple fact that readers and
clients will be drawn to the symbols that pertain to them.

That is a pragmatic approach. The Tarot may work simply because we expect it to
work—and because its symbols and structure are flexible enough to meet anyone's
needs.

In fact, people with a more cynical nature have even suggested that Tarot cards are so flexible that their message can apply to practically any situation. They point out that some people are so suggestible that they will believe any story, and find any way to apply cards to their own life.

Those skeptics have a point. Their explanation certainly accounts for the fact that con artists are sometime able to use Tarot cards to frighten and misguide vulnerable clients. But there are a number of other explanations for the cards' accuracy—and the possibilities they suggest are far more optimistic, enlightening, and intriguing.

Purely Academic

Some people pursue the Tarot as a purely academic pursuit. They find themselves embarking on a formal study of the cards' history and symbolism. Their explorations help them integrate a wide range of Western thought and tradition, including mythology, astrology, numerology, alchemy, philosophy, and Jungian psychology.

It is true that through training, education, and experience, anyone can learn what the cards mean. A trained Tarot scholar could even offer thought-provoking, illuminating readings based on nothing more than a strict review of the cards' historical significance and traditional interpretations.

Most Tarot readers, however, combine formal study with other, more mystical approaches.

Psychic Forces

Some experts believe that Tarot cards help them access their psychic ability. They use the cards as a tool to channel their psychic impressions and to help them tap into the underlying bond of energy, emotion, and shared experience that unites us all.

Three types of ability seem especially common among Tarot readers who consider themselves psychic: clairvoyance, clairsentience, and clairaudience.

Clairvoyance literally means "clear vision" or "clear sight." People who are clairvoyant have the ability to see things that are not physically there; they can visualize people and events with their mind's eye. Many Tarot readers, even those who don't consider themselves particularly psychic or clairvoyant, find that it soon becomes common for the static, two-dimensional images on Tarot cards to shimmer, move, and come to life before their eyes.

Clairsentience means "clear senses." People who are clairsentient can sense what's going on with another person or in another place. Many Tarot readers typically describe the information that comes to them as impressions or gut feelings.

Clairaudience means "clear hearing." People who are clairaudient often describe hearing sounds or voices that seem to come out of nowhere. People with clairvoyant experiences might hear an urgent shout of warning, for example, or footsteps in an empty house, or music in a quiet room. More common is the clairvoyant who describes a quiet voice inside their head. It isn't the same as a psychotic episode—it's just the odd phrase or suggestion that suddenly pops into your mind.

Tarot cards seem to trigger such messages in some readers who "hear" messages from the metaphysical or spirit world. You can use the cards to cultivate clairaudient experiences. First, relax and breathe deeply. Imagine that the borders of a Tarot card are a doorway. Picture yourself walking through that doorway and into the card. Approach the characters in the card and ask them for a message. You will probably be surprised by what you can hear. Many people who try this exercise report hearing background noise like wind, birds, and waves, as well as the voice of the figure in the card.

Some Tarot readers also believe that the unseen world of spirit directs them during readings. Some believe they are guided by ethereal guides, messengers, and occasionally, angels.

Whether or not you believe in psychic ability, you will probably find that Tarot cards free you to discover, trust, and explore your own intuition. The cards, after all, seem to be a neutral observer. When you read Tarot cards—whether for yourself or for someone else—it is possible to shed long-standing preconceptions and judgments and simply interpret information that seems to come from a higher source.

Synchronized Swimming

Some Tarot readers believe that *synchronicity*, a term that means "meaningful coincidence," guides their readings.

Carl Jung, the same psychotherapist who developed the concept of archetypes, also created the concept of synchronicity. Jung believed that, as humans, we are all born with access to the "collective unconscious"—a reservoir, of sorts, for all of our shared energy and experiences.

According to Jung's theory, the collective unconscious is like a cosmic, underground lake or stream. In fact, Jung said that our instinctive understanding of symbols, myths, and archetypes are all drawn from the well of the collective unconscious. He pointed out that artists, writers, and musicians regularly tap into the waters of the collective unconscious for inspiration and explanations of the human condition. Jung believed that the symbols, myths, and archetypes that regularly appear in our dreams, our myths, and our stories all spring from that same source, which explains why so many people and cultures share similar legends and make use of the same symbols, regardless of time and place.

When we experience synchronicity, or meaningful coincidences, we rediscover our connection to the collective unconscious. We may find ourselves thinking about a long-lost friend, for example, when a letter from that person arrives in the mail. We may be reminiscing about a favorite food from childhood, only to discover that it is the featured special at a restaurant that night. We may find ourselves experiencing overwhelming sensations of déjà vu when we visit a new place or meet new people. We may even find ourselves falling in love at first sight.

Synchronicity, many Tarot readers believe, explains why Tarot cards work. When we are concerned about love and the Lovers card turns up in a reading, it is not a meaningless coincidence. Cosmic forces are at work. Synchronicity reinforces the belief that we are tuned into the universe, and that we are part of a bigger picture than we can imagine.

Quantum Leaps

Some Tarot readers believe that the secrets of the cards lie in new discoveries about the physical universe—the revolutionary world of quantum physics.

The mysterious paradoxes of quantum physics all echo the mysteries that Tarot readers face on a daily basis. How can a seemingly random spread of cards pinpoint our thoughts, emotions, and experiences? How can the cards possibly reflect what is going on in the real world? The answer may be scientific, after all.

While most of us are used to thinking of the physical world in terms of the three dimensions of height, width, and depth—and in terms of linear time—some quantum physicists have suggested that there may be additional dimensions of space and time. It is possible, they say, that some of those dimensions may actually fold the universe in upon itself and connect dimensions of space and time that seem to be far apart. As a result, we may be able to tap into emotions and events that are far away from us, at least in our terms of space and time.

What's more, quantum physics would seem to indicate that our perception determines what is "real"—and that we may have the power to change and create reality. Some experts in quantum physics have proposed that reality actually consists of an infinite number of possibilities, and that all exist simultaneously—until we observe one of them or choose one of them, at which point the rest collapse in upon themselves or spiral off into unobservable (and thereby irrelevant) parallel universes.

In quantum physics, cause and effect are not necessarily linked in the usual way we think of them. Events of the past and the present do not always lead in a straight line to events in the future, and events that should be completely random can be predicted and even altered. In some experiments with very small, subatomic particles, it seems that the future actually reaches back into the past to influence and change the course of time.

You can choose any theory you like to explain the inner workings of the Tarot. As you become proficient with the cards, you might even develop your own explanation. No matter what you believe about how the Tarot works, its accuracy is often uncanny.

Chapter Six

Meet Your Match

Finding the perfect deck is a lot like finding the perfect partner. You'll probably have to shop around—and you really won't know if you've found "the one" until you spend some time together.

How to Choose a Deck

When it comes to finding a Tarot deck, there are cases of love at first sight. You may be wandering through your favorite bookstore, when suddenly you'll spot a new deck that seems to offer everything you want: smooth rounded corners, a glossy finish, and an attractive package. The sample images pictured on the box seem to whisper to you with promises of wisdom, sensitivity, depth, and perception. When you slip the cards into your hand, you feel a tingle. You could picture yourself walking into a party with that deck or introducing it to your friends and family.

But don't make a long-term commitment based on first impressions—or someday, you might find yourself sitting at the kitchen table with a Tarot deck that just doesn't speak to you.

When you go off in search of the ideal deck, try to visit a store that has sample decks on display. Look at all of the cards, not just the images that are pictured on the box. Make sure that all seventy-eight cards, Major and Minor Arcana alike, are fully illustrated. Look for art that appeals to you, in color, symbolism, and design. Examine the details. You should be able to recognize several of the artist's symbols—meaningful touches such as costumes, accessories, props, power animals, and astrological references. Don't forget to consider the back sides of the cards. Chances are you will be looking at them almost as much as you look at the front sides.

If you're torn between two or more decks, try a side-by-side comparison of several of the same Major Arcana, Minor Arcana, and court cards. You will have an easier time selecting your favorite.

At some point, you might find yourself infatuated with a rebellious new brand of Tarot—specialty decks based on myths, legends, hobbies, sports, and special interests. Those decks are enticing, especially if they parallel your special interests and experience. Beguiled, you may be eager to break tradition and run off to start a new life together.

If you are new to the Tarot, however, go slowly. Tarot readers who are older and wiser usually recommend that you begin with a standard deck like the *Universal* Tarot, or the *Robin Wood* Tarot, or the *Rider-Waite*. If you absolutely must have that new rebel deck, make sure that the card images reflect the standard interpretations found in traditional decks.

You can always play the field later on. The Tarot does not demand that you remain faithful to one deck or remain in a relationship that you have outgrown. You are free to change partners whenever you like or even use several decks at the same time.

How to Personalize Your Deck

Even after you have selected a Tarot deck, you will soon discover that the cards themselves are powerless until you imbue them with your own energy, your own thoughts, and your own understanding of the cards.

In real life, we get to know our new companions by spending time with them. That holds true with new Tarot decks, too. Some Tarot readers even dive right into a relationship with their new decks by sleeping with them—tucked under their pillows, of course.

To truly bond with your new deck, however, you will need to study each card and work with the deck itself.

You might want to begin your relationship with a "new deck" reading. Shuffle the cards and ask, "What will I learn from this deck?" Draw one card at random and interpret the answer.

You might want to start by reading the guide or booklet that comes with most decks.

You could even write your own handbook for the cards. It's not as difficult as it sounds. Simply take a few minutes to go through the deck, card by card. Jot down your initial observations and impressions about each one. If you dedicate a blank journal to your work with the cards, leave plenty of space for later. As time goes by, you will probably want to add details and new interpretations, as well as notes about readings you have conducted.

If you want to study and learn about your deck over time, try pulling just one card a day. Carry it with you, or leave it out in a conspicuous place—on your desk, near your phone, or on your refrigerator. As you notice the card during the course of the day, study it. Pay attention to its colors, its symbols, and its details. Think about its meaning and its significance.

How to Take Care of Your Deck

You might also want to personalize your deck by selecting—or creating—a unique storage container for your deck. Traditionally, decks are wrapped in black silk and stored in a wooden box above head level. Currently, however, readers use everything from luxurious cloth napkins to colorful polyester scarves to wrap and protect their decks.

There are three reasons for wrapping your Tarot deck in fabric. First, many readers believe that a deck should be wrapped to keep it from picking up psychic vibrations and energy that could play out in a reading. Second, wrapping your deck will help keep your cards together, should you accidentally drop them. Third, and perhaps most pragmatically, you can spread all of your cards on the cloth during your readings. A spread cloth will help keep your deck clean, especially if you read on a kitchen table or on any surface that might have crumbs, grease, or dirt on it.

Some readers like to store their cards only in natural materials, such as silk, cotton, or wood—not polyester or plastic. That's because some readers don't want to "suffocate" their cards, and some don't want to sully their decks with materials that aren't environmentally correct. Whether you use a hand-stitched satin pouch or a zippered plastic bag, however, the choice is yours.

Between readings, some readers put all of the cards back in order before they put them away. Many begin by sorting the Major Arcana, zero through twenty-one, and then they sort the Minor Arcana cards. Wands come first, then Cups, Swords, and Pentacles. The cards of each suit run from Ace through Ten, followed by the Page, Knight, Queen, and King.

Some Tarot readers believe they should cleanse their decks periodically by passing them through incense or storing them with crystals or herbs. Some like to charge their cards by leaving them overnight in the light of a full moon.

Some go to extreme lengths to keep their cards clean by refusing to let others handle their cards. They want their decks to be completely imbued with their own vibes, untainted by the thoughts, the hopes, and the wishes of other people. That hands-off policy, however, makes it difficult to do readings for other people, so the practice isn't widespread.

Ultimately, there are no hard-and-fast rules for personalizing, storing, or safeguarding Tarot cards. Remember that the cards don't have any intrinsic power of their own. They are simply pieces of paper, and you are free to handle yours in any way you like.

Chapter Seven

Get Ready to Read

Most of us primp and preen for a date with someone special. A date with destiny is no different—especially when your future is about to be revealed in the cards. Here are some simple suggestions for preparing your space, your self, and your reading partner.

Set the Mood

You can read Tarot cards anywhere you would like. A quiet room is ideal, but you can also read at a kitchen table, in a bedroom, or in the backyard. You should find a place where it is easy for you to concentrate and where you will be free from interruptions and distractions. Wherever you choose to read, it should be a place where you can immerse yourself fully in the cards—an area many Tarot readers refer to as "sacred space."

Naturally, your reading area should be clean before you begin. Most Tarot readers like to clean their reading spaces before they begin—not just by dusting and vacuuming, but also by clearing out stale or negative energy by lighting candles, burning incense, or even by burning sage, in a process called "smudging." Some Tarot readers even position a bowl of clean water nearby to serve as a repository for negative thoughts and emotions. (If you try this technique, make sure you throw the water away when you are done—preferably by flushing it down the toilet. Don't use it on your plants, give it to your dog, or try to use it for any other purpose.)

Setting the mood for a Tarot reading is a lot like setting the mood for a party. You can hold a party in practically any setting—your living room, a restaurant, or a park. Likewise, you can read Tarot cards anywhere you like—at the kitchen table, or in the den, or on a blanket in the backyard.

Just as you would decorate for a party, you might want to enliven your reading area with a few carefully chosen accessories. A few extra touches can add depth and significance, even to a routine reading, and they will help you clearly define your sacred space. Here are a few suggestions to inspire you.

Start with a spread cloth that is attractive and sensual. While black silk is traditional, you may want to find fabric that matches your cards. Solid colors are best, because busy prints can distract from the images and symbols on your cards.

It can also be fun to bring the Minor Arcana to life by displaying a real example of each suit: a wand, a cup, a sword, and a pentacle. Your wand might be a branch you find outside, carve, and decorate yourself. Your cup might be an antique teacup, a pewter goblet, or the champagne flute from your wedding. Your sword might be a letter opener or a pocketknife. Your pentacle might be a silver dollar. If you like, you can create specific examples of each symbol, based on the images in your favorite Tarot deck.

The four suits of the Minor Arcana correspond to the four ancient elements: earth, air, water, and fire. You might want to have a representation of each element on hand. A crystal, for example, might represent earth. (The crystal you choose might add another layer of meaning. Quartz crystals, for example, are said to offer clarity. Amethyst opens one's intuitive sense. And obsidian is a grounding stone.) A burning candle could do double duty as a representation of fire and air. Make it a floating candle, and you will incorporate water, as well. You might also like to have fresh flowers in water, or even a glass of water or tea to sip as you read.

Some Tarot readers like to decorate their space with artwork that reflects their work with the cards: prints and paintings of ancient people and places, for example, or sculptures of ancient gods and goddesses.

Don't forget the impact of soothing background music to help you relax and set the mood. Whether you like classical masterpieces or New-Age melodies, you might want to set aside a few favorite recordings to play during your readings.

If you know you're going to be conducting a romance reading, set a romantic mood. Start with your spread cloth. While a black silk scarf may be traditional, it isn't romantic. Dress your space, instead, with something unmistakably symbolic of love and romance—a red satin pillowcase, for example. You could go a step farther and spread your cards on the weddings and engagements page of your local newspaper. For an even more dramatic presentation, you could actually spread your cards on an evening gown, a wedding dress, or a flowing bridal veil.

Keep your eyes open for other accessories that can help set the mood for a romance reading, as well. Scatter a few rose petals on the table and scent the air with perfume. Collect some tokens that symbolize an evening out, like movie tickets or a restaurant menu. Decorate your reading space with the bride and groom from the top of a wedding cake.

Use the cards themselves for romantic inspiration. To symbolize the fiery passions of the Wands cards, light several candles. To symbolize watery emotions of the suit of Cups, serve champagne or sparkling cider in elegant crystal flutes. To symbolize the airy communications of the Swords cards, display a volume of romantic poetry, a collection of Valentine's Day cards, or a few elegantly scripted love letters—even if you have to write them yourself. And to symbolize the physical pleasures of the Pentacles, share a few chocolates as you contemplate the cards.

If you are reading for someone else, ask that person to add a romantic token of their own to the spread: a note, a phone number, or a piece of jewelry. If the person happens to have a photo of himself or herself with their beloved, incorporate it into the spread.

One note of caution: even if a Tarot reading concerns a troubled or broken relationship, use only positive symbols of love and romance. You will want to draw constructive energy into the reading to symbolize your hope for a brighter future. That way, a Tarot reading will help you break old patterns and make better decisions for future actions.

Prepare Yourself

Before a Tarot session begins, you will need to prepare a physical space that's conducive to a reading. It's just as important—if not more so—to prepare yourself for a reading, too. Many Tarot readers follow a few simple steps, typically known as cleansing, centering, grounding, and shielding. The process, which takes less time than you might think, will help you clear your mind of everyday worries and distractions. It will give your intuition a chance to warm up and make it easier for your conscious and unconscious minds to work together. You will find it easier to focus on the cards and tune in to anyone for whom you are reading. You may even find yourself slipping into a light trance, much like the feeling you get when you're daydreaming or relaxing on the beach. That's probably the best state to be in when you read Tarot, because it will help you read the cards smoothly, freely, and unencumbered by everyday concerns.

Cleansing is the process of shedding outside energy and contaminants, not only physically, but also spiritually. Cleansing will wash away any outside influences that could hamper your reading.

One easy and practical way to cleanse is to wash your hands with soap and water. As you wash your hands, visualize any cosmic and psychological "dirt" being washed away and running down the drain. If you aren't near a sink, you can simply imagine yourself being bathed by waves of pure white light.

Centering is the process of gaining control of your emotions and thoughts. Too often, most of us spend our days scattered in a dozen different directions. We all have a long list of things to do, people to see, and a wide range of tasks and chores to complete. When you are preparing to read Tarot cards, however, all of those troubles, worries, and concerns need to be packed up and tucked away—temporarily, at least—so that you can concentrate on the reading. Centering can also help you to be neutral and non-judgmental in your assessment of the cards.

A few minutes of deep breathing can help you center. Sit with your feet firmly on the floor and your back straight. Breathe in deeply through your nose. As you inhale, feel the air filling your lungs and oxygenating your entire body. Breathe out through your mouth. As you exhale, consciously release any tension along with your breath. Take a few moments to let go of anything that is weighing you down. Picture each one of your worries and concerns as a helium-filled balloon—then release them, one by one, and watch them float off into the sky.

Grounding is the process of creating a firm connection between yourself and the material world. In the physical world, an electrical current will flow through any available conductor until it reaches the ground. If you happen to be unfortunate enough to get in the way, electricity will use your body as a conductor. When you read Tarot cards, you run a similar risk of getting in the way of free-flowing emotional and spiritual energy. If you are properly grounded, however, you can avoid the shock of discovering that you are suddenly the recipient of someone else's problems, issues, and concerns. Grounding will help their energy flow through you, so you can remain relatively unaffected by the runaway emotions of other people.

One easy way to ground is to sit with your feet firmly on the floor. Place your hands in your lap, and become aware of your body. Close your eyes and imagine that you are a tree. Pretend that your feet have grown roots. Send those roots deep into the earth, down through the floor of the room you are in, down through the layers of bedrock beneath the building, down toward the center of the earth. Next, imagine that your arms are branches growing toward the heavens, reaching up into the sky, through the clouds, and into the bright sunshine. Imagine how stable you would feel, firmly planted in the ground, with your limbs free to sway gently in the breeze.

Shielding is the process of screening yourself from interference and unwanted energy. In the physical world, the air is filled with electrical energy. Some of that energy is naturally occurring. Some is emitted by electrical devices and appliances. And some is transmitted, like radio waves.

Each type of energy in the physical world has a counterpart in the spiritual world. If you are in the same room with another person, you will find yourself in their energy field. Some people emit their worries and concerns unconsciously, while others consciously transmit their issues to anyone within range. If you are planning to read Tarot cards for another person, shielding can help you make it clear that you are simply looking at their cards—and that you are not taking on their problems or assuming responsibility for their decisions. Shielding can help make those boundaries clear.

One way to shield is to picture yourself surrounded by pure white light. Imagine that the white light works like a force field, protecting you from any negative thoughts and emotions.

In addition to cleansing, centering, grounding, and shielding, many Tarot readers begin each session with a prayer for guidance from a higher power. Some use prayers drawn from their own spiritual traditions. Others use prayers or invocations that they write themselves, like this one by Aleister Crowley, who designed the Thoth Tarot deck: *I invoke thee, Lord, that thou wilt send the great Angel that is set over the operations of this secret Wisdom, to lay his hand invisibly upon these consecrated cards of art, that thereby we may obtain true knowledge of hidden things to the glory of thine ineffable Name. Amen.*

No matter what the source, opening visualizations and prayers are intended to help Tarot readers connect with a higher power, to draw strength and wisdom, and to clarify and communicate their intention—their ultimate goal of a productive Tarot reading.

Prepare Your Partner

When you read Tarot cards for yourself, you are both the reader and the *querent*—the person who has a question for the cards. (The word querent is derived from "query," which means "inquiry" or "question.") When you read cards for yourself, you will be actively engaged in a dialogue with the cards. When you read Tarot cards for someone else, however, a third voice will be added to the discussion. Your session will be, in essence, a three-way conversation. To some extent, you may be serving as a translator between the cards and the querent. For the most part, however, your session should be a joint effort between you and the querent, and you should actively solicit his or her input. No one knows your querents' own experiences, hopes, and fears as well as they do. Their insights and ideas can be a valuable aid in deciphering the cards.

When you are interpreting the cards for someone else, think of it as a working partnership—and make sure that both of you are reading from the same page. Before the reading begins in earnest, you may want to take a few minutes to explain how Tarot cards work and describe your method of reading the cards. Some of the people who ask you for a reading might be new to the Tarot, which can make them nervous or anxious about what they will hear. Many need reassurance and a general guide to the mystery that is about to unfold. Take time to describe the steps you will take together.

Before you start reading the cards, make sure that you are alone. Tarot readings are private, even intimate, events. They are not designed for family viewing or audience participation. While some Tarot readers don't mind onlookers, most do. For one thing, the mere presence of another person can confuse your reading. You might start to interpret cards for your querent, only to find that none of the cards or your explanations makes sense to him or her—until a nearby observer meekly announces, "I think that's about me." More commonly, bystanders can be distracting. Some may feel compelled to interject their own observations and volunteer their own interpretations of the cards. Their comments might be accurate, but they will also interrupt the flow of your own impressions. Spectators might also interfere with the course of the reading by suggesting new avenues of inquiry and exploration that don't originate with the querent. Especially assertive or aggressive bystanders may actually hijack the reading; they might as well elbow both the reader and the querent out of their chairs and take over. Occasionally, the presence of others may keep shy or modest querents from asking about issues that are on their minds. In the worst-case scenario, your querent might unexpectedly find his or her most intensely personal issues come to life in the cards, right there for nearby friends and family to see. It is your obligation as a Tarot reader to protect your querents' privacy and the confidentiality of your readings. If you are certain of your skill as a reader, you may be willing to take the risk of allowing spectators. As a rule of thumb, however, it's a good idea to keep your readings private.

Traditionally, Tarot readers sit directly across from their querents. By sitting face to face, you can see the querent clearly, gauge their reactions to the cards, and clarify any confusing or troubling cards. Unfortunately, that arrangement usually leaves the querent looking at a bunch of cards that are upside down. If you like, you can choose to sit side by side. It is a bit unorthodox, but it can be remarkably effective. Any way you choose to sit is fine, as long as you can see the cards clearly. Feel free to experiment until you find a seating arrangement that feels natural and works for you.

Chapter Eight

Tarot Ethics

Before you start throwing Tarot cards around the room, make sure you won't bruise any-body with your predictions. The cards are heavier than they look.

The Do's and Don'ts of Tarot Reading

The Tarot is a powerful tool for studying any situation. The cards can clarify your position, pinpoint your strengths and weaknesses, and demonstrate how events and other people could affect you. Tarot cards can show you the path you are currently on, as well as the course you are most likely to follow. Tarot cards can even pinpoint areas of your life that need attention, whether you realize it or not. What's more, Tarot can suggest a range of solutions to your problems and show you likely outcomes for each.

Obviously, the Tarot is a powerful tool that can do a lot of good. Like any tool, however, it can also do damage. Unfortunately, some practitioners have been known to use the cards to frighten and misguide. That's why first-rate Tarot readers abide by certain ethical guidelines in their use of the cards.

A conscientious Tarot reader, for example, will never predict death for anyone. For one thing, even the most experienced reader can occasionally misinterpret the significance of a card. Secondly, the future is always uncertain, and a seemingly bleak situation could turn around—perhaps because of a reading.

Likewise, experienced Tarot readers try not to alarm others with descriptions of catastrophic illnesses or injury. If you are reading cards for someone else and you feel that you simply must say something about a health problem or an injury, suggest that the querent see a physician for a routine checkup, get extra rest, or pay attention to any symptoms of poor health.

In fact, you should take great care to buffer any negative information you see in the cards. Instead, try to describe the positive forces that are at work, and point out steps that your querent can take to improve his or her situation.

To protect both yourself and your querent, don't use Tarot cards to dispense legal, medical, or financial advice. If your querents are facing life-threatening problems or challenges with far-reaching ramifications, encourage them to consult a specialist.

Likewise, try to discourage people from making important decisions solely based on a Tarot card reading. When it comes to life-altering choices, the cards should be just one factor out of many considerations.

While romance readings can be a remarkably effective way of analyzing your relationships and assessing your romantic prospects, they can also raise some troubling ethical issues. Instead of asking the cards about your own life, it is often tempting to skip over the information you already know and ask the cards about other people. Unfortunately, that could be a serious violation of other people's privacy—and it could even come back to haunt you.

You shouldn't read Tarot cards simply to find out what's happening in other people's private lives, and you shouldn't use Tarot cards to try to read someone else's thoughts or gauge their emotions. After all, you probably wouldn't want your friends and relatives looking into your personal life without asking you first. In fact, the very act of attempting to pry into other people's privacy will frequently set off a cosmic cause-and-effect chain reaction. You might even call it "instant karma." Once you start trying to peek into the private lives of other people, you might suddenly realize that others are suddenly trying to pry into your affairs.

If you have already made the mistake of asking questions about someone else without knowing you were crossing an ethical boundary, don't worry. If you really didn't mean any harm, you can just write it off as an innocent mistake. You probably didn't learn much from your session, anyway. For one thing, it's hard to get a clear reading about someone who isn't aware of a Tarot reading, isn't part of the dialogue, and can't give feedback. In addition, there are certain cosmic protections in place when it comes to metaphysical tools like the Tarot. Beginners usually have a hard time accessing any information that is off-limits.

It's best to limit your Tarot readings to questions that directly pertain to your own life and your own thoughts. There are times, of course, when you can ethically ask the cards about another person—as long as you are motivated by the right reasons, consider your questions carefully, and are willing to live with any repercussions. It is perfectly okay, for example, to use Tarot cards to look for ways that you can help others and improve your relationships with them.

You may wish to adopt or adapt the following code of ethics for your own work with the cards, which is loosely based on one code provided by the American Tarot Association.

A Tarot Reader's Code of Ethics

- I will treat you with respect.
- I will do my best to answer any questions you have during your Tarot reading.
- I will be open. I will not use Tarot cards to secretly pry into anyone else's private life.
- I will be objective. I will try to keep my own opinions and beliefs out of your reading.
- I will be truthful. I will not lie, exaggerate, or disguise what I see in the cards.
- I will be optimistic. I will use Tarot cards to show you how you can make the most of your current situation.
- I will be honest. I will not use Tarot cards to trick you or cheat you.
- If I charge money for a Tarot reading, I will charge a fair price based on my experience and expertise. I will also tell you the full cost of the reading before we begin.
- I will keep your reading confidential. Unless I have reasonable cause to suspect that someone's life, safety, or health is in danger, I will not discuss your reading with anyone.

Chapter Nine

Popping the Question

The best readings come from questions that are thoughtful, clear, and direct. The better you phrase your question, the better your answer will be.

The Heart of the Matter

When most people sit down for a Tarot reading, they ask questions that seem straight and to the point. Romance readings typically focus on a few tried-and-true inquiries, like "Who loves me?" "Is my partner faithful?" and "When will I find love?"

It would be great if you could answer questions as quickly and easily as some people expect. Just pick a card, and you could tell someone to check out the dark-haired accountant in the next cubicle, or get a divorce lawyer, or eat lunch at the deli on December 20, because that's where he or she is destined to meet his or her soul mate.

In the real world, however, it isn't that simple. While the Tarot can make the occasional prediction, its reputation as a fortune-telling device is greatly exaggerated. In reality, the Tarot is a mirror. The cards offer a thought-provoking way to discover and explore your avenues for change. They can even depict the most likely outcome of your current path. Sadly, however, they rarely give clear answers to quick questions.

The key to conducting an effective Tarot reading is to find the quest behind every question—the thinly veiled hopes and dreams that most people are too afraid or too self-conscious to voice aloud. Then you can help your querents put their quest into words. Once you discover which quest each querent is on, you can develop a question that will elicit a clear and specific response.

Take, for example, a common inquiry: When will I find love?

People who ask that usually aren't looking for a specific date to pencil into their appointment books. They are really asking about a whole range of related issues: Will I find love? Can I find love? Why haven't I found love? Don't I deserve to be loved? How do I find love? Where should I look? What will I find? And what do I do in the meantime?

Here is how you can get to the heart of the matter and discover the quest that is hidden in every question.

Start by gathering some background information. Ask your querent the reason for the question. Ask about the circumstances that have led up to the question. Ask why your querent decided to take action and get a Tarot reading today—rather than last month, or last week, or sometime in the future.

Then, even before you pull a single card, ask your querent what answer they want to receive. Ask what answer they think they will hear—and, finally, ask what answer they dread most.

Once you have explored the issues at the heart of their quest, you can help your client refine and rephrase their original question in light of the new information you have developed together. Avoid questions that might elicit yes-or-no answers. Instead, encourage your querents to ask about situations, and be as clear and specific as possible.

Rather than asking, "Will I find love?" for example, you will get more insight—and more information—from related questions like: What do I have to offer a partner? What do I want from a relationship? What should I expect from a relationship? How can I be more attractive to prospective partners? What should I do to find a partner? Where should I look for love? How can I be ready for love? and, of course, How can I be happily single in the meantime?

Don't be surprised to discover that your querents already know the answers to the questions you develop. A Tarot reading based on a thorough examination of the issues surrounding their initial question will help querents put their feelings into words, clarify their hopes, and make decisions and plans they can implement once the reading is done and the cards are put away.

Refining Common Questions

Here are some common questions about love and romance, along with suggestions for refining, expanding, and exploring those questions in a Tarot reading.

Instead of asking:	Try asking:
Will I find love?	How do I feel about love?
	How do I feel about the prospect of a new relationship?
	How would I feel if I were in a relationship?
	What do I want from a relationship?
	What do I expect from a relationship?
	What should I expect from a relationship?
	What should I look for in a partner?
Why haven't I found love yet?	What kind of people do I attract?
	What kind of people do I find attractive?
	Why have my other relationships ended?
	What lessons have I learned from my past relationships?
	How will those lessons help me with future relationships?
	What is keeping me from starting a new relationship?
	What relationship advice do I need right now?
When will I find love?	What do I have to offer a partner?
	What are my strengths?
	What are my weaknesses?
	What are my hopes?
	What are my fears?
	What do I expect from a relationship?

Instead of asking:	Try asking:
When will I find love?	What should I expect from a relationship?
	What should I do to find a partner?
	How can I be more attractive to prospective partners?
	Where should I look for love?
	How can I be ready for love?
	How can I be happily single in the meantime?
How does _____ feel about me?	Should I call _____?
What does _____ think of me?	Should I pursue _____?
	Should I date _____?
	How do I feel about _____?
	What role do I play in _____'s life?
	What role does _____ play in my life?
	What do I know about _____?
	What don't I know about _____?
	What should I know about _____?
	How would I feel if I were in a relationship with _____?
Which suitor should I choose? (1) or (2)?	What does (1) have to offer me?
	What does (2) have to offer me?
	How would I feel if I were with (1)?
	How would I feel if I were with (2)?
Are _____ and I compatible?	What first attracted me to _____?
Are _____ and I soul mates?	What did _____ first think was attractive about me?
	What keeps me in a relationship with _____?
	What keeps _____ in a relationship with me?
	What are our strengths as a couple?
	What are our weaknesses?
	How do we communicate?
	What do we give each other?
	What do we take from each other?
	How do we help each other?
	How do we hurt each other?
	How can we make the most of our relationship?

Instead of asking:	**Try asking:**
Does _____ love me?	How does _____ feel about me?
	How does _____ feel about our relationship?
Is _____ faithful to me?	How does _____ feel about me spiritually?
	How does _____ feel about me emotionally?
	What does _____ think about me intellectually?
	How does _____ view me physically?
	How does _____ feel about other people?
	How does _____ feel about his commitment to me?
	Why do I feel insecure?
Should I stay with _____?	What have I learned about _____?
Should I break up with _____?	What do I still need to learn about _____?
Do I have a future with _____?	What has _____ taught me about myself?
	What lessons have we learned as a couple?
	What lessons must we still master?
	How will I feel about _____ in six months?
	How will I feel about _____ in one year?
	How will I feel about _____ five years from now?
Will I be married?	How do I feel about marriage?
Should I be married?	How would I feel if I were married?
Will _____ propose?	What would I like about marriage?
Will _____ and I be married?	What would I dislike about marriage?
Should _____ and I be married?	How would I feel if I were married to _____?
	What would I like about being married to _____?
	What would I dislike about being married to _____?

No matter what question you choose, remember that the Tarot is not a mysterious, all-knowing oracle that reveals your inevitable fate. Rather, the Tarot is a way for you to discover your own best road to success. The Tarot can help you see your most likely future and give you the chance to change that future if you choose. Remember, it's the choices you make—perhaps as a result of a reading—that will determine the outcome of any situation.

Chapter Ten

Playing the Field

You have selected a deck. You have prepared your space, yourself, and your reading part-
ner. You have even decided what your question will be. Now it's time to cut the cards and
get to work. Here is a step-by-step method for reading Tarot cards that will work whether
you're looking at a single card or a seventy-eight-card spread.

Your Significant Other

Many Tarot spreads call for one card in the spread, the *significator*, to signify or represent the querent. The significator is usually the first card to be selected during a reading. There are a number of ways to choose a significator.

1. Let the deck choose

This is the simplest, fastest way to find a significator. Simply shuffle the deck for the
reading, as you would for any spread. Lay the first card down as the significator, and
proceed with the rest of the spread from there.

2. Follow your instincts

Either hold the deck in your hands or lay all the cards face down on a table. Mix the cards randomly, without looking at them, and pull one that "feels" right to you. You can also use a pendulum—a ring, a crystal, or any object hanging from a string—to find a significator. Simply hold your pendulum over the cards, without consciously trying to make it move, and it will swing back and forth over the card you should use.

3. Go by age

Historically, many Tarot readers have selected the significator based on the age of the querent. Use Pages for children, Knights for young men and women, and Queens or Kings for mature adults.

4. Look at your querent

You can also base your selection on physical appearance. Wands usually represent people with fair skin and blonde, red, or auburn hair. Cups stand for those with light-to-medium skin, light brown, blonde, or gray hair, and blue or hazel eyes. Swords are chosen for people with olive skin, brown or black hair, and light eyes, and Pentacles characterize people with dark skin, dark brown or black hair, and dark eyes. However, the appearance method only works if you happen to have a deck that mirrors the cultural background of your querent. If you are reading for a friend who happens to be Asian, and your deck is full of blonde, blue-eyed court cards, the selection process won't work very well. Happily, many Tarot decks on today's market are designed to be more inclusive, and some include images from a wide range of cultures. You might want to shop around for a deck that reflects your own cultural background, as well as that of the people you know.

5. Suit yourself

You can even ask your querents to choose their own significators. Simply let them look through the deck and choose the card they like best. Ask them to select a card that seems to depict their questions, concerns, or situations. Letting querents choose their own significator is remarkably effective, for three reasons: First, it acquaints querents with the deck and makes them feel more comfortable with the wide range of illustrations on the cards. Many people are a little afraid of the Tarot, because most people are only acquainted with the more frightening images they've seen on television or in the movies. Second, having the querent handle each card imbues the deck with their energy. Finally, because Tarot symbolism is so intuitive, the card they select often is a clear representation of the issue that concerns them most.

6. Follow the Sun

Tarot readers with a background in astrology commonly choose a significator based on the Sun sign of the querent. If you would like to try it, here is a handy outline of the Major Arcana cards and court cards associated with each sign:

Aries (March 21–April 20) The Emperor and the Queen of Wands

Taurus (April 21–May 20) The Hierophant and the King of Pentacles

Gemini (May 21–June 20) The Lovers and the Knight of Swords

Cancer (June 21–July 22) The Chariot and the Queen of Cups

Leo (July 23–August 23) Strength and the King of Wands

Virgo (August 24–September 22) The Hermit and the Knight of Pentacles

Libra (September 23–October 23) Justice and the Queen of Swords

Scorpio (October 24–November 21) Death and the King of Cups

Sagittarius (November 22–December 21) Temperance and the Knight of Wands

Capricorn (December 22–January 20) The Devil and the Queen of Pentacles

Aquarius (January 21–February 18) The Star and the King of Swords

Pisces (February 19–March 20) The Moon and the Knight of Cups

Mix It Up

Once you have determined what the question will be, shuffle the cards. Keep the question in mind as you work.

The most effective shuffle is a poker-style shuffle. Shuffle the deck seven times: not only is seven a mystical number, but it also randomizes the cards fairly well.

If you want to minimize the number of reversals in your spread, make sure both halves of the deck are facing the same direction when you shuffle them.

You may want to avoid bending the cards excessively by implementing an overhand shuffle. Use your dominant hand—which is usually the right hand—to pull a few cards from the deck and drop them back into your other hand. Simply mix the cards until you feel they are ready to read.

You can also use a slush pile to mix the cards. Simply put all of the cards face down on a table, and "stir" them with your hands.

Spread the Cards

Once the cards are shuffled, ask the querent to cut the deck into three piles. Typically, the querent then uses his or her left hand, which is associated with the unconscious, to cut the deck into three piles.

If you like, you can turn over the top card in each pile for a quick mini-reading: The three cards may represent the past, present, and future of the situation. The card on the bottom of each stack often represents unconscious factors and motivations that influence a reading or hidden or unseen forces that are at work.

Put the deck back together, and then lay out the cards, face down. Start with a basic three-card spread, or try one of the layouts in chapter 12.

Whether you use a simple three-card spread or a more complex Celtic Cross, you should know in advance what each card position represents and have a time line in mind for the response.

Read Out Loud

To read the cards, turn them over from right to left, just as you would turn the pages in a book. Try to avoid flipping the cards end over end. That way, upright cards remain upright, and reversals can be easily spotted. Most of the cards should be oriented toward you, so you're not looking at the images upside-down. After you examine the cards carefully, you can turn them around so your querent can have a better look.

As you turn each card over, say its name aloud. "This card," you might say, "is the Ace of Pentacles."

Many beginning Tarot readers feel embarrassed and worry about saying the wrong thing. Don't think about how you sound—just say anything and everything that comes to mind. Verbalizing your impressions will help you assess each card, and you may even surprise yourself with the accuracy of your insight and intuition.

If the card is from the Major Arcana, explain that it may represent forces beyond your querent's control, and discuss what you know about its archetype. Describe each figure's clothing, posture, expressions, and attitudes, and relate the image directly to the querent. If you are looking at the Hermit, for example, you might say, "This card depicts you as something of a hermit. You are wearing a cloak and a hood. You may be using the cloak to protect yourself from the weather, or you might be using it to seem more anonymous. Your long white beard shows that you have lived a long time, and you have probably accumulated some wisdom along the way. You hold a lamp high, to light your path and to show others the way."

If the card is from the Minor Arcana, summarize what you know about the suit. "Pentacles," you might say, "represent physical concerns. Pentacles are material. They can be seen, felt, touched, and put away. They can represent money or property. They can also symbolize spiritual and emotional treasures—the values we hold dear, the memories that are close to our hearts, the people and things we love most and carry with us always."

Now start describing the card. You can go on at some length in simply describing the images in each card. As you do, you will notice details you may never have seen before. Point out the symbols and images that strike you as especially important. A bird, for example, might represent freedom. A bright, sunny sky could indicate bright days ahead. Also, allow the cards to remind you of stories from your childhood, such as the biblical account of Adam and Eve, or Greek and Roman myths, or fairy tales. Don't be afraid to draw upon your expertise in specialized knowledge or field of interest, such as psychology, business, health care, or parenting.

Describe the landscape and the sky in the card. Is it morning or night? What time is it? What is the weather like? What is the temperature? What sounds would you hear if you were actually in the card? What would you smell? Where would you wander for a closer look?

Pay attention to the color schemes in the card. What are the predominant colors? What mood do they convey? What accent colors are used? What do they add to the card's meaning?

Look at the number assigned to the card, and discuss its relevancy. Remember that Minor Arcana cards run from Aces to Tens, beginning to end. Likewise, cards One through Seven in the Major Arcana may represent beginning phases, Eight through Fourteen the middle, and Fifteen through Twenty-one the culmination and conclusion of a series of events.

When you read Tarot cards for someone else, the process is collaborative. Your querent's insights and analysis can be a valuable addition to a Tarot reading. Some readers like the querents to comment and ask questions about each card during the course of the reading. Others would rather have the querents wait for the discussion, so that their initial impressions can flow uninterrupted. In either case, you can encourage querents to find a connection to the cards. Here are some questions you can try:

- What do you notice first about each card?
- What do you like about each one?
- What do you dislike?
- What do these cards remind you of?
- Who do these cards remind you of?
- How do these cards make you feel?
- How do these cards relate to your situation?

If you would like to add even more depth and drama to the reading, experiment with standing or sitting like the figures in the card. Simply assuming the posture will add new insight into the meaning and the message of the card.

Analyze This

Once all of the cards have been turned face up, take a slower, longer look. Go back through the spread to compile an overview description of the spread. You will want to note a number of issues:

1. Take attendance

Determine how many of the cards are from the Major Arcana, and how many of the cards are from the Minor Arcana. If most of the cards are Major Arcana cards, your querent is dealing with a period of powerful, cosmic forces and change. If most of the cards are Minor Arcana cards, you are probably looking at a quiet, routine period.

2. Suit yourself

Determine which suits are most prominent. Wands stand for spiritual matters, Cups symbolize emotional affairs, Swords represent intellectual concerns, and Pentacles represent material issues.

3. Do the math

Conduct a quick count of the numbers on each card. If most of the Minor Arcana cards in the spread have low numbers, such as Aces, Twos, and Threes, the querent is just beginning a cycle. If most of the numbers are Fours, Fives, and Sixes, the querent is in the thick of things. If the numbers are Sevens, Eights, and Nines, the querent is near the end of a phase. Tens signify successful completion and preparation for a new cycle.

4. Pair off

Describe and explain any significant pairs and combinations. Keep your eyes open for a preponderance of any one suit, or pairs, or runs, or even poker-style full houses. Look for obvious partnerships, such as the King and Queen of Swords or the Empress and the Emperor. Also, pay attention to diametrical opposites, such as the Devil and the Archangel of Temperance.

Astrologically, the Major Arcana cards that correspond to each of the twelve astrological signs and their ruling planets are powerful pairs:

- The Emperor (Aries) and the Tower (Mars)
- The Hierophant (Taurus) and the Empress (Venus)
- The Lovers (Gemini) and the Magician (Mercury)
- The Chariot (Cancer) and the High Priestess (the Moon)
- Strength (Leo) and the Sun (the Sun)
- The Hermit (Virgo) and the Magician (Mercury)
- Justice (Libra) and the Empress (Venus)
- Death (Scorpio) and Judgment (Pluto)
- Temperance (Sagittarius) and the Wheel of Fortune (Jupiter)
- The Devil (Capricorn) and the World (Saturn)
- The Star (Aquarius) and the Fool (Uranus)
- The Moon (Pisces) and the Hanged Man (Neptune)

Body Language

The body language of the figures in your Tarot deck can be an important key to the meanings of the cards. Look at the physical relationships of the characters in the spread.

Who is coming into the spread? Who is leaving the spread? Who is facing whom? Which ones are having a conversation? Which ones are saying the exact same thing? Which ones are contradicting the others? Who is avoiding whom?

Look for indications that some of the cards might be representing common interests. Which characters share similar expressions, poses, or costumes? Which characters seem to be in the same general setting, with similar landscapes and backgrounds? Which cards are similar in color or tone?

Reversal of Fortune

During the course of normal shuffling, cards are flipped upside down. Some readers never use reversals; they simply turn every card to its upright position. After all, every card in the deck can trigger both positive and negative reactions. You might be thrilled when the Knight of Wands rides into a reading, or he might be the last person you want to see. The moon might represent a mystical interlude, or it could mean you are in for a long, dark night of the soul.

If you choose to use reversals, you can also interpret them in a wide range of styles. While some people believe that reversed cards simply reverse a card's upright meaning, others believe that topsy-turvy cards are simply vaulting and somersaulting in order to get attention during a reading. In her 2002 book, *The Complete Book of Tarot Reversals*, noted Tarot expert Mary K. Greer has identified at least twelve ways to read upside-down cards. For example, they could represent energy that is being blocked, repressed, or projected onto others. Reversed cards might also describe energy that is either delayed or developing, absent or excessive, misused or misdirected, or even playful.

Read 'Em and Weep

Tarot readings are brutally honest. Sometimes there is no knight in shining armor, and sometimes that beguiling creature really is the Devil.

While we might cringe when the Three of Swords shows up in a reading, most of the fun and learning that comes from a Tarot reading is grounded in the cards' honesty and apparent objectivity.

Here are ten ways to make the most of the answers you didn't want to hear.

1. Deal with it
Nobody expects to hear all good news, all the time. Sometimes, negative cards are just a fact of life. A Pollyanna Tarot reading that only included shiny, happy cards wouldn't resonate with most people. It wouldn't seem believable, and it wouldn't necessarily apply to real life.

2. Be evenhanded
Get into the habit of discussing the positive and negative aspects of every card in the spread—not just the usual suspects, like Death and the Ten of Swords. The sun, for example, has the power to burn and dehydrate, not just shoot happy sunbeams all over the place.

3. Change your perspective
Recognize that Tarot cards reflect the full range of human experiences. They depict comfortable situations, as well as uncomfortable ones. For most people, challenges can be opportunities for learning, growth, and change.

4. Don't take it literally
Remember, the images in the Tarot cards are metaphors. They symbolize events that are happening on an emotional, spiritual, and intellectual level, as well as in the physical world. When was the last time you saw someone tied to a tree and blindfolded, anyway?

5. Tone it down
If there is any chance that a card could be literal, discuss it in terms of possibilities that might not be so shocking. The Tower card could simply refer to an oncoming thunderstorm, for example, that might knock out power for an hour or two.

6. Check the history books
Remember what other negative cards may have suggested in your previous readings, and look for parallels that might apply to your current situation.

7. Ask for clarification
Lay new cards on top of any cards that seem confusing or unclear.

8. Get advice

Pull additional cards for suggestions on how you can make the most of your existing situation.

9. Find the moral of the story

Ask the cards what lessons you will learn from a negative experience. Even when the cards predict a less-than-desirable outcome, the surprisingly frank cards can shock us into facing reality and acknowledging the difficulties we face.

10. Keep your sense of humor

Sometimes, Tarot cards simply like to pull your leg. If you're not sure that they're serious cards, check them again in a day or two.

Happily Ever After

Try to end each reading on a positive note. If you are reading for someone else, offer a final summary of the spread, and make sure they have understood everything you've said during the reading.

Also, look for specific action that you can take as a result of the reading. You don't have to make any life-changing decisions, but plan to do one thing based on the advice of the cards—like go to the movies or take a walk under the full moon.

Once your session has concluded, you might want to make a note of it for your own records. Keep a journal of your readings and your reactions to the cards.

You may want to develop a specific ritual for ending each reading, as a signal both to your subconscious mind and to your querent that the session is done. If you have a candle burning during your readings, for example, blow it out when you are done.

Put your cards away. Some Tarot readers return each card in the deck to an upright position. Some "seal" the deck by placing favorite cards on the top and bottom. Some wrap their cards in silk or place them in a special wooden box, traditionally stored above head level, to protect the cards from unwelcome psychic vibrations.

Finally, stand up, stretch, and leave the room. The reading is ended; go in peace.

Chapter Eleven

The Dating Game

We all want to know when something will happen. From the time we can talk—as small children, riding in the backseat—we want to know when we'll get to our destination.

The Clock Is Ticking

Once you have seen a happy future in the cards, you probably want to know when you can expect it to arrive. When will that Knight of Swords come to your rescue? When will the girls in the Three of Cups cast a wry glance your way? When will your life change inexorably for the better?

Unfortunately, there is no proven way to determine the timing of any given event—in part, because the Tarot is symbolic, not literal. The Tarot is from another realm—a world where time is not always linear. The cards are from a parallel reality, a dream-world that is separate from our physical existence. Events speed up and slow down on behalf of our souls, not our Timexes.

What's more, the Tarot describes trends, not certainties. People have free will; you might even change course because of a Tarot reading. You can make decisions that will alter your path, so that even the most likely outcome of any given situation will change.

However, if you would like to determine when events will unfold, there are several techniques you can try. Obviously, there is no guarantee, but they might help you make an educated guess about when the Tarot's predictions will come true. Just don't set your watches by them.

1. Include a time frame in your query

Ask questions that refer to a specific period of time, such as next week, next month, or next year. If you forget to specify a time frame and ask an open-ended question, you might get a vague and confusing answer that could either be accurate next week—or twenty years from now.

2. Check the numbers

Look at the numbers of each card in question. A Two may indicate an occurrence in two days, two weeks, two months, or two years.

3. Look at planetary symbols

Illustrations of the moon, which waxes and wanes over the course of twenty-eight days, often signify a period of about a month. The appearance of the Sun card might suggest an event that will happen in a year, or at the same time as a birthday, anniversary, or other annual event.

4. Determine the season

Look for symbols and illustrations that clearly depict spring, summer, fall, and winter.

5. Follow suit

Wands cards correspond to spring, Cups cards correspond to summer, Swords cards correspond to fall, and Pentacles cards correspond to winter.

6. Use a linear spread

Lay your cards in a row, and read them from right to left. The farther you go down the line, the farther an event will be in the future.

7. Look to the stars

One of the most precise ways to determine timing in the Tarot is to use astrological correspondences.

Aries: The Emperor, the Two, Three, and Four of Wands, and the Queen of Wands correspond to the sign of Aries, from March 21 to April 20.

Taurus: The Hierophant, the Five, Six, and Seven of Pentacles, and the King of Pentacles correspond to Taurus, from April 21 to May 20.

Gemini: The Lovers, the Eight, Nine, and Ten of Swords, and the King of Swords correspond to Gemini, from May 21 to June 20.

Cancer: The Chariot, the Two, Three, and Four of Cups, and the Queen of Cups correspond to Cancer, from June 21 to July 22.

Leo: Strength, the Five, Six, and Seven of Wands, and the King of Wands correspond to Leo, from July 23 to August 23.

Virgo: The Hermit, the Eight, Nine, and Ten of Pentacles, and the Knight of Pentacles correspond to Virgo, from August 24 to September 22.

Libra: Justice, the Two, Three, and Four of Swords, and the Queen of Swords correspond to Libra, from September 23 to October 23.

Scorpio: Death, the Five, Six, and Seven of Cups, and the King of Cups correspond to Scorpio, from October 24 to November 21.

Sagittarius: Temperance, the Eight, Nine, and Ten of Wands, and the Knight of Wands correspond to Sagittarius, from November 22 to December 21.

Capricorn: The Devil, the Two, Three, and Four of Pentacles, and the Queen of Pentacles, correspond to Capricorn, from December 22 to January 20.

Aquarius: The Star, the Five, Six, and Seven of Swords, and the King of Swords correspond to Aquarius, from January 21 to February 18.

Pisces: The Moon, the Eight, Nine, and Ten of Cups, and the Knight of Cups correspond to Pisces, from February 19 to March 20.

Chapter Twelve

Spreads and Layouts

The first Tarot card spread we have on record is the layout that Casanova's young lover Zaira used, back in 1765. When she wanted to know what Casanova was up to, she consulted twenty-five cards laid out in five rows of five cards each.

Spread Your Wings

Most Tarot card spreads—the layouts, patterns, or designs we use to arrange the cards for a reading—are designed with a specific purpose in mind. Some spreads are intended to offer a specific question. Others are designed to offer an overview of a situation.

Spreads and layouts can be as simple or as elaborate as you like. Some spreads call for just a single card, while others incorporate ten or fifteen cards. One spread even uses every card in a seventy-eight-card deck.

You can use traditional Tarot spreads, or you can create your own layouts. Just make sure that you know what each card in the spread will signify, before you start to read. That way, you will be able to interpret the cards' messages clearly.

Past, Present, Future

One of the most common spreads is a three-card past, present, and future spread that presents each image as a single moment in time. Simply shuffle and cut the deck into three separate piles or deal the top three cards off the top. Read the cards from left to right, just as you would read words on a page.

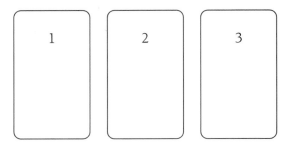

In a romance reading, the first card will represent the past. It can help you review previous relationships, release old regrets, and review the lessons you have learned from your mistakes.

The second card, which represents the present, can help you evaluate your current situation. It can also help you assess your wants and needs, as well as the characteristics and gifts that you could offer someone else in a relationship.

The third card, which offers the most likely outcome of your current path, represents the future. Look to it for concrete suggestions that can help you take control of your destiny and put yourself in the right place at the right time to reach your goals.

Elements of a Relationship

Because the four suits of the Minor Arcana offer insight about every area of your life, a spread based on the four suits can give you a good overview of any romance or relationship issue.

Just as in the Minor Arcana, the card in the first position—the Wands card—will represent your spiritual life. The second card, in the Cups position, will depict your emotional life. The third card, in the Swords place, will symbolize your intellectual life, while the fourth card, the Wands position, will represent your physical existence.

You can even double it up for couples' readings.

Ideally, partnership readings should include both partners, so the cards can serve as the basis of a discussion. Use the cards to help clarify your priorities and to communicate those needs and expectations to a partner. Focus on your strengths and weaknesses as a team—and don't use the cards to attack your partner, pass judgment, or cloak your own attitudes, opinions, and "suggestions" for improvement. The cards, after all, are nonjudgmental, and they can be excellent tools for examining a relationship from both points of view.

The Court Card Consultation

If you like the Elements of a Relationship spread, you can take it a step further and use it solely in conjunction with the court cards.

Court cards frequently represent the facets of your personality or projections of other people in your life. There is much more to the court cards than meets the eye, however. In fact, the court cards are the embodiment of family matters, partnerships, and marriages. The court cards are the de facto relationship experts of the Tarot deck—and they can become your allies in conducting romance readings. You might want to base your next romance reading on this innovative, courts-only spread.

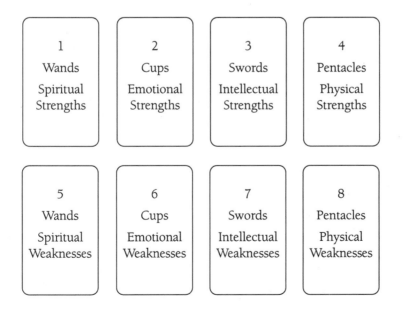

1	2	3	4
Wands	Cups	Swords	Pentacles
Spiritual Strengths	Emotional Strengths	Intellectual Strengths	Physical Strengths

5	6	7	8
Wands	Cups	Swords	Pentacles
Spiritual Weaknesses	Emotional Weaknesses	Intellectual Weaknesses	Physical Weaknesses

First, pull the sixteen court cards out and set the rest of the deck aside. Shuffle them and deal them into two rows of four cards each. The first row will represent your strengths—the gifts and talents you bring to relationships. The second row will represent your weaknesses—or, to be more tactful, the areas in which you have room to improve.

The four cards in each row will each relate to the four suits of the Minor Arcana. The first card in each row will represent spiritual gifts, which are usually represented by the fiery suit of Wands. The second card in each row will represent emotional affairs, which typically correspond to the watery suit of Cups. The third card in each row will represent intellectual issues, like the airy suit of Swords. The fourth card in each row will embody physical matters, the realm of the earthy suit of Pentacles.

Turn over the cards one by one, and assess each one in terms of its traditional significance along with its place in the spread. Pages, for example, symbolize youth, enthusiasm, and an unbounded capacity to learn; they are students and messengers. If the first card in the first row is the Page of Wands, for example, you have a gift for developing the spiritual side of a relationship.

Likewise, Knights are adventurers, eager to embark on sacred quests, defend the helpless, and rescue those in jeopardy. Queens are mature women, gracious and wise in the ways of the world and ready to safeguard and nurture those in their realms. Kings are seasoned, experienced men who have successfully completed the quests they began as knights. They have grown to become authoritative rulers and strong protectors.

Normally, you won't find that a Wands card has fallen in a "Wands" position or that any of the cards fall into their corresponding places in the spread. If a card does fall in its own realm, however, you can probably be assured that the traits associated with it are clear-cut and well-defined.

The Celtic Cross

When Arthur Edward Waite designed his Tarot deck more than a century ago, he developed a corresponding Tarot card layout. Since then, the Celtic Cross—which is pronounced "Keltic," by the way—has become a perennial favorite. It is highly adaptable, and it offers a well-rounded overview of any situation. Here is one version of the classic Celtic Cross:

1. **Significator:** This card represents you.

2. **Covering Card:** This card represents your situation.

3. **Crossing Card:** This card represents the energy of the moment and the forces that are affecting your situation.

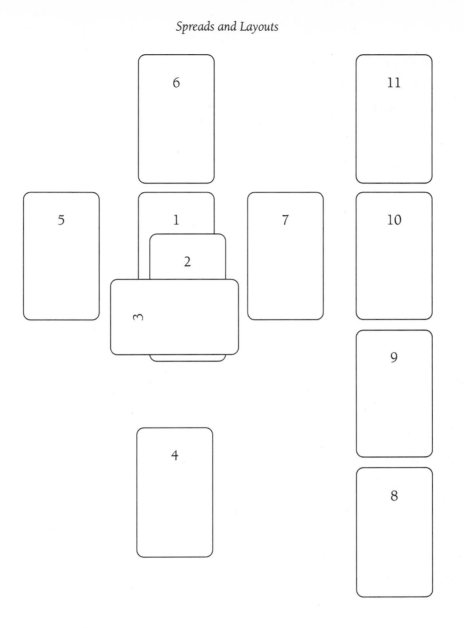

4. **Foundation Card:** This is the foundation of your situation.

5. **Recent Past:** This card represents the last six months to a year.

6. **Crowning Card:** This card represents the most ideal outcome of your current situation.

7. **Near Future:** This card represents the next six months to a year.

8. **Self-image:** This is how you see yourself.

9. **Public Image:** This is how others see you.

10. **Hopes and Fears:** This card represents the dreams you almost don't dare to dream, your hopes and fears, which are two sides of the same coin.

11. **Most Likely Outcome:** This card represents the most likely outcome of your current path, if nothing changes.

Zodiac Spread

Tarot and astrology are inexorably linked. Many practitioners who combine both arts like to use a Tarot card spread based on a horoscope chart, in which each card represents a separate sign of the Zodiac. Lay the cards out in a circle (see spread, next page). Start at the nine o'clock position, and work your way clockwise around the wheel.

1. **Aries:** Your public image and the first impression you make

2. **Taurus:** What you value in a relationship

3. **Gemini:** How you communicate your wants, needs, and desires

4. **Cancer:** How you nurture your partner

5. **Leo:** How you feel when you are the center of attention

6. **Virgo:** How you guard and protect your physical health

7. **Libra:** How you relate to a partner

8. **Scorpio:** How you express your sexuality and physical drives

9. **Sagittarius:** Your philosophy of love and romance

10. **Capricorn:** Your ambition; your public image

11. **Aquarius:** How you visualize the future and express your free-spirited side

12. **Pisces:** The secrets and mysteries of your subconscious; your intuition

Selective Spreads

People who want romance readings are frequently unhappy with their love lives. Their relationships are failing, broken, or nonexistent. Often, they find themselves at a dead end. They don't have a clear picture in mind of what they want for themselves. They only know that they are not happy with their current situation.

Traditionally, Tarot readers have consulted the cards by shuffling and dealing the cards facedown. The cards fall as they will, and a questioner's fate hangs on the luck of

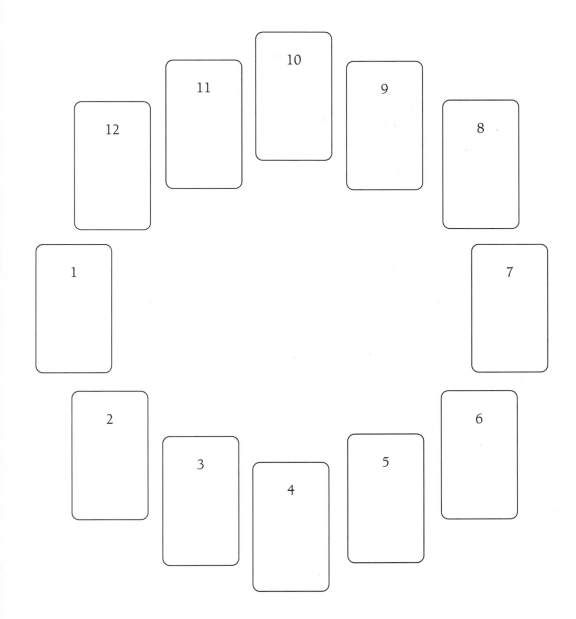

the draw. Until each card in a spread is turned faceup, no one knows what secrets or truths the cards will reveal. The Tarot offers an independent analysis of any situation and an impartial answer to any question.

However, there is no rule that says the cards must be dealt facedown. In fact, it can be just as instructional, insightful, and intuitive to deliberately *choose* the cards you want to appear in the spread.

The process is an extension of what Tarot expert James Wanless terms "fortune creation," rather than "fortune telling." It's active, not passive. It's optimistic and enlightening, and in many ways, it's more interesting than readings that rely upon the luck of the draw.

You can try a selective reading with any spread, from a basic Past-Present-Future layout to the more complex Celtic Cross.

The process is deceptively simple. Shuffle the cards as you focus on your situation. But don't just deal the cards. Instead, go through the deck, faceup. Look at each card, and choose the card you like best for each position in a spread.

Start with a basic past, present, and future spread. First, choose any card you like to represent your past. Generally speaking, it's fairly easy to choose cards to represent the past. Old patterns of behavior are very recognizable in the Tarot. Next, choose a card to depict your present. Finally, choose a third card to illustrate the future you want most.

While the process is simple, a selective reading can be just as time-consuming as traditional readings. That's because selective readings demand a degree of honesty, reflection, and creative visualization that most of us aren't used to. Selective readings can also be just as effective and enlightening as a traditional reading—especially when you are dealing with issues of love and romance.

In selective readings, just as in regular readings, it's important to rely on your intuition. Don't edit yourself. Don't limit yourself.

In fact, the process can be liberating. Rather than meekly waiting for the future to unfold, you can start to visualize the future for yourself and create your own destiny. You can be proactive, rather than reactive. It's easier to fill a void with a positive than a negative. By clarifying in your own mind and heart what you want most, you will be better prepared to spot opportunities, people, and possibilities.

Part II

What's in the Cards

0. The Fool: A Leap of Faith

A young vagabond strolls dangerously close to the edge of a cliff. He seems oblivious to the danger he's in; his face is turned to the sky, and he's gazing far off into the distance. A little white dog nips playfully at his heels. His right hand holds a walking stick, slung nonchalantly across his shoulder, with a small knapsack dangling from the end of the stick. In his right hand, he clutches a red rose. The Fool wears a green cap with a red feather, a black tunic and a long-sleeved white undershirt, yellow leggings, and soft leather boots. Above him, a bright yellow sun fills the sky with illumination and warmth. In the distance, there is a series of snow-capped mountain peaks and a green valley.

While there are twenty-two cards in the Major Arcana, only twenty-one of them are numbered. In most standard Tarot decks, the Fool card stands alone, without a number and without a set place in the order of the cards. Despite the fact that the Fool card is unnumbered, however, many Tarot readers think of it as the first card in the Tarot deck. In that respect, the Fool is a symbol of new beginnings, new journeys, and new adventures.

Some Tarot experts say that the Fool is both the beginning and the end of the Major Arcana. Like the Alpha and the Omega, the first and last letters of the Greek alphabet, the Fool represents the be-all and end-all of the Major Arcana—and every card in between.

Ultimately, the Fool also represents each one of us. The Fool is a new and willing participant in the game of Tarot, as well as the game of life.

In most decks, the Fool is pictured on the edge of a cliff, eyes cast toward the heavens, apparently unconcerned about where his next step will take him. While mountain peaks beckon in the distance, he doesn't seem to notice their existence. Unworried about everyday concerns, he ambles along. He has no set course in mind and no specific goals. He lives for the moment, and he is the original happy wanderer.

In fact, the Fool is an original, a freethinker, an eccentric. He is a vagabond, an adventurer, a drifter, and an explorer. He is impulsive, courageous, fearless, and trusting. His inexperience even makes him naïve, idealistic, and childlike. After all, fools rush in where angels fear to tread, and they rarely look before they leap.

If the Fool takes one more step without looking, however, he may fall—or he may fly. By any account, however, the Fool is about to take a leap of faith. His leap may even symbolize the process of a human soul entering the body. In many traditions, the Fool also represents the physical nature of human existence. As he steps off the cliff, he illustrates the descent of spirit into matter. The image also illustrates the concept that all people embody a spark of the divine and that all of us are a part of God and have a place in the divine plan. It even suggests that our own creations, artistic or not, are divinely inspired.

In most depictions of the card, the Fool wears a feather of victory in his cap, which symbolizes success, acclaim, and praise.

The Fool also carries a red rose in his hand that symbolizes passion, and he slings a knapsack haphazardly over one shoulder. Some experts suggest that the sack contains the Fool's karma—the accumulation, good and bad, of his earthly deeds. If it is the culmination of his existence, it doesn't seem to weigh much. Others suggest that the sack holds symbols of three of the suits of the Minor Arcana: a cusp, a sword, and a pentacle. The walking stick in the Fool's hand represents the suit of Wands. The four tools symbolize everything he'll need to experience a rich, full, and rewarding life.

The white mountain peaks in the distance represent future travels and obstacles to be overcome. The sun overhead represents light and illumination, often from a higher source.

The dog nipping at his heels is a loyal and faithful traveling companion. It may be his conscience, or his subconscious, warning him of danger and heeding him to pay attention. The dog may also represent the taming influence that society has on most of us, transforming us from savage, primal beasts into tame, well-bred creatures of habit.

The Fool's Journey

Many Tarot experts describe the sequence of Major Arcana cards as the "Fool's Journey," because the unnumbered Fool is free to travel through the rest of the deck. As the Fool moves through the sequence of cards, he can step into each one. Like an actor in a play, he can try on the costumes of each of the figures, assume their mannerisms and characteristics, and perform their parts.

In that sense, the Fool serves as a stand-in for the rest of us. We are all playing the lead role in the drama of our own lives. Studying the Fool's Journey makes it easier for us to examine the roles we have already performed. It also makes it possible for us to try out for new parts and even practice our lines for upcoming appearances in future productions. Like the Fool, we are free to skip randomly through the procession or set a straight course through each of the cards.

When you see the Fool card in a romance reading, you may be about to take a giant leap of faith in your current relationship—or fall in love with someone new.

Falling in love is a leap of faith. Falling in love is also a risky proposition. You may make a fool of yourself, or you might find yourself being fooled.

If you are looking for romance, you are beginning a great adventure. It is one small step for a man, but a giant leap for mankind. A journey of a thousand miles begins with a single step—if you are willing to put one foot in front of the other and set out. Even so, you might want to look before you leap.

As an archetype, the Fool might be compared to the simpleton, the trickster, the clown, or the joker. At times, he is naïve, idealistic, and childlike. Sometimes, however, he represents the wise fool—the inverse counterpart to the king. In some royal courts, only the court jester could criticize the king openly and honestly, so many truths were told in jest.

Traditionally, the Fool is known as the spirit of ether, and the card corresponds to the first letter of the Hebrew alphabet, *Aleph*, which means ox.

Astrologically, the Fool is associated with Uranus, the planet of rebellion, as well as the element of air.

I. The Magician: The Power of Love

With one arm raised toward the heavens, the young, dark-haired magician uses his entire body to draw energy from the outside world—and then transforms it through the sheer power of his mind and the force of his will. In a single, swift motion, he points his other arm toward the earth and channels that cosmic energy back into the world.

The Magician is clearly a compelling showman. Even without the impressive costume—a white tunic, belted at the waist and topped with a red cape—his piercing gaze would transfix any audience. He stands behind a wooden table, where he has placed the props he will need for today's show: a golden pentacle, a hefty chalice, a gleaming silver sword, and a heavy wooden bough. Over his head, a lemniscate, the figure-eight symbol of infinity, seems to float in midair.

Audiences are naturally drawn to magicians and fascinated by their performances. Ask people if they want to see a card trick and you'll probably have their complete attention. The art of stage magic, however, is the art of illusion and misdirection. The Magician in the Tarot practices "real" magic, because he literally transforms the world around him.

The Magician in the card might be an older, more experienced version of the Fool. At this stage, he represents an individual in control of life's tools and techniques. He has unpacked his knapsack in order to perform with the tools of his trade—the wand, the cup, the sword, and the pentacle from the Minor Arcana. They foreshadow the four suits of the Minor Arcana, which symbolize spiritual life, emotional life, intellectual life, and physical life.

The lemniscate, the figure eight shape that symbolizes infinity, floats over his head as a constant reminder of the cycle of life. (The lemniscate symbol reappears throughout the deck. It's especially obvious in most versions of Strength and the Two of Pentacles.)

The Magician raises one hand over his head to draw power from the heavens above and channel it into the world below. He loudly chants, "As above, so below," and makes magic happen. His very posture is a reminder that our earthly existence reflects a spiritual reality. With one simple gesture, the Magician reminds us that we have the power to manifest our dreams and ideals to materialize our fondest hopes and wishes, and to create our own reality.

Most stage magicians use wands to direct the attention of their audiences. Their wands are, of course, simply extensions of their arms, and hands, and fingers. We all point when we want others to look at something. Even though the Magician holds a classically proportioned wand—the same length as the distance from his wrist to his elbow—he actually uses his entire body to direct and redirect the cosmic energy that surrounds him. In fact, the atmosphere around the Magician is positively charged with energy and potential.

The Magician is talented and skilled. He is an expressive performer, whose witty banter reveals his self-confidence. He can be crafty and cunning. His hand is quicker than the eye. He is also adaptable and dexterous.

When you see the Magician in a romance reading, there is magic in the air—and, like the Magician, you have the power to control the flow of energy in your relationships. You also have a natural stage presence. When the curtain rises and the spotlight shines on you, you come alive. You've got a few tricks up your sleeve—even if they happen to be Tarot cards. You are comfortable making lively banter and small talk, and you are good at keeping the show moving.

What's more, you cast a powerful spell. In fact, that is one meaning of the word "spell." Historically, only the most powerful people could read and write, because they were the educated, wise ones. When they wrote something down, it carried weight. Their words had power. They changed things. Even today, writing can be a magical act.

When you focus your thoughts and write down your wishes, dreams, and plans, you are actually casting a spell. You're spelling out your intentions. That simple act will help make them real. It pulls them from the ethereal realm of hopes and dreams and gives them a physical existence on the material plane, where they exist as ink on paper. It is one step in literally manifesting your hopes and dreams.

If you are in a relationship, you understand the importance of an assistant when you're performing the big tricks. When you have locked yourself into a box, your assistant offers the audience a distraction as you wriggle your way free.

If you are looking for romance, don't underestimate the importance of your costume. You might want to dress more like a magician, in attractive colors and designs that will let you move. Once you have amazed and astounded your audience, don't give away any of your tricks—because once the secret is out in the open, the magic is gone.

As an archetype, the Magician is often compared to Mercury, the god of speed and communication. He knows how to think clearly, communicate well, move between worlds, and manage multiple realities.

Traditionally, the Magician is sometimes known as the Juggler or the Magus of Power. The card corresponds to the second letter of the Hebrew alphabet, *Beth*, which means house.

Astrologically, the Magician is associated with Mercury, the planet of thought and communication. Some versions of the card incorporate the astrological glyph for Mercury, which depicts the twin serpents entwined around Mercury's *caduceus*, or wand.

II. The High Priestess: Silence Is Golden

A beautiful woman sits quietly. Her face is serene, unlined by worry or concern. She is seated in front of two massive columns: one dark, one light. Between them, a curtain is emblazoned with ripe pomegranates and tall palms. She wears a lunar headpiece with a representation of the waxing, full, and waning moon. A cross hangs from the slender chain around her neck. Her gown is purple, and her cloak is green. Moreover, tucked partially beneath the cloak, she holds a rolled-up scroll in her lap. Just four letters are visible: TORA.

The High Priestess card is often associated with two fascinating legends. According to some Tarot readers, the High Priestess card depicts the fabled Pope Joan—a legendary ninth-century woman who disguised herself as a man and rose through the ranks of the church. Using the name John Anglus, she was elected to the throne of St. Peter, where she served as pope for two years, five months, and four days. Apparently, no one realized that the pope they knew and loved was actually a woman—until, during a procession, she collapsed on the road near St. Peter's and gave birth. She reportedly died within hours. Some say she died of childbirth; others say she was torn apart by a vengeful crowd.

The myth of Pope Joan is difficult to verify, because there are no official church records of her existence. A related story, however, seems to have historical backing. At the end of the thirteenth century, a Guglielmite nun named Sister Manfreda Visconti was elected papess of her order. It was a radical feminist move that her followers hoped would serve to depose Pope Urban VIII. Sister Manfreda was set to usher in a new, feminine age of the church—until the orthodox papacy of Rome put an end to those plans by burning her at the stake in 1300. Her short-lived reign, however, was immortalized in the High Priestess card of the *Visconti-Sforza* Tarot deck that was painted as a wedding gift for her distant cousin, Bianca Maria Sforza.

Obviously, there is a long, rich history of myth and tradition behind the High Priestess card—a history almost as mysterious as the High Priestess herself. In fact, the High Priestess card usually symbolizes the great mysteries of life.

Most versions of the card usually depict an enigmatic young woman with a Mona Lisa smile. She sits between the two pillars of Solomon—one black, one white—with a veil stretched between them. The veil is decorated with palms and pomegranates, symbols of male and female fertility. It represents the curtain that hung in the Temple of Solomon, symbolically separating this world from the next. The High Priestess, however, has the ability to penetrate that veil. She is psychic. She can see into the next world and into the future, and like the ancient Sybils, she has the gift of prophecy. She makes an excellent teacher and guide into the world of spiritual enlightenment.

The High Priestess wears a veiled crown on her head with two crescent horns and a circular orb that depict the waxing, full, and waning moon. Another moon is lying at her feet in the folds of her gown. The moon is commonly used as a symbol of reflection, intuition, and the cyclical nature of life.

The scroll in her lap is the Hebrew Torah, or book of the law. Part of it is hidden under her cape, indicating that some things can not be revealed. Interestingly, the letters can be rearranged to spell "Tarot."

When you see the High Priestess card in a romance reading, you are also naturally intuitive. You seem to have a sixth sense. As a result, you may find that others are naturally drawn to you for guidance and advice. You are able to share the wisdom of your own experience. You see the big picture. Like the High Priestess, you must have your own space—a sacred space where you can read, write, and reflect.

If you are in a relationship, you are probably less dependent on romance than others seem to be. That doesn't mean, however, that you don't value a relationship. You are simply self-reliant, which frees you to take part in relationships with other advisors, counselors, and naturally empathic people.

If you are looking for romance, you could find it where other scholarly, reflective people can be found: a library, a bookstore, a writer's group, a discussion group, an organization of like-minded individuals who share similar experiences.

As an archetype, the High Priestess is often compared to Isis, the Egyptian goddess of love, or Diana, the Roman goddess of the moon.

Traditionally, the High Priestess is sometimes known as the Priestess of the Silver Star. The card corresponds to the third letter of the Hebrew alphabet, *Gimel*, which means camel.

Astrologically, the High Priestess is associated with the Moon, the planet of reflection and intuition.

III. The Empress: Mother Nature

A young blonde woman reclines on a cushioned chair in the middle of a cultivated field. There is a verdant meadow and a grove of budding trees in the background. A clear blue stream winds its way past her. She is wearing a headpiece and holding a scepter; a heart-shaped pillow with the symbol of Venus leans against the base of her chair.

The Tarot's Empress is visibly pregnant—apparently in her fifth or sixth month of pregnancy. That period is a golden time for most women: the morning sickness of the first trimester has abated, they can feel the baby stir and kick with regularity, and they haven't grown too large to move around comfortably herself. Before long, the Empress will celebrate the joy and excitement of birth. Unfortunately, she will also undergo an equal measure of sorrow.

The experience comes as a surprise to most new mothers. From the moment a child is born, a certain amount of loss begins. Suddenly, nine months of joy and anticipation are a thing of the past, replaced by the pain of labor and the demands of a newborn. For the next few weeks or months, it's not unusual for new mothers to mourn the loss of their sleep, their former physical selves, their independence, and their time alone with partners and friends.

Naturally, the joy of giving birth and raising a child outweighs those losses, and most mothers eventually get used to the mixed feelings of joy and sadness they experience as their children grow. Ultimately, a mother's struggle to reconcile those extremes of emotion leads to a profound transformation. The Empress will grow and mature as much as her children do.

When you see the Empress card in a romance reading, you face a similar metamorphosis. For the most part, the Empress symbolizes fertility, creativity, productivity, and fruitfulness. Her appearance promises happiness, pleasure, joy, and success. You will be stronger, wiser, and more compassionate—but your growth will come at a price.

When you see the Empress card in a romance reading, you may soon discover that you have a healthy, attractive glow and that people will be physically drawn to you. Like the Empress, you will have both the energy and the inspiration to produce tangible works of art. At the same time, however, you might also experience the prospect and the pain of losing those you hold dear—if only incrementally. You may be compelled to release your creations. You may want to show them to other people, which could leave you open and vulnerable to their appraisals and criticisms. You might also need to release them, at some point, to make room for new projects.

If you are in a relationship, you may find that your partnership imbues you with the power to create an entire world of relationships.

If you are looking for love, you will probably find it in someone who shares your sense of beauty and creativity. Perhaps Mother Nature herself will draw you to another, at a garden, a park, or a nature preserve. You might find a kindred spirit at an art show, a gallery, a film festival, a craft show, or a museum. While the Empress's creativity refers to creations of all kinds—writing, painting, drawing, and sculpting—it can also indicate that a real, physical pregnancy is a distinct possibility.

As an archetype, the Empress might be compared to Mother Earth or, occasionally, the Virgin Mary. She is frequently associated with Demeter, Greek goddess of the harvest, whose daughter Persephone was kidnapped by Hades, the lord of the underworld. Furious and bereft, Demeter refused to allow crops to grow until Persephone was returned.

Traditionally, the Empress is sometimes known as the Daughter of the Mighty Ones. The card corresponds to the fourth letter of the Hebrew alphabet, *Daleth*, which means door.

Astrologically, the Empress is associated with Venus, the goddess of love and emotion. Some versions of the Empress card incorporate the astrological glyph for Venus, which depicts the mirror of the goddess of beauty.

IV. The Emperor: Solid as a Rock

In a barren desert valley, a burly emperor is seated on a massive, rough-hewn throne. He is an imposing figure: his shoulders are broad, and his bulk is solid muscle. Like a child's drawing of God, he wears a crown and a long, white beard. His face is stern. His eyebrows are heavy and dark, and his gaze is harsh. He wears a tunic, armored epaulets, and a purple robe. In his right hand he holds an ankh, the Egyptian cross that signifies the balance between male and female. Rams' heads are carved into the back and arms of his throne. Behind him, two icy mountains rise.

Caesar. Augustus. Caligula. Claudius. Nero. Charlemagne. Napoleon.

History's most powerful emperors are all known by a single name—because their commands changed the world. While ordinary kings ruled nations, emperors commanded entire groups of nations.

The Emperor in the Tarot is a direct descendant of those authoritative leaders. He is an ambitious ruler, a tireless commander, a ruthless conqueror, and a charismatic visionary. He is willful and stubborn, confident, courageous, and strong. He rules through logic, reason, and will. He is forceful, energetic, firm, and paternalistic. An archetypical father, the authoritative Emperor brings order out of chaos so that civilization can prosper.

In a reading, the Emperor often represents the search for authority, structure, and control.

His very throne is an emblem of his power. It is a massive, concrete structure, a tangible example of the stability of a cubic solid. Four carved rams' heads surround him, a direct reference to his Aries drive and leadership, as well as his similarity to Mars, the god of war.

When you see the Emperor card in a romance reading, it's a sign that you need structure and stability in a relationship. Security in a relationship is also important to you. You may be attracted to powerful people, people who are in command, because they reflect some aspect of your own personality. You recognize that power is an aphrodisiac. You are fascinated by the ways in which other people use—and abuse—their own power.

If you are in a relationship and you find yourself pitted against other people or circumstances that seem to threaten or interfere with your goals, you adopt a "take no prisoners" attitude. For you, all is fair in love and war. Even without meaning to, you may find that you easily dominate others who are less focused on the end game.

If you find yourself in a bad relationship, you quickly develop an exit strategy. For you, love can be a battlefield, and you are more than willing to fight for the relationship you want and deserve. You can easily set a goal and draw up a battle plan for achieving those goals. Then, once you have conquered, you can take off your armor.

If you are looking for romance, you are not afraid to make decisions, and you don't mind making the first move. You are a natural leader. You don't want surprises; you want control. If you can't be in control, you at least want to know who is in charge. You are rarely caught off-guard.

Traditionally, the Emperor is sometimes known as the Son of the Morning. The card corresponds to the fifth letter of the Hebrew alphabet, *Heh*, which means window.

Astrologically, the Emperor is associated with Aries, the first sign of the Zodiac. In addition to the rams on the Emperor's throne, some versions of the card incorporate the astrological glyph for Aries, which depicts a ram's head and horns.

V. *The Hierophant: Tradition, Tradition*

From his papal throne, the Hierophant raises his right hand in blessing over two kneeling acolytes. In his left hand, he displays a golden triple cross. Like the miter on his head, its three divisions represent the triple god: Father, Son, and Holy Spirit. The back of his throne is arched, like a doorway. He sits before two massive columns with the crossed keys of Saint Peter at his feet. His feet are bare, and both of them are flat on the floor. The acolyte on the left wears a robe embellished with red roses of passion; the one on the right wears a robe embellished with white lilies of purity. Both bow their shaved heads in reverence and obedience to their teacher and guide.

In ancient Greece, the Hierophant was a priest who guided his followers through the sacred rites of the Eleusinian mysteries. Each year, the Hierophant would lead his people through a reenactment of the goddess Persephone's kidnapping by Hades, god of the underworld—as well as her eventual return. The ritual symbolized the annual cycle of death and rebirth, as well as the immortality of the soul. It could even guarantee a participant's admission into the afterlife of the Eleusian Fields.

Today, the role of the Hierophant lives on in every spiritual teacher and guide who leads his or her followers through long-standing ritual and tradition. The word hierophant shares the same origin as the word hierarchy, an organization with varying levels of authority—and a hierophant is the final authority on matters of faith. Hierophants have the power to speak on behalf of God, to explain the teachings of divine wisdom, and to serve as a bridge between this world and the next.

Typically, the Hierophant card symbolizes teaching, tradition, inspiration, and revelation. The Hierophant may be a professor, a priest, a confessor, or a psychiatrist.

When you see the Hierophant in a romance reading, you are a traditionalist. You are an old soul, and you look for equally evolved individuals to be your companions. More often than not, you are attracted to people who have something to teach you—a mentor, a teacher, or a guide. You are comfortable with authority figures, and you don't mind serving as one yourself.

If you are in a relationship, being with a partner is an essential step toward developing your own spirituality. While you don't enter into romantic relationships lightly, you are comfortable with commitment—and the appearance of the Hierophant card could even symbolize a marriage. You appreciate the simple beauty and grace of daily rituals. You appreciate the deeper significance of routines that others miss. Sharing meals and spending time together becomes a way for you to establish deep bonds.

If you are looking for romance, the Hierophant card implies a certain level of political posturing and campaigning in your relationships. You believe there is a right way and a wrong way to do almost everything, but you have an innate understanding of the subtle maneuvers one must make to keep a relationship flowing smoothly. You are also not above appealing to a higher source—or even speaking on behalf of that higher source—when you believe that you are right. You may risk becoming preachy and dogmatic in your relationships. You may even find yourself denying your physical nature in favor of developing your own spirituality.

As an archetype, the Hierophant is often compared to the pope.

Traditionally, the Hierophant is sometimes known as the Magus of the Eternal Gods. The card corresponds to the sixth letter of the Hebrew alphabet, *Vav*, which means peg or hook.

Astrologically, the Hierophant is associated with Taurus, the sign of the bull. Some cards feature the Taurus glyph that depicts the horns of a bull or fallopian tubes and a uterus, as well as the union of the sun and the crescent moon.

VI. The Lovers: Opposites Attract

Like Adam and Eve, a man and a woman stand nude in a garden. The woman stands in front of an apple tree—the Tree of Knowledge of Good and Evil. A long serpent has wound its way up the trunk of the tree, and it seems to be whispering into the woman's ear. The man stands before the fiery Tree of Life. A low-lying gray cloud hovers ominously between them. Above the cloud, a radiant sun fills the sky with its rays, and Raphael, the archangel of love and healing, spreads his wings and raises his arms, as if to shield the pair from the burning sun.

An appearance by this couple could encourage any hopeless romantic. Yes, the Lovers card is exactly what it appears to be. It is the card of love and romance, of passion and desire, the merging of two bodies and the union of two souls. But while the Lovers card is an inspiring and hopeful card, it involves much more than simply falling head over heels and living happily ever after. That's because the Lovers card is, first and foremost, a card about making choices. Adam and Eve were thrown together by chance, but when they each tasted the forbidden fruit, they made a choice to stay together, come what may.

Finding a partner is also a matter of choice. You choose how you will present yourself to others. You choose what type of person you would like to pursue or attract. Once you are in a relationship, you choose every day how you will treat your partner and what course your relationship will follow.

Traditionally, historic versions of the card often depicted a young man standing between two women, looking befuddled. One was old, the other young. Interpretations of the women's presence often varied; some believed that the older woman was wealthy, while her younger counterpart was beautiful. Which would he choose—wealth or winsomeness? Other accounts suggested that the older woman was the mother of the bride—or possibly the groom. How could he keep both women happy?

For the most part, the Lovers card represents duality, balance, and wholeness. It depicts dualities, polarities, and the attraction of opposites—the balance of yin and yang, give and take. It can symbolize love, romance, and marriage, as well as peace, happiness, friendship, and cooperation.

If you are in a relationship, the Lovers card might be addressing the issue of communication. How do you communicate your ideals, your dreams, your visions, your goals? What do you want? And if you don't know, how do you expect someone else to guess?

If you are looking for romance, you may find yourself suddenly facing a difficult choice. Do you choose the energy, beauty, and promise of youth—or the experience, wisdom, and stability that come with age?

As archetypal characters, the Lovers can be compared to Adam and Eve, Romeo and Juliet, Anthony and Cleopatra.

Traditionally, the Lovers are sometimes known as the Children of the Voice Divine. The card corresponds to the seventh letter of the Hebrew alphabet, *Zain*, which means dagger.

Astrologically, the Lovers are associated with Gemini, the sign of the twins. Some versions of the Lovers card feature the Gemini glyph, which depicts twins in an embrace or the Roman numeral II.

VII. The Chariot: Driven to Distraction

A Roman chariot stands perfectly still, just outside the walls of a fortified city. A pair of sphinxes—one black, one white—lay at rest in front of the vehicle. They make a mysterious team. There are no harnesses and no reins, so if it's their job to pull the chariot, they move it through sheer willpower. A serious young man stands inside the coach. He is brawny and strong, and his armor accentuates his muscled torso and forearms. Both hands rest on the front of the chariot; he holds a long, silver spear in his right hand. The top of the chariot is covered by a blue canopy with white stars. The front of the chariot is embellished with the emblem of a winged disc and a shield.

Oedipus Rex, the hero of the classic Greek tragedy written in 430 B.C., was the victim of a terrifying prediction. When Oedipus was born, his father—King Laius—went to the Oracle of Delphi to inquire about the baby's fate. The Oracle told him that Oedipus was destined to kill his father and marry his mother. Horrified, King Laius left the baby in the wilderness to die. However, a shepherd discovered the abandoned infant and brought him to the childless King Polybus to raise.

Oedipus grew. Eventually, he learned that he had been adopted, and he headed off in his chariot to find his biological father. Along the road, Oedipus met King Laius.

They didn't recognize each other, of course—and after an ugly confrontation, Oedipus killed the traveling king.

Oedipus continued on his way, completely unaware that he had just murdered the very man he was looking for. Before long, Oedipus happened to encounter a sphinx, who refused to let him pass unless he could answer a riddle: What is it that goes on four legs in the morning, two legs in the afternoon, and three legs in the evening? The answer, of course, was man, who crawls on four legs as an infant, walks on two legs as an adult, and walks with a cane in his old age. Enraged at Oedipus's cleverness, the sphinx turned to stone.

The illustration on most versions of the Chariot card depicts Oedipus at that point—young, smart, strong, and in search of his heritage and his birthright. He doesn't yet realize that he has already begun to fulfill his monumental destiny.

Traditionally, the Chariot card represents triumph, victory, success, vengeance, and providence. The young charioteer is in full command of his physical and emotional drives. Unfortunately, he is also inexperienced and somewhat immature.

When you get the Chariot in a romance reading, your love life is headed in the right direction. You are off and running, and you are in full control of your speed and direction. However, you might need to examine issues regarding direction, speed, and competition. You might also need to reign in some of your preconceived ideas about relationships.

If you are looking for romance, you are attracted to other movers and shakers like yourself. You like people who know where they're going and how to get there. You like drive and forward motion. You also like things to move quickly.

As an archetype, the Charioteer can be compared to Oedipus, of course, as well as related heroes and seekers, like Odysseus.

Traditionally, the Chariot card is sometimes known as the Lord of the Triumph of Light. The card corresponds to the eighth letter of the Hebrew alphabet, *Cheth*, which means fence.

Astrologically, the Chariot is associated with Cancer, the crab. Some Chariot cards feature the Cancer glyph, which depicts a crab's claws, the sideways movements of the crab, and nurturing female breasts. Cancer is ruled by the Moon. Both are symbolized by the color silver.

VIII. Strength: Brute Force

In a field outside the fortressed walls of a medieval castle, a young woman in servant's garb gently holds the jaws of a powerful lion, calmly soothing the savage beast. The lion is backing up on its haunches, and its eyes are fixed on the woman's face. It isn't clear whether the woman is opening or closing the lion's mouth. She has one hand on its nose, the other on its bottom jaw. The lion's tongue is hanging out, and its fangs are clearly visible. The two are standing in a field. There is a hill behind them with the fortressed walls of a medieval castle standing on top of it.

Every now and then, you might read a newspaper article or see a television show about courageous heroes who risk their lives to save others. For the most part, however, they don't think of themselves as particularly strong, brave, or fearless. "Courage," John Wayne once said, "is being scared to death—and saddling up anyway." General George S. Patton agreed. "Courage is simply a matter of fear holding on one minute longer," he said. Eleanor Roosevelt described the true nature of courage. "You gain strength, courage, and confidence by every experience in which you really stop to look fear in the face," she said. "You must do the thing which you think you cannot do."

The Strength card, which switches places with Justice in some decks, illustrates the courage everyone must find within himself or herself. It is a card of fortitude and force, willpower and nerve, grit and determination. It is also the card of energy, action, and passion.

When you see the Strength card in a romance reading, you have the heart of a lion. You have the courage of your conviction, and you have mastered your wild, animal nature. Your courage, self-control, and quiet confidence can sooth the most savage of beasts. You may not think of yourself as courageous. You are probably as nervous and afraid as everyone else feels in new, potentially threatening situations. What sets you apart is your ability to move forward despite your doubts, and your willingness to take action even when your worst fears are looking you straight in the face.

If you are in a relationship, your partner has probably discovered that your ferocious roar simply disguises the fact that you are really a pussycat—and maybe even something of a sex kitten. Once you have found someone who can make you purr, your hunting days are usually over for good, and you are quite content to become domesticated. You might spend much of your time curled up on the most comfortable chair in the house, waiting to be petted.

If you are looking for romance, the Strength card is a reminder that you have what it takes to master the wild kingdom. Take pride in your accomplishments, and don't diminish your abilities. You might even want to take a cue from Strength's association with Leo and get a new hairstyle.

As an archetype, the Strength card is often compared to the Greek god Hercules, who killed the Nemean lion, despite the fact that its skin could not be penetrated by spears or arrows. After he strangled the lion with his bare hands, Hercules wore its skin as a cloak. The Strength card can also relate to the New Testament stories of the Christians who were fed to the lions, and Daniel who was rescued from the lion's den. It can even be compared to the fairy tale of Beauty and the Beast.

Traditionally, Strength is sometimes known as Force, Fortitude, Lust, or Daughter of the Flaming Sword. The card corresponds to the ninth letter of the Hebrew alphabet, *Teth*, which means snake.

Astrologically, Strength is associated with Leo, the lion. The Strength card almost always features a lion. Some cards also feature the Leo glyph, which looks like a lion's mane or tail. Leo is ruled by the Sun. Its colors are fiery red, orange, yellow, and gold.

IX. The Hermit: A Solitary Life

High atop a barren mountaintop, a middle-aged man in a full-length cloak raises a lantern in his right hand. His left hand grasps a rustic walking stick. His black goatee is flecked with gray. He wears a gray hooded tunic and simple sandals on his feet. His head is bowed, and he seems to be studying something further down the mountainside.

Out of the swirling mists of time, the solitary Hermit ventures forth. High above the busy world below, he reflects on spiritual concerns. He carries a lantern of wisdom, both to light his path and to serve as a beacon to others.

Some Tarot historians point out that very early renditions of the card were known as "Time." Their illustrations featured Saturn—also known as Father Time—holding an hourglass instead of a lantern. Today's Hermit, however, seems to resemble the Greek philosopher Diogenes. His philosophy, cynicism, revolved around the precepts of self-control and self-sufficiency. He believed in leading—and living—by example, as he attempted to expose vice, conceit, and the errors of conventional thought.

Diogenes also believed in living according to nature. He was a master of self-control and abstinence who weathered extremes of heat and cold with only a coarse cloak to protect him from the elements. He carried a walking stick and, according to legend, he also carried a lantern during the daylight, as he searched in vain for an honest man.

The card is generally thought to represent wisdom, prudence, and illumination. It illustrates the concepts of solitude and silence, as well as philosophy, introspection, and meditation. The Hermit is the old man of the mountain, a recluse, and a guide. He may even be an older, wiser version of the Fool, standing on the same mountain he started from.

If you are in a relationship, you are no clinging vine. It is important to you to have time to yourself, to collect your thoughts and contemplate. It's easy for you to remove yourself from the hustle and bustle of everyday life—spiritually and intellectually, if not physically. Just make sure your partner understands that you are climbing away to contemplate, not to hide, and that you are not retreating simply to avoid interaction.

If you are looking for romance, you will probably be most attracted to fellow thinkers. While you like to seclude yourself, you don't mind being found. You will gladly share your insights and observations with others. In many ways, you are a groundbreaker; you have blazed a trail up a mountainside and, from your vantage point, you have a clear view of the hustle and bustle below. The climb—and your current vantage point—have made you humble. You know that you are in a unique position to shed light for those who follow in your path.

As an archetype, the Hermit is often compared to Merlin, the reclusive and hidden magician.

Traditionally, the Hermit is sometimes known as the Magus of the Voice of Light. The card corresponds to the tenth letter of the Hebrew alphabet, *Yod*, which means hand.

Astrologically, the Hermit is associated with Virgo, the virgin. Virgos are quiet, hardworking, and unassuming. Some Hermit cards feature the Virgo glyph, which looks like three ears of corn or the initials of the Virgin Mary.

X. The Wheel of Fortune: Spin Again

Suspended in midair, where fluffy white clouds dot a blue sky, there is a giant orange disk. In the disc's outer rim, the letters T, A, R, and O are alternated with the Hebrew letters Yod, Heh, Vau, and Heh—which are sometimes pronounced as "Jehovah," the name of God. A sword-bearing sphinx sits on top of the wheel. A jackal-headed Anubis seems suspended from its right side, and a slithering serpent is dangling along the right side. There are four winged creatures in the four corners of the card: an angel, an eagle, a lion, and a bull. All four creatures are reading books.

> Fortune can, for her pleasure, fools advance,
> And toss them on the wheels of Chance.
> —Juvenal (AD 55–AD 127)

Early versions of the Wheel of Fortune card were frequently illustrated with an image that was almost cartoonlike. At the top, there was a king with a little talk balloon coming out of his mouth. "I am reigning!" he exclaimed. Another monarch was pictured falling off the Wheel, sadly commenting, "I have reigned." Riding the Wheel to the top, however, was a third sovereign, proudly proclaiming, "I will reign!"

The Wheel of Fortune is a graphic reminder that our lives—and our positions—are constantly changing. In fact, as they say, nothing is certain but change itself, and what goes up must also come down. It even refers to the idea of karma and the belief that what goes around, comes around. The Wheel of Fortune is the wheel of life and the spinning wheel of fate.

The letters around the rim of the wheel spell "TAROT," as well as "ROTA," the Latin word for "wheel." The letters are interspersed with the Hebrew letters Yod, Heh, Vau, Heh—the origin of the word Jehovah, the unspeakable name of God. In the four corners of the card are the four fixed creatures of the Zodiac: Aquarius the Water Bearer, Scorpio the Eagle, Leo the Lion, and Taurus the Bull; the four beasts of the Apocalypse; and the symbols of the four evangelists Matthew, Mark, Luke, and John.

In most Tarot readings, the Wheel of Fortune is generally considered a good omen, because it portends a turn for the better. It symbolizes good luck, good fortune, prosperity, abundance, and success, as well as interrelated notions of destiny, fate, chance, and probability. The card can also represent motion, evolution, and the inevitable cycles of life.

When you see the Wheel of Fortune in a romance reading, your love life is about to change for the better.

If you are in a relationship, this isn't your first time around the wheel. You have ridden up, and down, and around again—maybe more times than you'd like to count. This time, however, you are definitely on the way up. You will obviously be sharing the ride with your partner. While you're waiting in line, however, you might want to take a few moments to reflect back on your shared history. Because the Wheel often refers to cycles of time, it's a vivid reminder that those who don't remember the past are condemned to repeat it.

If you are looking for romance, others won't be able to resist your optimism and enthusiasm. Now is the time to take risks. You can't win if you don't play, and this time you've got nothing to lose. In fact, fortune is smiling on you.

No matter what, enjoy the ride. Maintain your playful attitude. But, as always when you climb on board the Ferris wheel of love, follow the safety rules. Wear your seat belt. Keep your hands inside the car at all times. And don't eat too much cotton candy.

Traditionally, the Wheel of Fortune is sometimes known as the Lord of the Forces of Life. The card corresponds to the final letter of the Hebrew alphabet, *Kaph*, which means fist.

Astrologically, the Wheel of Fortune is associated with Jupiter, the planet of luck and expansion.

XI. Justice: The Balance of Nature

The goddess of justice sits on an elevated platform between two white columns. She holds an upraised sword in her right hand and a perfectly balanced set of scales in her left. Her red robes are topped with a green cape; her head is crowned with a solid gold crown. Her feet are bare; her left foot is positioned slightly behind the right, as though she's about to stand up and announce her verdict.

Most of us say we want justice to be done—especially when we feel wronged and feel other people need to be set straight. The prospect of facing justice ourselves, however, is less exciting. Our secret fear is that we might actually get what we deserve. Justice holds a two-edged sword—a reminder that fairness cuts both ways.

Happily, the goddess of justice pictured in the Tarot is open-minded and fair. While the blindfolded goddess is a prominent figure in many courtrooms, the goddess of justice in the Tarot has her eyes wide open. She represents cosmic and karmic justice, which is not necessarily the same as legal justice, or even punishment. She is eminently fair, even to those who make a few honest mistakes.

In some decks, the Justice card is sometimes switched with Strength. It represents balance, fairness, reason, and equity. It could indicate your involvement in legal issues, such as contract and license issues, lawsuits, and arbitration. The Justice card may indicate that major action in your life will come to a halt until a decision is made.

When you see the Justice card in a romance reading, you might be reminded of your past relationships. When partnerships end, it's not unusual for them to conclude with bitterness and animosity on both sides. The Justice card, however, is a reminder that relationship problems are never one-sided. With the passage of time, you will be able to see more clearly and rationally. You will be able to weigh your own role in relationships more fairly. You will make better decisions, and better judgments, in future relationships.

If you are currently in a relationship, you may be judging your partner—perhaps harshly—in an effort to avoid being judged yourself. Alternatively, you may be feeling judged. Whatever the case, try to make more of an effort to be fair, both to your partner and to yourself.

If you are looking for romance, the Justice card could also indicate that you are in the process of making decisions, weighing your options, evaluating your possibilities, and judging your prospects on a trial basis.

Because of the card's association with Libra—symbolized by the scales—the Justice card also portends an upcoming period of parties and socialization. Other people will find you charming and gracious.

As an archetype, the Justice card is often compared to the Greek goddess Themis, the guardian of the infant Zeus. Themis had the gift of prophecy, but she resigned from the shrine of Delphi to become the Greek goddess of justice. The Justice card is also associated with Maat, the Egyptian goddess who weighed the hearts of the dead for honesty, truth, and goodness. On her scales, a pure heart would weigh no more than a feather.

Traditionally, the Justice card is sometimes known as Adjustment or the Daughter of the Lord of Truth. The card corresponds to the thirtieth letter of the Hebrew alphabet, *Lamed*.

Astrologically, Justice is associated with Libra, the scales. Some cards feature the Libra glyph, which depicts the scales of balance.

XII. The Hanged Man: Swept Off His Feet

From the crossed branches of a living tree, a young man is suspended by a rope wrapped around his right ankle. He wears soft gray boots, brown tights, and a gold tunic belted around the waist. His hands are behind his back; his left leg is bent at the knee and tucked behind his right leg. While he is completely upside-down, his face is calm and re-laxed. There is a glowing yellow nimbus, or aura, completely encircling his head.

More than three thousand years ago, the people of Northern Europe used a magical, mysterious alphabet called the runes. According to legend, the runes were actually dis-covered by the Norse god Odin. In a supreme act of self-sacrifice, he hung upside-down from the World Tree for nine days and nights, much like the Tarot's Hanged Man. At the end of his ordeal, his transcendent act of self-sacrifice was rewarded with the gift of written language—in the form of the runes, one of the first written alphabets.

For centuries, Odin's runes were carved on stone, etched into metal, and burned into wood. Runes had the power to charm, to curse, and to spell—in both senses of the word. Each rune had both a literal meaning and a closely related symbolic signifi-cance. Every letter was imbued with a symbolic meaning that could be used to invoke the power of the Norse pantheon of gods through poetry, inscriptions, and invocations. They could even be used for divination. Today, runes still have the power to counsel, to clarify, and to communicate, and many Tarot readers use them in conjunction with their cards.

The Hanged Man card offers a new perspective. He sees the world from a viewpoint that is radically different from the norm. All of the blood is rushing to his head; he can think of radical new solutions to old problems. His aura is illuminated and bright, and his intuition is keen. Ultimately, the Hanged Man is a mystic. He is undergoing a spiritual initiation through a symbolic death and resurrection.

When you see the Hanged Man in a romance reading, you may need to change your perspective about your relationships. You may have a number of outdated attitudes and beliefs hanging around.

If you are in a relationship, you may need to sacrifice some of your comforts on behalf of your partner. Don't worry—a reward will follow.

If you are looking for romance, you may find yourself in a period of suspension and delay. Sometimes, the Hanged Man is compared to an unborn child, who is suspended upside-down in water before birth. Occasionally, the card may also represent sacrifice, trials, punishment, suffering, loss, defeat, or failure.

As an archetype, the Hanged Man is sometimes compared to Christ, who allowed himself to be hanged as an ultimate act of sacrifice. Occasionally, the Hanged Man is also associated with traitors, who were historically hung upside-down. Some versions of the card even depict Judas, the disciple who betrayed Jesus, with his thirty pieces of silver falling out of his pockets.

Traditionally, the Hanged Man is sometimes known as the Spirit of the Mighty Waters. The card corresponds to the Hebrew letter *Mem*, which means water.

Astrologically, the Hanged Man is associated with Neptune, the planet of mystery and illusion, as well as the element of water.

XIII. Death: The Kiss of Death

The Grim Reaper, a skeletal figure in heavy black armor, rides a white horse. He holds the reins in his right hand. In his left hand he carries a black flag with a five-petal white rose. The horse is in the process of stepping over the body of a dead king; he lies flat on his back with his royal red robe spread out around him and his gold crown lying in the dirt next to his head. In fact, Death rides for all—king, bishop, woman, child—with no regard for power or status.

The old gypsy looks at you, lays down a card, and gasps aloud. Her crooked finger of fate points to the image on the table, and you know that all is lost—for she has dealt the card of Death.

No, wait . . . That's only in the movies. Unlike the foreboding card of imminent doom that most of us expect, Death is a card of new beginnings and fresh starts. You aren't going to keel over in your chair. In fact, you're going to rise up and be better than ever.

The Death card is usually a good omen. In the Tarot, Death makes it possible to let go of old habits, old patterns, and old relationships that are no longer healthy. It is the card of transformation and change, metamorphosis and rebirth. It doesn't represent the loss of energy. Instead, it symbolizes a conversion, like the Phoenix, the mythical bird that burns and then is reborn from its own ashes. The Death card foretells the completion of one stage of life and the exciting beginning of a new phase.

Death is rarely sudden, and seldom unexpected. It is a fact of life that most people—and some relationships—die slowly, over time. For the most part, death comes because of naturally progressing illnesses and conditions that can be readily observed.

When you see the Death card in a romance reading, there is nothing to fear. In fact, if you have been suffering through a painful period in your life, the Death card can even come as something of a relief.

The Death card simply means that the end is in sight and a new beginning is imminent. The transformation will be as natural and predictable as a change of seasons. Just as winter turns into spring, the Death card portends new life springing from the remnants of the old.

If you are in a relationship, the Death card could occasionally portend the end of your relationship—but it's not that cut and dried. The card could also indicate that either you or your partner is undergoing a radical transformation, which could revitalize your relationship.

If you are looking for romance, the Death card could be telling you that it is time to rethink your approach. You have been killing your chances. See what needs to change, and transform yourself.

As an archetype, the figure in the Death card is often compared to the Grim Reaper.

Traditionally, the Death card is sometimes known as the Child of the Great Transformers. The card corresponds to the Hebrew letter *Nun*, which means fish.

Astrologically, Death is associated with Scorpio, the scorpion. Scorpio is the catalyst of the Zodiac, ruled by the planet Pluto, the god of the underworld. Some cards feature the Scorpio glyph, which looks like the feet, tail, and stinger of a scorpion.

XIV. Temperance: Mix and Match

Michael, the Archangel of Temperance, is pictured with one foot in the watery world of the subconscious and one foot on the dry land of consciousness, where a bed of wild irises is blooming. Michael's wings are spread wide behind him; the golden emblem of the sun is on his forehead. As the sun rises over a distant mountain peak, he mixes the contents of two golden chalices.

The Temperance card is obviously a card of balance and moderation. The Archangel Michael is sometimes said to be cutting wine with water, an ancient practice designed to keep drunkenness to a minimum. The word temperance usually refers to abstinence from alcoholic beverages. Temperance is the last of the four cardinal virtues, too, following prudence, justice, and fortitude.

There is more to the Temperance card than meets the eye, however. In fact, the card is one of the most meaningful and romantic cards in the Tarot deck.

Just as Michael is blending water and wine, he is mixing the elements: fire and water, earth and air. While most Tarot cards depict extremes—between black and white, day and night, hot and cold—the Temperance card symbolizes the importance of merging and combining opposing forces, including the ultimate blend of two separate individuals. To some degree, the card also illustrates the principle of alchemy, a magical philosophy concerned with the transmutation of base metals into gold. That is exactly the transformation that can occur when two people meet and become better for it. The two chalices in Michael's hands may symbolize the sun and the moon, which symbolize a man and a woman. The water flowing between them represents a shared bond and an exchange of energy.

The Archangel Michael is straddling the shoreline near a pair of blooming irises. In Greek mythology, Iris was the goddess of the rainbow. Rainbows symbolized a bridge between heaven and earth, which probably inspired Iris's role: she served as a messenger from the gods to humankind. She also helped keep peace among the gods: whenever the gods argued, Zeus would also send Iris to the underworld to fill a golden jug with water from the River Styx. Each god was required to drink from the jug. If he or she had lied, they would immediately fall over breathless for a year and, subsequently, be cut off from councils and feasts for the next nine years.

When you see the Temperance card in a romance reading, opposing forces are about to combine in new and rewarding ways. Temperance is a card of action and reaction, adaptation and accommodation, and realization.

If you are in a relationship, you may be entering a period of renewed harmony with your mate. Old differences will be reconciled, and you will be able to integrate your past differences into a better, more productive relationship.

If you are looking for romance, you might find it at the seashore or on the beach.

Temperance is sometimes known as Art, and sometimes it is called Alchemy. Traditionally, the card is also known as the Daughter of the Reconcilers. The card corresponds to the Hebrew letter *Samekh*, which means tent post.

Astrologically, Temperance is associated with Sagittarius, the archer. Sagittarius rules the hips and the thighs. Half-man, half-horse, the archer is powerful and ready to gallop. Like a racehorse, the typical Sagittarian can't stand still. Their far-ranging travels—both intellectual and physical—tend to make them wax philosophical. They shoot arrows to see where they land. Some cards feature the Sagittarius glyph, which looks like an archer's bow and arrow.

XV. The Devil: Face Your Demons

Grinning malevolently, a giant, red-skinned demon taunts and torments the man and the woman chained to his perch. They are surrounded by inky darkness, but the demon is holding a torch in his clawlike hands, which provides enough light to make out the frightful details. Two gnarled horns, like a Ram's, protrude from his knobby bald head. His forehead is furled, and his pupils are dilated like a cat's. He has pointed ears and a long, pointed chin that ends in a wiry goatee. Two hideous bat wings sprout from his shoulders. While his upper body is slim and sinewy, his legs are covered in fur, like a goat. Instead of feet, he has talons that grasp the pedestal on which he is perched. A nude woman and a naked man are bound to that pedestal, with chains that are loosely wrapped around their necks. They hold their hands behind their backs as if they are handcuffed.

If you were looking for the Lovers card in your Tarot reading, you have found at least one version of it here—a grotesque mirror image, in which the Lovers have been entrapped and enslaved by their own misplaced priorities. Like an evil puppet master, the Devil knows how to pull their strings. Meanwhile, the young couple looks a little demonic themselves. Their tails are burning, and the flames seem eerily reminiscent of the trees that stood behind them in the Lovers card.

The Devil is often compared to Pan, the god of music, nature, goats, sheep, and shepherds. He had the body of a man and the hindquarters and horns of a goat. He could inspire panic, but for the most part his adventures were actually somewhat amusing. For centuries, Pan has symbolized the wild side of human nature. Over time, the horny creature has also come to represent the Devil.

As a result, the card has more than its share of negative interpretations. The Devil can represent the wickedness of slavery, entrapment, violence, fraud, trickery, and schemes that cause harm to others, although it just as frequently describes the inherent evil in allowing oneself to be trapped in a web of illusion. Look carefully at the couple in the card: they are not chained tightly, and they could free themselves if they wanted to. They are trapped by their own misconceptions, shame, guilt, denial, and inhibitions. The Devil card might also represent people who are repressing their emotions, their passion, and their ambition. The word devil is "lived," spelled backward.

Perhaps the Devil card's most negative real association is its connection with drinking and the abuse of intoxicating substances. Pan was a close associate of Dionysus, the god of wine. As a result, the Devil card occasionally represents temptation, materialism, and addiction.

When you see the Devil card in a romance reading, look for the positive qualities that the card represents. Thanks to his association with Pan, the Devil can symbolize erotic pleasure, wild behavior, and unbridled desire. It can represent mirth, playfulness, instinct, and carnal desires. It can represent a passion pit. In many ways, the Devil card may awaken you to the possibilities of a devil-may-care attitude.

Even so, you've got to give the Devil his due. If you are in a relationship, the Devil card could indicate trouble—possibly with a former lover. After all, hell has no fury like a woman scorned.

If you are looking for romance, you might want to adapt a more playful, devilish attitude. Just remember, however, that your decisions could have lasting repercussions. You can't shake hands with the Devil and say you're only kidding.

Traditionally, the Devil is sometimes known as the Lord of the Gates of Matter. The card corresponds to the Hebrew letter *Ayin*, which means eye.

Astrologically, the Devil is associated with Capricorn, the goat. Obviously, the image of the Devil incorporates many goatlike features. Some Devil cards also feature the Capricorn glyph, which depicts the head and horns of a goat attached to the tail of a fish.

XVI. The Tower: A Bolt from the Blue

As a thunderous lightning bolt strikes the top of a tall stone tower, fire rages through the structure and a royal-looking couple plunges head-first through the air. Arms flailing, their gowns and capes billow like the gray clouds that swirl behind them. Sparks rain down from the night sky. The couple is headed for certain doom on the rocky cliff at the base of the tower.

The Tower card is not a gentle card. It depicts, in graphic detail, the forceful expulsion of a young, attractive couple from their comfortable existence in their ivory palace. Struck by a bolt from the blue, they are shaken to their very foundation.

At the same time, however, they may have been released from a prison of their own making.

The Tower card is an unmistakable illustration of the shock we experience during times of crisis and change. It is a card of sudden, drastic transformation. It is a surprise ending, a dramatic twist, a rude awakening. On rare occasions, the Tower even symbolizes punishment on a biblical scale, like the retribution God inflicted on the builders of the Tower of Babel.

The Tower is usually associated with Mars, the god of war, and the destruction and havoc he can wreak. The card may symbolize anger, upheaval, destruction, and ruin. Just as frequently, however, the Tower represents enlightenment, inspiration, and release. Ultimately, the Tower experience is one of purification, as an old structure is torn down so that renovation can begin.

When you see the Tower in a romance reading, the dramatic symbol takes on an entirely new layer of significance. The Tower is a distinctly masculine symbol, which frequently refers to potency and sexual energy. It may signal a passionate, romantic interlude—one that could even culminate in pregnancy.

If you are in a relationship, you may be in for a period of upheaval. You and your partner may move to a new home, or you may simply move to a new level in your liaison. In rare cases, the Tower card can indicate a divorce—but usually, the Tower describes a breakup that has already occurred, rather than one that looms in the future.

If you are looking for romance, the Tower card could indicate that you will find it when you least expect it. You could be struck, suddenly and without warning. You may find yourself attracted to a strong, aggressive individual.

As an archetype, the Temperance card is often compared to the Tower of Babel, the ivory towers of academia, and the fairy tale *Rapunzel*.

Traditionally, the Tower is sometimes known as the House of God or the Lord of the Hosts of the Mighty. The card corresponds to the Hebrew letter *Peh*, which means mouth.

Astrologically, the Tower is associated with Mars, the god of war.

XVII. The Star: A Match Made in Heaven

A golden yellow star with eight rays fills most of a blue sky, the center of a cosmic display that features seven smaller, silver stars. All of the stars have eight rays. Bathed by their shimmering light, a powerfully built woman kneels on the shore of a clear, deep lake. She holds two clay pitchers, and she pours water from both. She's pouring one directly into the lake; she's pouring the other onto the grassy meadow, where it puddles and then streams into several directions. Wildflowers bloom all around her. There is a low-slung mountain range in the distance and a solitary tree. In its branches, a silver ibis spreads its wings.

For centuries, people have looked to the night sky for guidance. Sailors navigate by the North Star. Small children make wishes on the evening star. Young lovers watch for shooting stars, so they can make wishes for their happiness.

Since the dawn of time, storytellers have gathered around campfires and used the stars as a launching point to describe our most secret hopes and dreams. Every constellation in the night sky is associated with a corresponding myth or legend. Aquarius, the sign most closely associated with the Star card, is reputed to be Ganymede, the handsome young cupbearer of the gods. He lived with them on Mount Olympus, where he kept their cups filled with ambrosia—the water of life, the nectar of the gods, and the drink of immortality

According to some traditions, each star in the night sky is an unborn or departed soul. In fact, the light of every star in the night sky has traveled vast distances across the centuries to reach us. Each one is a twinkling reminder of our shared history and myth. The stars and the signs of the Zodiac have helped shape our very understanding of the human psyche.

When you see the Star card in a romance reading, it may be time for you to experience the stories they carry, firsthand. You might find that the next phase of your life will find you experiencing the fundamental truths that make up each tale: find your quest, take risks, develop and change as a person, and reap the rewards, whether you seek romance or anything else.

If you are in a relationship, the Star card could indicate that you are the center of your own universe. Stars are, after all, distant suns, each encircled by their own orbiting solar systems.

If you are looking for romance, others will be dazzled by your star quality. The twinkle of the constellations will merely reflect the sparkle in your eyes.

In either case, you may need to be more proactive in your own work to manifest your dreams. Like the ancient Greeks, who transformed the musings of a few sky-gazing shepherds into legends that would last for centuries, you may need to develop your own story. Flesh out your dreams and desires by discussing them with others. Find other people with dreams and desires that parallel yours, and develop them together.

As an archetype, the Star is often compared to the Star of Bethlehem, which heralded the birth of a new era in human civilization.

Traditionally, the Star is sometimes known as the Daughter of the Firmament. The card corresponds to the Hebrew letter *Tzaddi*, which means fishhook.

Astrologically, the Star is associated with Aquarius. The card usually incorporates some version of a Water Bearer. Some versions of the Star card also feature the Aquarius glyph, which depicts waves of water or sound.

XVIII. The Moon: Some Enchanted Evening

The man in the moon—or possibly the woman in the moon—seems to bow her head in reverence above an ancient stone gateway. Twenty-four moonbeams illuminate the full length of a country lane that winds its way from distant hills through the gateway and to the rocky, weedy shores of a shimmering lake. A colossal crab is emerging from the lake. A floppy-eared dog guardedly watches the crab's ascent, while a second dog begins to rear back on his haunches to howl.

For eons, the golden sun has pursued the silver moon endlessly around the globe. Masculine and feminine, radiant and reflective, conscious and subconscious … The sun and the moon are the primordial couple, and their heavenly partnership has given birth to countless tales that parallel our own romantic escapades.

While the sun may generate heat, the moon inspires romance. Bathed in its mystic glow, all harsh edges disappear. Everything looks softer and more dreamlike.

Occasionally, moonlight can also make shadows seem to lengthen, and it can cloak some truths in its darkness. The moon has a dark side—the secrets and mysteries that may not be understood or even recognized.

For the most part, however, the moon is a useful marker to chart the cycles of our lives. The moon is closely linked to pregnancy and childbirth, because its phases so clearly match the pregnant female form: slim, then round and full, then slim again.

When you see the Moon card in a romance reading, all of your romantic hopes and dreams may seem bathed in a celestial glow. Your passions may seem to rise and swell like the tides; you may make choices for reasons you don't fully understand.

If you are in a relationship or if you are looking for romance, use the cycles of the moon to gauge your own progress and to time your short-term plans. When the moon is new, it is a good time to begin new projects. They should reach their culmination as the moon reaches its own fullness. As the moon wanes, you can tie up any loose ends, reflect on your success, and prepare for your next new proposal.

As an archetype, the moon is often compared to Artemis, the moon goddess, who chased playfully through the skies with her brother Apollo, god of the sun. The moon was also known as Diana, the goddess of the hunt. Diana was frequently said to run through the countryside at night, in the company of her two pet dogs.

Traditionally, the moon is sometimes known as the Ruler of Flux and Reflux. The card corresponds to the Hebrew letter *Qoph*, which means the back of the head.

Astrologically, the moon is associated with Pisces, the visionary twelfth sign of the Zodiac, ruled by Neptune. Some cards feature the Pisces glyph, which depicts two fishes, either kissing or joined by a chain.

XIX. The Sun: Your Time to Shine

Underneath a bright yellow sun, a beaming, naked toddler spreads his arms open wide. He's the original fair-haired child, chubby and cherubic, with a mass of golden curls. Like Adonis, god of the sun, he rides bareback on a muscular white horse. There is a red banner blowing and swirling nearby, and a field of ripe, full sunflowers just behind a wall. Just like a child's drawing, the sun looks happy.

Once a year, the sun returns to the same place in the sky that it was on the day of your birth. When it reaches that point—your Solar Return—you are once again, for a brief moment in time, back where you started. You may feel renewed, recharged, invigorated. Throw in some cake and ice cream, and it is no wonder that birthdays make us feel like we are the center of the universe.

Obviously, the sun is the marker of annual events, like birthdays and anniversaries. The sun also represents a wide range of related concepts. The sun, for example, is the center of our solar system. In astrology, the Sun represents the true center of every individual's universe—ourselves. We can only see the world from the center of our own existence. As a result, the sun symbolizes consciousness, self-awareness, and ego. It illustrates our need to shine—and our need to find a moonlike companion that can reflect our rays.

For thousands of years, people believed that the sun traveled around the world. Because the sun was reborn with every dawn, it became the god of rebirth. Even today, we worship the sun—at least from our favorite spot on the beach. The sun is the giver of life. Its perfect blend of light and heat make it possible for life to exist on earth. On an individual level, the sun describes our own need to create and give life to our ideals.

The sun is masculine and active, as opposed to the feminine and receptive aspects of the moon. The sun radiates the energy and heat that the moon reflects.

While the sun usually represents brightness, radiance, energy, and optimism, the Sun card could burn too brightly in our lives. It can cause sunburn and blindness, drought and devastation. The sun is a perfect example of the wide range of symbolism present in every Tarot card.

For the most part, the Sun is a good sign in any Tarot reading. When you see the Sun in a romance reading, you will find illumination and enlightenment.

If you are in a relationship, you might pay special attention to upcoming birthdays, anniversaries, and other important dates. Find reasons to celebrate. Make a few dates with your loved one.

If you are looking for love, others will be drawn to you. You will seem to radiate energy and optimism. Don't be afraid to shine.

As an archetype, the sun is often compared to Apollo, the god who pulled the sun through the sky in his golden chariot. His travels were emulated by Roman charioteers, who pursued a course based on the cosmic cycle of the sun.

Traditionally, the sun is sometimes known as the Lord of the Fire of the World. The card corresponds to the Hebrew letter *Resh*, which means head.

Astrologically, the Sun card is associated with the Sun. Some versions of the Sun card incorporate the astrological glyph for the sun that depicts the wheels of the sun god's celestial chariot.

XX. Judgment: Last Call

The Archangel Gabriel blows his horn and, awakened by the sound, an entire cemetery full of people rise up out of their graves. Arms outstretched, they reach out to embrace a second chance at life, restored to youth and health. The angel is larger than life. He floats above the clouds, and his outstretched wings fill the sky.

Get up! Get moving! The Judgment card is a call to action—a clear indication that you need to be up and about. God's angel himself is sounding the alarm. It's time for you to face the music.

The Judgment card, of course, has its origins in the biblical story of the end times. To Christians, God's last judgment will bring this world to an end and determine the fate of every human soul. When you see the Judgment card in a Tarot reading, don't worry about being called to account for past misdeeds. The Judgment card is the card of forgiveness and release. It's a card of rejoicing and celebration. In a reading, the Judgment card often represents a willingness to be judged on our merits, and it reminds us to forgive ourselves for errors along the way.

When you see the Judgment card in a romance reading, it is time to let go of old wounds, release the past, and rise up for a better tomorrow. It can also be a reminder not to judge others, lest you be judged yourself.

If you are in a relationship, the Judgment card could signal that a secret is about to be revealed. Like the naked people in the card, someone—or something—could be exposed. You may need to forgive your partner for old sins. You might also be called to forgive yourself, as well.

If you are still looking for romance, don't panic. The angel is blowing his horn, but the fat lady won't sing until you get to the next card. You still have plenty of time to find a partner and begin a new life together. You might want to try new and creative ways to find romance, however. Like the figures in the card, you should think outside the box as you move toward your destiny.

Traditionally, the Judgment card is sometimes known as the Spirit of Primal Fire. The card corresponds to the Hebrew letter *Shin*, which means fang.

Astrologically, Judgment is associated with Pluto, the planet of death and regeneration.

XXI. The World: Last Dance

Encircled by a wreath of glory—a world with no beginning and no end—a young woman has shed her inhibitions . . . and her clothes. She might even have been resurrected; some Tarot readers believe that the garment swirling around her is actually a shroud, a traditional, winding sheet that was wrapped around the dead. In the four corners of the card, the four fixed creatures of the Zodiac make their last appearance in the Major Arcana.

Well, now you've seen everything—and what a long, strange trip it's been. Like the wandering Fool, you have journeyed from one end of the Major Arcana to the other, and come to the final card in the series. You are a seasoned traveler and a citizen of the world. You have broadened your horizons, and the truth has set you free. You have finally reached the last stop on the Fool's Journey—the World.

A card of completion and success, the World symbolizes your maturity and your achievements. Like the joyful, self-assured, young woman in the center of the card, you can celebrate the successful completion of your adventure. In a Tarot reading, the World card usually indicates that you have attained a state of wholeness, balance, and unity. Your body, mind, and spirit are one.

Occasionally, the World card is called the Universe and traditionally, the World is sometimes known as the Great One of the Night of Time. The card corresponds to the Hebrew letter *Tav*, which means sign. Astrologically, the World is associated with Saturn, the planet of limitations and restrictions. It's a final reminder that the boundaries that confine us also define our world.

In a romance reading, the World could signify that you and your traveling companion have arrived at the station together.

And if you're still looking for romance, you have come to the right place.

Of course, there is the question of the four creatures in the corners of the card: Aquarius the Water Bearer, Scorpio the Eagle, Leo the Lion, and Taurus the Bull. The four represent the four dimensions: width, length, height, and time. They symbolize the four cardinal directions: north, south, east, and west. They are reminders of the four seasons, the four winds, the four phases of the moon, and the four ages of humankind: infancy, youth, adulthood, and old age.

And most importantly—at least for our purposes—the four creatures also symbolize the four elements and the four suits of the Minor Arcana.

Actually, maybe your trip isn't over yet. You've still got fifty-six cards to go. Maybe the World card is just your ticket into the next half of the deck.

Show your card to the conductor, and have a seat.

The Ace of Wands: Light My Fire

The Ace of Wands—a single, massive branch with budding leaves still sprouting from its tip—emerges from billowing gray and white clouds. A strong and steady hand holds it aloft. Is it God's hand? Or are we simply seeing a close-up view of the Magician's hand, as he picks up the tools from his table? Below, there is a solitary dwelling in the heart of a grassy, green valley and a low ridge of blue mountains along the horizon.

The Ace of Wands is the first card in the suit of Wands, the suit that corresponds to the ancient element of fire. In that respect, the Ace of Wands is the embodiment of creative inspiration. Like a match, it lights and ignites the rest of the Minor Arcana cards. It is the spark that starts the fire, the lightbulb that goes off over your head whenever you get a bright idea, and the proverbial twinkle in your father's eye.

When you see the Ace of Wands in a romance reading, prepare for a sudden surge of energy, of drive, of passion, and vitality. Get ready for action, and expect to be impressed.

That energy could come in any number of guises, but you'll recognize the same physical power and bulk that is depicted in the card. Picture a cave dweller wielding a massive club. Remember the legend of Thor, an ancient Norse god who carried a mighty hammer to intimidate his adversaries and defeat his opponents. The Ace of Wands conveys quick, powerful, dramatic action, not long conversations or protracted negotiations. Think of Harry S. Truman, who advised his people to speak softly and carry a big stick.

Ultimately, the Ace of Wands is a uniquely masculine symbol that represents force and power, potential and virility. The Ace of Wands may be an impressive physical specimen—or, if it falls reversed in a reading, it could represent a shriveled, dried-up, disappointing little twig or a limp little sprout.

One word of warning: when you see the Ace of Wands in a romance reading, remember that you could be playing with fire. Be careful: don't get burned, and don't spark an inferno that will rage out of control.

Traditionally, the Ace of Wands is known as the root of the power of fire. That means it is the source of all that fire represents.

The Two of Wands: In Control

An enterprising young nobleman holds a globe in his left hand and gazes out past a battlement. Two tall branches have been mounted onto the low wall, like torches. He grasps one of them, absentmindedly, with his right hand. He has dressed casually in soft, fringed leather boots, a belted tunic, a cape that is draped across one shoulder, and a jaunty red cap. The wall is decorated with a St. Andrew's Cross: two crossed staffs, one with white lilies, the other with red roses. Only a portion of his view is visible: a low rise of green hills in the distance.

Traditionally, the Two of Wands is known as the card of dominion. The well-dressed businessman in the card epitomizes that role: he holds the power to dominate—to master—all that he surveys. Look at the card: he literally holds the whole world in his hands.

What you don't see, however, is that carrying the weight of the world can be a heavy burden. Without a corresponding measure of sound judgment and self-control, the enterprising young man in the illustration might even be crushed by the weight of his own authority. After all, power corrupts—and ultimate power corrupts absolutely.

In the Tarot, the number two usually symbolizes duality, partnerships, and the meeting of minds. The Two of Wands may hint at a mutual stirring of interest. It may indicate a developing partnership, a strategic alliance, or a merger.

When you see the Two of Wands in a romance reading, you might be surprised to discover that you are in a position of command and control. You do far more than merely influence others—you actually have the power to dictate the terms of your relationships.

But do you really want to be a dictator? For every action, there is an equal and opposite reaction. Think carefully about your goals. Take time to clarify your own wants and needs, as well as your own personal code of ethics.

Astrologically, the Two of Wands is associated with the starting point of the Zodiac, the first ten degrees of Aries, where Mars, the god of war, can devote his energy to setting goals and preparing for victory.

The Three of Wands: Third Time's the Charm

A middle-aged nobleman is standing with his back to us, as he gazes out over a low stone wall across a vast sea. He's standing on a sandy surface, with one foot resting on a small boulder. Three sapling trees frame him, and he's holding on to one of them with his left hand.

Traditionally, the Three of Wands is known as the card of established strength. The figure in the card has established his stronghold, which is symbolized by the three firmly rooted saplings.

It's a good card to find in any Tarot reading. Three represents a synthesis, the result of a thesis and an antithesis. The presence of the Three of Wands indicates that you have found a way to successfully combine two opposing forces in your life. You were faced with a problem: you had two options, but they were both extreme. They were each as different from the other as day and night. To others, your situation looked as though it was a simple matter of black and white and that you would have to choose either one or the other. You found a compromise, however. Through skillful negotiation, you found a way to blend the two extremes, and now you're ready to move ahead with your hopes, your dreams, and your plans.

When you see the Three of Wands in a romance reading, a new relationship may recently have been formed. It could indicate that the energies of two people have blended and combined. The seeds of a promising partnership have not only been planted—they also have sprouted and taken root.

Where that relationship is headed is still a matter of conjecture, of course. The saplings are still young, and the figure in the card is still watching and waiting to see what develops.

Astrologically, the Three of Wands corresponds to the second ten degrees of Aries, where the Sun leads the way.

The Four of Wands: The Wedding Dance

A young couple sits and sorts through a woven bushel basket filled with grapes. There is an arbor of four wands nearby with a garland of grapevines fastened to the top. The couple is a matched pair. Both have dark hair, both are wearing full-length, long-sleeved tunics, and both are wrapped in long, flowing capes. The man, on the left, has a blue cape; the woman, on the right, has a red cape. They are sitting in a courtyard with the walls and turrets of a medieval citadel behind them.

The Four of Wands is one of the most positive relationship cards in the Tarot. In many Tarot decks, the card depicts a couple celebrating their marriage. The couple is outdoors, which symbolizes a connection to nature and fertility, and they are saying their vows under a leafy arbor or *chuppa*, a Jewish wedding canopy. The four wands that support the canopy symbolize the structure and stability of a home with four corners, while the canopy itself represents protection from the elements, as well as blessings from heaven.

Four is the number of wholeness and stability. That's because, geometrically speaking, four points combine to form a solid. There are four dimensions in the physical world, four corners to a room—or a house—as well as four seasons, four cardinal directions, four evangelists (Matthew, Mark, Luke, and John), four elements, and four suits in the Minor Arcana.

When you see the Four of Wands in a romance reading, you are probably dealing with a relationship based on a traditional foundation. The fact that the couple is being married in an official ceremony implies an adherence to convention and the recognition of a legally binding social contract.

Religious and spiritual traditions play a role in most weddings. Christians are often reminded that Jesus' first reported miracle was performed at a wedding celebration, when he transformed water into wine. That story reminds us that weddings are occasions for momentous—and public—transformation that can be celebrated with great joy and fanfare.

The fact that the wedding couple is out in public also implies that they have the blessing and support of their family and friends. They are not like Romeo and Juliet, who were forced to hide their romance from their warring families.

It is interesting to note that no officiate—no rabbi, priest, or minister—is pictured. That's because, according to many religious traditions, a true marriage is believed to be entered into solely by the bride and groom. The ceremony may be conducted by a third party, but, in fact, the two people actually marry each other. If there are guests and witnesses present, their role is to support and encourage the couple to keep their vows, not to validate the wedding or make the marriage legal.

Traditionally, the Four of Wands is known as the card of perfected work. That's one thing to keep in mind, especially if you can relate to the planning and preparation of a wedding ceremony. For many couples, wedding planning can be a nightmare—and then nothing seems to go according to plan, anyway. Right up until the ceremony begins, details are overlooked, mistakes are made, and family members panic and argue. Yet, somehow, every bride looks beautiful, and every wedding seems to go off without a hitch.

Astrologically, the Four of Wands is associated with the third ten degrees of Aries, where Venus, the goddess of love and beauty, casts a romantic glow over an otherwise single-minded sign.

The Five of Wands: Lost in the Crowd

Five young men hoist long branches over their heads. All of the branches—and all of the participants—are getting tangled up. No one seems to be aware of what the others are doing, and their efforts seem to be getting lost in the crowd.

The Five of Wands, traditionally known as the card of strife, has a disorganized, disjointed quality. The five figures in the card are trying to work together, but it's not going smoothly. Each member of the group is struggling to find his place and to cooperate with the others. As outside observers, we can see that they're just a few steps away from forming a star-shaped design with their wands. Because they're not communicating well, however, the resulting conflict seems to be leading them into competition and chaos.

Clearly, they could use a hand. They need guidance and direction from someone who can see the big picture and help them work together to construct a form of beauty and symmetry.

When you see the Five of Wands in a romance reading, it may be time for you to step back and try to see the big picture, too. You may discover that you are struggling unnecessarily, and that a few well-timed words and thoughtful moves will make it possible for you to develop a workable structure for your own relationships.

Part of the problem is the sheer number of participants in the card. Four young men with four pieces of timber would have no problem joining forces to devise a square. The introduction of that fifth element, however, offers a challenge to most builders.

The five figures in the Five of Wands may symbolize your five senses—sight, sound, touch, taste, and smell—that work together to help you make sense of the outside world. The five figures might also represent the other people in your life.

Whenever you see a Tarot card with several figures in it, ask yourself what their relationship to each other might be. Are they from the same social class? Are they colleagues, competitors, or combatants? What drives each individual, and what has brought them together? What weaknesses divide them? What strengths does each have to contribute? And what are they trying to show you?

When you see the Five of Wands, think about the motivations, strengths, and weaknesses that are at play in your relationships. Are you at odds—perhaps even with yourself? Are you using all of your senses? Are you using your gifts and talents? Are you communicating clearly?

Astrologically, the Five of Wands is associated with the first ten degrees of Leo. It depicts the energy of Saturn, the planet of limits and restrictions, in the fiery, self-centered sign of Leo.

The Six of Wands: A Hero's Welcome

A conquering hero rides his valiant steed through a crowd of cheering, shouting people. They are celebrating because he has won the war, and he has brought peace and prosperity back to them. There are no visible reminders of the struggle he overcame—only signs and symbols of victory, as the teeming horde celebrates his success and their good fortune.

The Six of Wands is one of those cards you can practically hear when you look at it. At a glance, you can see that it's noisy: children run and shout with excitement, horses' hooves clatter in the street, and musicians fill the air with the sound of drums and bugles.

When you see the Six of Wands in a romance reading, it's your turn to feel victorious. You'll find that you have triumphed over obstacles, and your partnership is about to experience a period of peace and prosperity. You have proven yourself in battle, you have the support of powerful allies, and you can conquer any enemies who threaten the peace and harmony of your relationships.

Be ready, however, for the dark side of success. Pay attention to the fact that even though the hero in the card is being publicly honored and acclaimed, he is above the crowd—not part of it. Everyone else literally looks up to him. He can never again blend in and be an ordinary man.

On a practical level, that could mean that others might be jealous of you. Some of your long-standing partners might call on you to return favors. Some of your newfound allies might claim credit for your victory. Some might even want a piece of you and your success. And you'll always have to keep a wary eye open for the opponents you vanquished, because they might come back for revenge.

All in all, though, the Six of Wands is a good card. Six is generally considered to represent the human being, because God created man on the sixth day. Six also symbolizes your sixth sense—your psychic ability—as well as the six directions of space (left, right, forward, backward, up, and down).

Traditionally, the Six of Wands is known as the card of victory. Astrologically, it corresponds to the second ten degrees of Leo, where Jupiter, the god of luck and expansion, can enjoy his own good fortune.

The Seven of Wands: King of the Hill

At the edge of a steep cliff, a bearded knight in full armor stands his ground. His feet are firmly planted; he is in command. However, he is compelled to stand in place, to defend his turf against a half dozen oncoming aggressors. The invaders are not visible, but they are clearly attempting to scale the side of the cliff. Despite the fact that the knight is outnumbered, he is undeniably in a more defensible position. He does not shirk; he meets his opponents head on.

The Seven of Wands is highly charged. While our hero may be king of the hill, his continued success is not necessarily assured. It will take courage, fortitude, and perseverance to continue to fend off his attackers.

When you get the Seven of Wands in a romance reading, it's not the time to rest on your laurels. Rather, your relationship will probably be facing a number of challenges. The oncoming wands may represent an imbalance brought about by misunderstanding, doubt, fear, and embarrassment, as well as a lack of self-confidence.

Happily, you will be able to see each of those challenges clearly, and your courage, determination, will, and sense of perseverance will be unrivaled. In the meantime, however, it wouldn't hurt to muster any resources and reinforcements at your disposal.

Seven is an exceptionally mystical number. Classically, there were seven days of creation; seven gifts of the Holy Spirit (wisdom, understanding, counsel, fortitude, knowledge, piety, and fear); seven deadly sins (envy, sloth, gluttony, wrath, pride, lust, and greed); seven virtues (faith, hope, charity, fortitude, justice, temperance, and prudence); seven corporal works of mercy (feed the hungry, give drink to the thirsty, welcome the stranger, clothe the naked, visit the sick, visit the prisoner, and bury the dead); and seven heavens. There are seven visible planets, seven musical notes, and seven chakras, or energy centers, of the body. To randomize your Tarot deck fully before a reading, shuffle it seven times.

Traditionally, the Seven of Wands is known as the card of valor. Astrologically, it corresponds to the third ten degrees of Leo, where Mars, the all-powerful god of war, finds the courage and determination to win any battle.

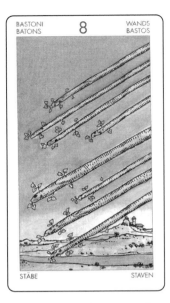

The Eight of Wands: It's Electrifying

Eight leafy branches soar through the air like arrows, all flying parallel to each other at a forty-five degree angle. It isn't clear, from the illustration, whether the wands are landing or taking off. They are traveling over a nearby river, within the sight of anyone in the hilltop castle in the background.

Historically, the Eight of Wands has usually signified speed, travel to distant lands, and messages that come from faraway places. As times have changed, the meaning of the card has become even more relevant. Nowadays, we all send news and messages to distant friends and associates via phone, fax, and e-mail. Our bulletins travel long distances across the airwaves, as surely and as speedily as the eight wands fly through the air.

One thing that has not changed, however, is the Eight of Wands' essential meaning. Its appearance in any Tarot reading signals the speedy onset of new developments, new messages, new transmissions of thought and intention, and new communications coming over the transom.

When you see the Eight of Wands in a romance reading, don't be surprised to hear news that has traveled some distance to reach you. You might find yourself traveling or sending new messages in return. The wands pictured in the card might even be Cupid's arrows. You could find yourself involved in a long-distance relationship, in which you will need to take advantage of technology and electronic communication to stay in touch.

Traditionally, the Eight of Wands is known as the card of swiftness. Astrologically, it corresponds to the first ten degrees of Sagittarius, where Mercury, the messenger of the gods, is equipped to cover long distances quickly and easily.

BASTONI BATONS 9 WANDS BASTOS

STÄBE STAVEN

The Nine of Wands: Sadder but Wiser

A middle-aged, mustached man stands sheltered with his back protected by a wall of wands. His back is stooped, his posture is guarded, and his eyes are open and alert, as though he is expecting—and dreading—someone's approach.

The lone figure in the Nine of Wands, a wounded warrior, stands with his back against a wall. He is battle-hardened, wary, and on edge. At the same time, however, he is determined, wise, and cagey, and he has found a place where he can fall back, regroup his thoughts, regather his strength, and prepare for whatever may come.

When you see the Nine of Wands in a romance reading, you may feel as though your back is against the wall. You may feel weary and under attack. You may feel the need to protect yourself and your resources.

The good news is that you will live to fight another day. While the Nine of Wands might seem like a test, it clearly suggests that you have the perseverance, determination, and strength to overcome obstacles. You have the courage of your convictions.

Traditionally, the Nine of Wands is known as the card of strength in opposition. Astrologically, it is associated with the second ten degrees of Sagittarius, where the goddess of the moon can shed her light on those who seek solutions to complex problems.

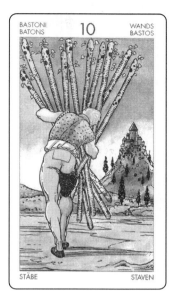

The Ten of Wands: Carry On

Stooped and bent over with the weight of his burden, a strong young man struggles to carry an armload of heavy wooden branches. The path ahead of him is straight and smooth, but he seems to be moving toward rockier terrain, as he heads for his home on a nearby hill.

It can be easy to recognize yourself in the Ten of Wands. Everyone has felt overworked, burdened, and occasionally bent over with the weight of everyday responsibilities, thoughts, and concerns.

When you see the Ten of Wands in a romance reading, however, the consequences become more serious. You aren't just looking at someone who has too many meetings to attend or someone with too many dirty dishes in the sink. When you see the Ten of Wands in a romance reading, it is time to acknowledge the fact that you seem to be doing all of the heavy lifting in your relationship.

You might not even realize that the situation has gotten so far out of control. You may simply have been strolling along on a quiet country lane, picking up the pieces of your life together. Once you had most of the load in your arms, you got so busy trying to balance it that you haven't even noticed that your partner is nowhere in sight.

Happily, this leg of your journey is coming to an end. Ten is the number of completion and perfection, and you are almost home. In a short time, you will be able to lay down your burden. At that point, however, you will need to decide how you want to continue. You can choose any number of options. At first, you may simply need to rest—but you could also throw all of the logs on the floor and decry the unfairness of your relationship, or burn them in the fireplace. You could head back out on the road and look for more branches to pick up. You could leave, or you could negotiate a new agreement with your partner, one in which the division of labor is more equitable.

The good news is that your work to this point has not gone to waste. You have a good handle on the problems in your relationship, and carrying them around has made you a stronger person. You are headed for a conclusion: how you reach it will be up to you.

Traditionally, the Ten of Wands is the card of oppression. Astrologically, it is associated with the third ten degrees of Sagittarius, where a malicious Saturn, god of boundaries and limitations, puts obstacles and roadblocks in front of those who long to travel freely.

FANTE DI BASTONI VALET DE BATONS — KNAVE OF WANDS SOTA DE BASTOS

BUBE DER STÄBE — STAVEN SCHILDKNAAP

The Page of Wands: Playing with Fire

With an expression of determined optimism, a regally dressed bearded man stands in an arid desert with both hands holding firm to a long, leafy branch. He is healthy, young, and strong, and brimming with confidence and self-assurance.

The bright young Page of Wands is the personification of fire—the embodiment of the fiery energy that connects the suit of Wands to the world of spirit and creativity. In other words, the Page of Wands is a graphic example of how fire can take human form.

All of the Pages in the Tarot deck embody the elements they represent. Elementally speaking, the four Pages of the Tarot are all earthy, physical creatures. They simply combine the element of earth with the element of their suit. The Page of Wands personifies fire, the Page of Cups personifies water, the Page of Swords personifies air, and the Page of Pentacles personifies earth.

The Page of Wands, who personifies fire, is arguably the most mesmerizing of the four.

Like all Pages, the Page of Wands is youthful, with childlike enthusiasm and an unbounded capacity to learn. Filled with energy, ambition, and drive, he is daring and courageous. He is quick to fall in love and equally quick to lash out in anger. Like fire itself, he can be warm and passionate. Without a safe place to burn, however, he can also rage out of control, and he could become unstable, violent, and destructive.

When you see the Page of Wands in a romance reading, he usually reflects a facet of your own personality. If you don't like or acknowledge the Page of Wands side of yourself, however, you might find yourself projecting all of his qualities onto someone else in your life—and you'll either love him or hate him. In either case, your relationship with the Page of Wands will be passionate, fiery, and hot.

During the Renaissance, pages were the youngest members of the royal court. Pages would frequently serve as messengers; it was their job to take news from one person to another. Because they were young, pages were students learning their future roles through apprenticeships.

Because pages are students and messengers, his appearance in a romance reading might also be telling you that important lessons or messages are coming your way regarding the spiritual side of your love life.

Pages are purely elemental; they are not associated with any astrological sign.

CAVALLO DI BASTONI   KNIGHT OF WANDS
CHEVALIER DE BATONS   CABALLO DE BASTOS

RITTER DER STÄBE   STAVEN RIDDER

The Knight of Wands: Fire and Lightning

A young knight on a galloping steed rides through a desert and past three ancient pyra-
mids. He's wearing a yellow tunic emblazoned with salamanders, the elemental creatures
of fire. Underneath the tunic, he's dressed in full battle armor. His helmet is topped with
a fiery red plume.

Single women often joke about waiting for a knight in shining armor. Happily, when
you conduct a Tarot reading, you can actually see when those knights are on the way.

When you see the Knight of Wands in a romance reading, you might think he's
about to ride out of the pages of a fairy tale and into your life. No one would blame you
for hoping. After all, everybody knows that knights are young and charismatic. They
are highly skilled in the courtly arts of love and romance. And they're chivalrous, which
means they're ready and willing to fight on behalf of the weak and helpless.

Unfortunately, as we so often find in fairy tales, there is a catch. For one thing,
you're not weak and helpless. What's more, that knight in shining armor might not be
coming from a faraway kingdom. In fact, that Knight of Wands in your romance reading might simply be a part of your own personality, waiting to ride out of your subconscious mind.

It might help to take a closer look at the legendary tale of the knight. Stories about knights are actually stories about transformation. In most renditions, a knight is on a quest for a mystical object, like the Holy Grail. As he pursues his mission, he encounters—and overcomes—a series of obstacles, which have all been deliberately contrived to test and challenge him. By the conclusion of his quest, the knight has learned that the mystical object he sought was never really the true goal of his adventure. Rather, the mission was actually one of self-development and change.

The same holds true for most of us who are in search of love and romance. Our quest isn't really to find a partner, although that can sometimes seem like our ultimate goal. While a partner can be a wonderful companion on the journey, what we really seek is the Holy Grail of self-transformation. No knight in shining armor can do the hard work for us. No crusading hero can truly change who we are inside, no matter how much we wish that it were so, and no one else can rescue us from ourselves.

If you are lucky enough to meet a real-life Knight of Wands, however, you'll recognize him immediately. The Knight of Wands, like all of the court cards in his suit, is fiery and energetic. He is witty, flirtatious, and romantic. He is a wanderer, a traveler, an adventurer, and a crusader. He can be fierce, sudden, impulsive, and impetuous.

Traditionally, the appearance of the Knight of Wands in a Tarot reading would sometimes indicate a move to a new home.

Elementally speaking, the four Knights of the Tarot are all fiery. They simply combine the element of fire with the element of their own suit. In that regard, the Knight of Wands embodies the passionate combination of fire with fire.

Astrologically, the four Knights of the Tarot are also associated with the four mutable signs of the Zodiac. The Knight of Wands represents the mutable fire sign of Sagittarius, which makes him outgoing and adventurous.

The Queen of Wands: Steam Heat

Quiet and intense, the Queen of Wands sits on her high-backed throne. It's carved with a design of sunflower stems and leaves, an obvious allusion to the sunflowers growing alongside the queen. She is dressed in bright yellow, orange, and magenta, and a heavy crown seems to sit weightlessly on her head. The queen's black cat, like a witch's familiar, sits knowingly at her feet.

The Tarot's four Queens are all examples of ideal women. Each one represents the watery, emotional side of feminine nature by combining the element of water with the corresponding element of her suit. In that respect, the Queen of Wands embodies the steamy combination of water with the fire, energy, passion, and heat of the Wands cards.

Like all of the Tarot's Queens, the Queen of Wands is a mature woman, gracious and wise in the ways of the world. A fiery redhead, she is also one of the most charismatic figures in the Tarot deck. She is physically fit, energetic, and strong. Traditionally, she is also known as a smart, savvy businesswoman who loves money and success.

Queens, of course, are rulers—but customarily, their rulership is based on the feminine principles of safeguarding and nurturing their realms. When you see the Queen of

Wands in a romance reading, she is probably there to safeguard and nurture you on a spiritual level (that's because Wands symbolize the spiritual realm of our existence). Look for the influence of a bright, outgoing, enthusiastic personality. She might be someone you know, or she might be a reflection of your own personality. Actually, you might recognize her by her flirtatious nature, which, occasionally, can also lead to fickleness and periods of infidelity.

Astrologically, the four Queens of the Tarot are associated with the four cardinal signs of the Zodiac. The Queen of Wands represents the cardinal fire sign of Aries, which makes her a natural leader.

RE DI BASTONI / ROI DE BATONS — KING OF WANDS / REY DE BASTOS

KÖNIG DER STÄBE — STAVEN KONING

The King of Wands: Hot, Hot, Hot

We see the King of Wands only in profile, as he sits on his throne deep in thought. He is not relaxed. He leans forward, legs apart, as though he could leap to his feet at any moment. His crown consists of a wreath of golden leaves, and he wears a chain-mail hood under his red tunic and cape. A small salamander, the elemental creature of fire, scurries across the base of his throne.

Like all of the Kings in the Tarot deck, the King of Wands is a seasoned, experienced man. He has successfully completed the mission he undertook as the former Knight of Wands. He was rewarded with the keys to the kingdom, and he now rules the entire realm, as well as its armies that defend and conquer in the name of the throne.

The King of Wands is a strong, spirited leader. He never rests, as you can tell by his inability to sit still, even in the card. He is a tireless and ardent defender of the persecuted and oppressed, even if it means that he will be forced to use violence. He is honest, courageous, and strong. And he is generous, almost to a fault.

When you see the King of Wands in a romance reading, you can expect long-term success in your relationship. That's because the King of Wands is traditionally thought to be a happily married man. You might also find yourself taking a more active role in defending your relationship or being helped by a strong, authoritative man.

Elementally, the four Kings of the Tarot are all airy intellectuals. They simply combine the element of air with the corresponding element of their suit. In that regard, the King of Wands embodies the heady combination of air with fire.

Astrologically, the four Kings of the Tarot are also associated with the four fixed signs of the Zodiac. The King of Wands represents the fixed fire sign of Leo, which makes him a confident, courageous monarch.

The Ace of Cups: Your Cup Runneth Over

An open hand, larger than life, balances a golden chalice on its outstretched palm. A white dove soars directly over the chalice, about to dip a communion wafer into the contents of the cup. From inside the cup, four streams of water rise up like a fountain and flow over the sides, into the blue waters of a lake below.

The Ace of Cups is the first card in the suit of Cups, the suit that corresponds to the ancient element of water. In that respect, the Ace of Cups is the source of all the water in the subsequent cards in the suit.

When you see the Ace of Cups in a romance reading, get ready to be showered with blessings. Your cup, as they say, is about to overflow with happiness. The dam is about to burst, and new love will wash over you.

Cups, of course, have long been used to symbolize the joy of romance, the contentment of companionship, and the celebration of community. Drinking from a shared cup plays an important role in many religious ceremonies, including weddings.

It is also important to note that cups can hold any number of liquids with powerful symbolic meanings. They can hold water, for example—the elixir of life. They can hold ritual wine, celebratory champagne, or even a beverage as mundane and healthful as chicken soup.

Like all of the Aces, the Ace of Cups sometimes represents the potential for creation. Occasionally, the Ace of Cups can even indicate a pregnancy. The cup is a feminine symbol that represents the womb, while the dove and the host represent the joining of a spirit and a physical body. Whether the pregnancy is literal or symbolic is a matter for interpretation: the Ace might simply be referring to the birth of a new project or creative pursuit.

The Two of Cups: A Toast to Romance

A young, dark-haired man and a beautiful, blonde woman stare into each other's eyes and pledge their love. They're in the courtyard of an ancient garden, surrounded by pillars, columns, and statues—some intact, others in ruins. The winged head of a lion, with a somewhat human-looking face, hovers over both of them.

The Two of Cups bodes well in any Tarot reading. It is the very picture of partnership, love, romance, and affection. Twos symbolize duality, partnerships, choices, and combinations. Twos can also symbolize an antithesis, a counterpoint, or a conflict.

However, the true meaning of the Two of Cups is much deeper than it seems at first glance. Like the Lovers card—and all of the Twos in the Tarot—the Two of Cups is a reminder of all of the elements that make up a successful partnership.

First and foremost, the card depicts the importance of clear communication in a successful relationship. For the most part, you should see eye to eye with your partner. Even in those instances where you disagree, however, the Two of Cups reminds you that there must be give-and-take in any relationship and that a balanced exchange of energy is a requirement for any relationship to take root and grow.

Some people say that opposites attract. In this case, it's obviously true: one is dark, the other fair. One is a man, the other is a woman. The differences between the couple reflect the duality of the world: the contrast between dark and light, male and female, delicate and strong.

The image also suggests an inherent balance in the universe, even though circumstances may differ. While the couple in the card is as different as night and day, they are equal. They stand face to face, looking into each other's eyes and sharing the moment.

When you see the Two of Cups in a romance reading, take heart. After all, the card is traditionally known as the card of love. A romantic partnership is practically guaranteed.

You might want to take note, however, of the winged lion that is rising over the young couple in the card. The lion is an alchemical symbol that signifies an unborn soul, waiting and hoping for a physical vehicle to enter this world. In other words, there could be a new baby waiting in the wings.

Astrologically, the Two of Cups is associated with the first ten degrees of Cancer, where Venus, the goddess of love, can help young lovers establish a happy home together.

The Three of Cups: Girls' Night Out

Under the leafy branches of a vineyard in full bloom, three young women scamper, frolic, and dance, each with an upraised goblet held high over her head. They celebrate the coming harvest and the richness of the fruit of the vine, and they toast the transformation of grapes into celebratory wine.

The Three of Cups is a card that celebrates friendship. Three young women dance together, holding their glasses high over their heads. A bountiful grape harvest means that there will be even more wine and feasting to come.

According to some Tarot readers, the three women pictured in the card are goddesses. Some see them as the embodiment of the three stages in every woman's life: maiden, mother, and crone (which in this case, means wise old woman). Others see them as the three fates who weave the fabric of every individual's life: one spins the thread, the second weaves it, and when each person's life is over, the third goddess snips the thread.

Sometimes, the number three symbolizes the combination of body, mind, and spirit. It frequently symbolizes past, present, and future, as well as the course of human existence:

birth, life, and death. Three also carries a religious connotation: many beliefs describe a holy trinity, such as Father, Son, and Holy Spirit.

In any event, the Three of Cups is a joyful card, and it's a good omen in any Tarot spread. When you get the Three of Cups in a romance reading, you can expect to have the support, encouragement, and help of your friends in finding and keeping the perfect partner.

Traditionally, the Three of Cups is known as the card of abundance. Astrologically, it is associated with the second ten degrees of Cancer, where Mercury, the messenger of the gods, brings news of plenty and prosperity to the home.

The Four of Cups: Opportunity Knocks

At first glance, the figure in the Four of Cups seems glum and disenchanted. He sits under the branches of an ancient tree, as leaves begin to change color and fall to the ground. There are three golden cups in front of him, just out of his reach. He doesn't seem to notice that a cloud has formed to his right. A ghostly arm is emerging from the vaporous mist. It holds a new, fourth cup in its outstretched hand.

Obviously, there is more to the Four of Cups than meets the eye—especially for the guy under the tree. He seems drained, listless, and uninspired. The party's over, and weariness has set in. Boredom and discontent are sure to follow.

When you see the Four of Cups in a romance reading, you may need to open your eyes to new possibilities. You are being offered a great gift—a new friendship, a new romance, or a new attitude. Either you don't see it, or you're working hard to ignore it.

You might be distracted by other factors. You might be avoiding new opportunities, because they don't fit into your current existence. Growth can be uncomfortable, and you are used to the way things are. Change is hard work, and it can even be a little bit frightening. On some level, you may even be enjoying your malaise. There are times when all of us like to spend some time alone with a favorite tearjerker on television or a sad song on the radio.

You can choose to accept the new cup of emotion that is being offered to you or decline it, for now. You have the luxury of time, and you are in no hurry.

Traditionally, the Four of Cups is known as the card of blended pleasure. Astrologically, it is associated with the third ten degrees of Cancer, where the goddess of the moon leads her followers through cycles of emotion and reflection.

The Five of Cups: Crying over Spilled Milk

Head bowed, a young man stands on the dusty banks of a river under a cloudy gray sky. There are three cups beside him, all on their sides, with their contents spilling and streaming away. There are two cups behind him, however, still standing upright. An arched bridge in the distance spans a flowing river leading to a fortress on the other side of its banks.

"Better to have loved and lost, than never to have loved at all."

That's what Alfred Lord Tennyson said—and he was probably right, although you'd never know it to look at the Five of Cups. It is a graphic image of loss and sorrow.

When you see the Five of Cups in a romance reading, you may be facing a loss of your own, such as the breakup of a love affair or a broken engagement. You may feel disappointed, disheartened, mournful, and sad. You might even feel regretful, because the spill might have been your fault. You might have stumbled, or turned too quickly, or somehow knocked all three cups over onto the ground.

The key to interpreting the Five of Cups is in acknowledging your loss, no matter what caused it. After all, there is no use crying over spilled milk. What's done is done. Everyone has made mistakes, taken a wrong turn. And everyone—at least if they're lucky—has a failed relationship in their past. While it might seem tragic at the time, we learn from our mistakes, and those early losses help prepare us for a relationship that can last.

For now, you can pick up the cups that have spilled and figure out a way to refill them. In the meantime, you should take care of the two cups that haven't tipped over.

Traditionally, the Five of Cups is known as the card of loss of pleasure. Astrologically, it is associated with the first ten degrees of Scorpio, where Mars, the natural ruler of the sign, can mourn with intensity.

The Six of Cups: Childhood Sweethearts

Two very young children enjoy a collection of cut flowers in six golden vases. The boy is wearing a red cape and a blue tunic; the girl is wearing a finely stitched gown and matching bonnet. Behind them, a heraldic shield hints at their heritage and the people who built their home.

The winsome young pair in the Six of Cups is the picture of innocence. They embody everything we like to remember about our first forays into romance—the eagerness to be with a newfound soul mate, the unexpected joy that comes with giving, and the thrill of receiving the gift of love from someone else.

Granted, it is a nostalgic picture, one that might as well be sepia-toned and slightly out of focus. But when you see the Six of Cups in a romance reading, it's time to reminisce. You may find yourself becoming reacquainted with someone from your distant past. Someone you have known since childhood might also introduce you to a new partner. A brother or a sister might be instrumental in giving you guidance. The Six of Cups may even refer to a soul mate, someone you were destined to connect with during your lifetime.

Ultimately, the Six of Cups is a sentimental reminder of how it felt to experience love and romance for the first time, and its appearance in a Tarot reading is an encouraging sign that you should be prepared to experience those sensations anew.

The number six is generally considered to represent the human being, because God created man on the sixth day. Six also symbolizes the sixth sense, psychic ability, as well as the six directions of space—left, right, forward, backward, up, and down.

Traditionally, the Six of Cups is known as the card of pleasure. Astrologically, it is associated with the second ten degrees of Scorpio, where the Sun radiates joy and optimism.

The Seven of Cups: Dream Lovers

A muscular man stands with his back turned toward us. He seems to be looking in amazement at a swirling bank of clouds, where seven golden cups seem to materialize out of thin air. Each cup holds a separate, symbolic offering: a woman, a veiled figure with outstretched arms, a snake, a castle, glittering jewels, a laurel wreath, and a dragon.

The Seven of Cups offers a glimpse into the world of the daydreamer, where seven separate possibilities flicker in and out of view.

The seven cups all relate to the seven Major Arcana cards, which in turn correspond to the seven visible planets. The woman is the Empress, which corresponds to Venus. The veiled figure is the High Priestess, which corresponds to the Moon. The serpent relates to the Magician, who traditionally wears a serpent belt, which corresponds to the planet Mercury. The castle on the hill is the Tower, which corresponds to Mars. The shimmering jewels are the good fortune promised by the Wheel of Fortune, which corresponds to Jupiter. The wreath is the oval wreath that surrounds the dancer in the World card; it corresponds to Saturn. And the fire-breathing dragon is an alternate manifestation of the horse from the Sun card.

The seven cups seem to hover, tantalizing, just barely out of reach. To pluck one out of thin air and make it materialize would involve a fair amount of effort. What's more, pursuing one dream would mean that the other dreams would have to be let go—at least temporarily. For many dreamers, to choose only one path seems too limiting.

To add insult to injury, the seven options are not merely fantasies. According to tradition, they each could lead to one's downfall, through lust, deception, lies, unfulfilled promises, vanity, illusionary success, and drunkenness.

When you see the Seven of Cups in a romance reading, it's time to quit daydreaming. Pick a reasonable goal, and pursue it.

You will still be able to dream. In fact, a certain amount of visualization and planning is necessary in order to plan and to prepare for the future you desire. But right now, it's time to get your head out of the clouds and get back to earth.

Traditionally, the Seven of Cups is known as the card of illusionary success. Astrologically, it is associated with the third ten degrees of Scorpio, where Venus, the goddess of love, lends a mystical, transcendent quality to romantic relationships.

The Eight of Cups: Looking for Love

In the foreground, eight golden cups are stacked in two rows, with five cups on the bottom and three cups on the top. Between a gap in the second row, we can see a solitary, stooped figure, leaning on his walking stick, in the process of turning away. He seems to be headed toward a crevasse in a nearby mountain range.

The Eight of Cups depicts someone who seems to have it all: those eight cups, neatly stacked, represent an orderly, prosperous existence. However, something is obviously missing. There is a void, an empty space in the collection—and the absence is enough to compel that figure in the card to turn his back on everything he owns and begin a quest for the missing piece.

When you see the Eight of Cups in a romance reading, others might think your life is complete. To outside observers, it looks as though you have it all. Your ducks are lined up in a row. Your life seems complete.

Nevertheless, you know that something—or someone—is missing, and you won't be able to rest until you have filled that void in your life.

You know that there is a risk in wanting more. You might even be tempting fate. Why turn your back on everything you already have, just so you can chase a dream?

What's more, you know that there is no guarantee that everything will stay in its place while you are out searching. Still, in your heart, you know that you must take a risk. "Good enough" isn't good enough, at least for you.

The Eight of Cups will often reaffirm what you already know: it is time to begin your quest and move toward completion. The Eight of Cups is not a card that usually offers specific advice, however. If you don't know how to begin your quest, pull another card for clarification. Before you pull that card, ask, "How do I take that first step?" or "What should I do next?"

Traditionally, the Eight of Cups is known as the card of abandoned success. Astrologically, it is associated with the first ten degrees of Pisces, where Saturn longs for unity with others.

The Nine of Cups: Love Potion #9

A giant bear of a man with a full beard and long curly hair reclines on a carved marble bench. He is the picture of contentment: he wears a satisfied smile, and he leans comfortably with his back against a bar. Nine golden cups are lined up on top of the bar, just above the man's cap-covered head.

Love can be intoxicating. Just like a drink or two, romance can smooth out our rough edges, free us from our inhibitions, and make us feel less self-conscious. After a few glasses of wine, we all feel a little more talkative, more intelligent, and more interesting than our usual selves. We even dance better! Come to think of it, everyone else at the party seems a little more attractive, too.

Unfortunately, love—like booze—can also cloud our thinking and impair our judgment.

When you see the Nine of Cups in a romance reading, you might want to sober up a bit. You can still enjoy the heady intoxication that love can bring—but drink responsibly. While that good-natured fellow at the bar offers a quick and easy escape from the cares of the workday world, you might regret it in the morning. His kiss might be sweeter than wine—but then again, you might also be better off drinking to each other only with your eyes. At any rate, make sure you have a designated driver, so at closing time you don't find yourself at the mercy of passing charioteers with fast cars.

Traditionally, the Nine of Cups is known as the card of material happiness. Astrologically, it is associated with the second ten degrees of Pisces, where Jupiter, the god of luck and expansion, occasionally seeks good fortune at the bottom of a bottle.

The Ten of Cups: Love and Marriage

A husband and wife stand together, side by side. The man has his left arm wrapped comfortably around the woman's waist, as their two young children dance and play nearby. The whole family is standing on the banks of a lake or a stream, not far from a snug, cozy cottage. Overhead, ten golden cups seem to shimmer in the arc of a colorful rainbow that arches across the entire sky.

In the Ten of Cups, we see a young married couple quietly basking in their happy life together. Their children are dancing for joy, and a colorful rainbow portends an equally joyful future together. The card represents the ultimate goal of a romantic partnership: the contentment of a happy home, a loving family, and a sense of togetherness.

There are four members of the family, a nod to the four elements and the four suits of the Major Arcana. They complement each other, and they complete each other. After all, when it comes to the Tarot, ten is the number of completion and perfection.

The children in the card symbolize the productivity that can result from a successful partnership. It doesn't matter whether the children are actually living offspring or simply the tangible results of the couple's relationship. In an ideal marriage, a husband and a wife will each enhance the other's creativity and productivity.

The cozy cottage in the background is an obvious illustration of a happy home. It's a warm and comfortable refuge from the outside world. It's not a castle—but it's not a shack, either. Meanwhile, the rainbow overhead symbolizes a bright future and the promise of God's protection.

When you see the Ten of Cups in a romance reading, expect a partner who can help you be more productive. You can celebrate your successes together and help each other be more productive. Together, you can give birth to projects and successes that will outlive you both.

Traditionally, the Ten of Cups is known as the card of perfected success. Astrologically, it is associated with the third ten degrees of Pisces, where Mars, the god of energy and aggression, becomes gentle and supportive.

FANTE DI COPPE   KNAVE OF CHALICES
VALET DE COUPES   SOTA DE COPAS

BUBE DER KELCHE   BEKERS SCHILDKNAAP

The Page of Cups: Message in a Bottle

A colorfully dressed adolescent gazes with amusement as a fish peers out from the cup in his right hand. He wears a wide-brimmed hat, a ruffled collar and blousy sleeves, a vest, and oversized pink bloomers. He's standing on a beach; behind him, waves roll toward the horizon.

The sensitive young Page of Cups is the personification of water—the embodiment of the fluid undercurrents that connect the suit of Cups to the world of emotion. In other words, the Page of Cups is a graphic example of how water can take human form.

Actually, all of the Pages in the Tarot deck embody the elements they represent. Elementally speaking, the four Pages of the Tarot are all earthy, physical creatures. They simply combine the element of earth with the element of their suit. In other words, the Page of Wands personifies fire, the Page of Cups personifies water, the Page of Swords personifies air, and the Page of Pentacles personifies earth.

The Page of Cups, who personifies water, is arguably the most romantic of the four.

Like all Pages, the Page of Cups is youthful, with childlike enthusiasm and an unbounded capacity to learn. He is extremely sensitive, however. He is gentle and kind, dreamy and imaginative. He is a poet, an artist, a dreamer, and he is still innocent and inexperienced enough to be completely optimistic.

When you see the Page of Cups in a romance reading, he usually reflects a facet of your own personality. If you don't like or acknowledge the Page of Cups side of yourself, however, you might find yourself projecting all of his qualities onto someone else in your life, and your relationship with that person will be emotional.

During the Renaissance, pages were the youngest members of the royal court. Pages would frequently serve as messengers; it was their job to take news from one person to another. And because they were young, pages were students learning their future roles through apprenticeships. When you see the Page of Cups in a romance reading, you may soon be receiving important lessons or messages about the emotional side of your love life.

Pages are purely elemental; they are not associated with any astrological signs.

The Knight of Cups: Prince Charming

A serious-looking knight, in full battle armor, seems to raise his cup in salute as he and his white horse stand on the banks of a wide, crystal-clear river. Fed by a rushing water-fall, the river spills over a towering, rocky cliff.

The Knight of Cups, like all of the court cards in his suit, is watery and emotional. He is gallant, graceful, and generous. He is imaginative—even visionary. More than anything, he is a romantic idealist who believes that beauty is truth, and truth is beauty. Unfortunately, the Knight of Cups is so romantic that he will fall in love with every beautiful woman who crosses his path. He will leave you with a long, lingering kiss on your doorstep, and he'll promise to call. He'll mean it, too—but once he's back on his horse and another beautiful woman crosses his path, he'll simply forget.

Traditionally, the appearance of the Knight of Cups in a Tarot reading would sometimes indicate a visit from a friend, who might even bring money.

Elementally speaking, the four Knights of the Tarot are all fiery. They simply combine the element of fire with the element of their own suit. In that regard, the Knight of Cups embodies the steamy combination of fire with water.

Astrologically, the four Knights of the Tarot are also associated with the four mutable signs of the Zodiac. The Knight of Cups represents the mutable water sign of Pisces, which makes him sensitive and introspective.

REGINA DI COPPE   QUEEN OF CHALICES
REINE DE COUPES   REINA DE COPAS

KÖNIGIN DER KELCHE   BEKERS KONINGIN

The Queen of Cups: Queen of Hearts

From her seashell-shaped throne, apparently carved from mother of pearl, the Queen of Cups gazes contemplatively into the depths of her golden chalice. Her silvery, satin gown flows gracefully, much like the flowing waves of her golden hair. She is surrounded by water, with a reflective, clear lake both behind and in front of her.

The Tarot's four Queens are all examples of ideal women. Each one represents the watery, emotional side of feminine nature by combining the element of water with the corresponding element of her suit. In that respect, the Queen of Cups embodies the pure blend of water with the emotional depth of the Cups cards.

Like all of the Tarot's Queens, the Queen of Cups is a mature woman, gracious and wise in the ways of the world. She is also one of the most well-balanced women in the Tarot deck. She effortlessly balances marriage and family and, indeed, she is the perfect wife and mother. She is creative and artistic, loving and caring. She is also remarkably intuitive. At times, she is prone to psychic prophecies and mystical visions.

Queens, of course, are rulers—but traditionally, their rulership is based on the feminine principles of safeguarding and nurturing their realms. When you see the Queen of Cups in a romance reading, she is probably there to safeguard and nurture your emotional life. Look for the influence of an intuitive, artistic personality. She might be someone you know, or she might be a reflection of your own personality. Actually, you might find her in the kitchen. She's an accomplished cook who seems to specialize in hearty soups and stews, along with a wide range of fresh-baked cookies, cakes, and pies.

Astrologically, the four Queens of the Tarot are associated with the four cardinal signs of the Zodiac. The Queen of Cups represents the cardinal water sign of Cancer, which makes her a natural-born wife and mother.

RE DI COPPE / ROI DE COUPES / KING OF CHALICES / REY DE COPAS / KÖNIG DER KELCHE / BEKERS KONING

The King of Cups: Still Waters Run Deep

Legs crossed, brow furrowed, the King of Cups seems lost in thought. He leans forward on his floating throne, which is carved with a seashell and seahorse motif. He's wearing a fish-shaped pendant, a blue tunic, and a long, flowing, gold cape. He holds a golden scepter in his left hand and a golden chalice in his right. Behind him, a merchant sailing ship glides across the waves, and a dolphin leaps high above the seafoam.

Like all of the Kings in the Tarot deck, the King of Cups is a seasoned, experienced man. He has successfully completed the mission he undertook as the former Knight of Cups. He was rewarded with the keys to the kingdom, and he now rules an entire watery realm, as well as its armies that defend and conquer in the name of the throne.

The King of Cups is a fiercely intelligent leader. He is frequently schooled in business, law, science, or divinity. His quiet, calm demeanor disguises a fierce and passionate nature.

When you see the King of Cups in a romance reading, you might want to be somewhat wary of men in positions of power. According to tradition, the King of Cups can be something of a hypocrite, someone who will offer help without intending to follow through. In modern interpretations, however, the King of Cups might also be considered a fitting counterpart to the Queen of Cups, in which case he may be a loving, caring husband and father.

Elementally, the four Kings of the Tarot are all airy intellectuals. They simply combine the element of air with the corresponding element of their suit. In that regard, the King of Cups embodies the vaporous combination of air with water.

Astrologically, the four Kings of the Tarot are also associated with the four fixed signs of the Zodiac. The King of Cups represents the fixed fire sign of Scorpio, which makes him an intensely passionate individual.

The Ace of Swords: Straight to the Point

From an arching cloud bank, a massive hand thrusts forth with a gleaming, gold-hilted sword. The hilt is decorated with gemstones. The tip of the spear is thrust through a golden crown. The left side of the crown has a leafy branch and the right side, a red feather.

The Ace of Swords is the first card in the suit of Swords, the suit that corresponds to the ancient element of air. In that respect, the Ace of Swords is the embodiment of intellectual thoughts and ideals.

The airy Ace of Swords cuts to the heart of any issue. It represents the essence of thought and intellectual understanding. It symbolizes your ability to communicate your thoughts through words, either written or spoken. The sword also represents your ability to cut through any clouds of confusion and to pierce through any veil of mystery or misunderstanding.

One of the Ace's most useful functions is that of a tool that you can use to promote and protect your ideas. As either a weapon of attack or a means of defense, the Ace of Swords cuts both ways.

When you see the Ace of Swords in a romance reading, it's time for you to think clearly about your relationships—and to express your opinions. It may be a good idea for you to clarify your thinking, perhaps through writing. You can be quick and to the point. You are given the gift of communication.

Like all of the Aces, the Ace of Swords sometimes represents the potential for creation. Occasionally, the Ace of Swords can even indicate a pregnancy. The card depicts the tip of a sword penetrating the base of a crown, which could represent the physical act of impregnation. The sword is an obviously masculine symbol. Whether an actual pregnancy is in the cards is anyone's guess. The card could simply suggest that a new idea is about to be conceived.

Traditionally, the Ace of Swords is known as the root of the power of air.

The Two of Swords: Second Chances

Under a crescent-shaped waning moon, the woman in the Two of Swords is in a precarious situation. Perched on a slippery, wet rock, she maintains a tenuous equilibrium by balancing two heavy swords against her shoulders. She can't see anything because she's blindfolded. But she can feel the cold wind at her back and the waves lapping at her feet. She is seated on the seashore, where rocks jut from the shallow water behind her.

The Two of Swords is one of the strangest images in the Tarot deck. Who blindfolded that woman? Who handed her the swords? Why is she sitting there? What could she possibly be thinking?

No one really knows—except you. When you see the Two of Swords in a romance reading, you are that woman on the rock. Now you have to figure out how you got there and what you're going to do next.

You may need to muster up your courage for whatever comes next. Obviously, you have to take some sort of action. You have to figure out a way to take your blinders off and either lay down your weapons or come out fighting.

Because the number two represents partnerships, choices, and combinations, you may find yourself facing a difficult decision—possibly between two partners or two relationships.

The Two of Swords is a serious, somber, contemplative card. You will need to weigh the consequences of your choices carefully. This is not a card that indicates an easy middle ground. It is an either/or situation, with only two options—black or white—and you must choose between them. You might want to pick up your own sword—a pen—and write down a list of pros and cons, advantages and disadvantages, before making any final decisions. Once you've made your peace, you'll be able to live with your decision.

Traditionally, the Two of Swords is known as the card of peace restored. Astrologically, it is associated with the first ten degrees of Libra, where the goddess of the moon lends a sense of balance to relationship decisions.

The Three of Swords: Heartbreak

The specter of a beating heart, stabbed repeatedly by three razor-sharp swords, hangs in the air. Beneath the heart, an anguished, dark-haired man lays sprawled on the wet grass. His hands are covering his face, and he seems to be consumed by grief.

There is no mistaking what's happening in this image. The Three of Swords is the proverbial card of broken hearts. The Three of Swords doesn't depict a friendly parting of ways. No one is shrugging or saying, "Things just didn't work out." When you see the Three of Swords in a romance reading, someone has suffered a painful loss. It may symbolize betrayal, infidelity, separation, or divorce.

Because there are three swords, the card may indicate the presence—or the possibility—of a third person in a relationship. It is important to note that the card doesn't indicate how that third person is involved. Maybe the querent is looking around. Perhaps one partner is unfaithful. It's even possible that a third party is an uninvited guest, taking advantage of a weakness in the relationship or trying to cause problems.

That's the bad news. Fortunately, there's good news, too.

For the most part, the Three of Swords tends to show up in the "past" position of most readings—and those who draw the Three of Swords recognize it immediately.

Those Three of Swords experiences are unforgettable and instantly identifiable in the cards.

Even if the Three of Swords shows up in a future position, however, it usually doesn't come as a surprise. Broken hearts don't happen suddenly. There is usually plenty of warning.

Often, the question is whether a broken heart is inevitable. Sometimes it is, but the future is never etched in stone. Sometimes, when you see a negative card as graphically illustrated as the Three of Swords, you can make changes in your life that will lead to a brighter conclusion.

If your heart has already been broken, however, the Three of Swords is a vivid reminder that healing may simply take time. There will be scar tissue, of course, and where the scar tissue grows your heart will be just a little bit harder and a little less flexible. In other words, you'll probably be a little less innocent and a lot less naïve.

The alternative—to refuse to heal, to become a bleeding heart—is actually less pleasant. After all, everyone experiences a Three of Swords at some point in life. With any luck, the experience will save you from making the same mistakes again, and it will better prepare you to make good decisions and forge a better partnership the next time.

If you happen to get the Three of Swords as the outcome card, don't end the reading on that note. Throw an additional card or two for clarification and advice. Explore the issue on a deeper level, and figure out how you can use the experience to grow as a person.

Traditionally, the Three of Swords is known as the card of sorrow. Astrologically, it is associated with the second ten degrees of Libra, where Saturn longs for perfection—and suffers greatly when he fails.

The Four of Swords: Sleeping Beauty

Under the soft glow of a stained-glass window, a young knight sleeps, arms folded in a prayerlike gesture across his chest. There are three swords hanging on the wall; a fourth sword is lying across his lap.

The Four of Swords is a card of retreat, rest, and recuperation. The figure is that of a knight or a soldier in effigy, carved into the lid of a casket in a medieval church. His expression is peaceful.

Obviously, the card might depict a traditional view of the afterlife. The battle has been won; now the soldier rests in peace and awaits his resurrection. The worries and concerns of the world, symbolized by the three swords overhead, are in a state of suspended animation. The battle is won, and final victory is just a matter of time.

When you get the Four of Swords in a romance reading, it indicates that you, too, could use a period of rest and recuperation in your relationships. You might be pushing things too hard. Relax: your issues, problems, and concerns won't go anywhere, but you could certainly use some time off. When you arise, rested and refreshed, you can pick up again right where you left off.

Four is the number of wholeness and stability. That's because, geometrically speaking, four points combine to form a solid. There are four dimensions, four corners to a room (or a house), four seasons, four cardinal directions, four evangelists (Matthew, Mark, Luke, and John), four horsemen of the Apocalypse, four elements, and four suits in the Minor Arcana.

Traditionally, the Four of Swords is known as the card of rest from strife. Astrologically, it is associated with the third ten degrees of Libra, where Jupiter, god of luck and expansion, finds new life through his relationships.

SPADE
EPEES

5

SWORDS
ESPADAS

SCHWERTER

ZWAARDEN

The Five of Swords: Spoils of War

A victorious fighter collects the swords he has won from two vanquished opponents who walk away, heads bowed, toward the horizon. The knight watches them leave, a smug, self-satisfied smile on his face. Billowing, fast-moving clouds fill the sky.

Some say that true love is worth fighting for—and they are probably right. Even so, however, true love can usually stick up for itself. Hardly anyone who looks at the Five of Swords is impressed by the fighter pictured in the card, who is so pleased with his victory that he can hardly stop gloating. One can only hope that there is no young woman standing nearby, waiting for him to add her to his winnings.

Unfortunately, when you see the Five of Swords in a romance reading, there is probably someone in your life who thinks of love as a competition. People who think in those terms will stop at nothing to win, and they will justify their aggressive behavior by claiming that all's fair in love and war. If they are cunning or lucky enough to vanquish a heart or two, they simply add their hapless conquests to their collection of winnings—the spoils of war.

True love is not a battlefield, and it's your job to stand your ground against anyone who might think otherwise. You can use the best defensive weapons you have at your disposal—the sharp sword of your intellect. Pay attention to how those around you conduct themselves, both in times of war and in times of peace, and don't get involved with anyone who plays by a different set of rules than you.

The number five frequently represents an unstable element in any equation. While it often symbolizes the five senses, the five appendages (head, hands, and feet), five fingers, and five vowels, the number five also is hard to balance. It is not stable, like a four-sided square.

Traditionally, the Five of Swords is known as the card of defeat. Astrologically, it is associated with the first ten degrees of Aquarius, where an idealistic Venus, goddess of love and romance, is repulsed by deception.

The Six of Swords: Crossing Over

In the Six of Swords, a ferryman deftly steers a small craft across the surface of a winding river toward a distant shore. His passenger is seated quietly, clothed from head to foot in a hooded robe. Six swords stand upright, like silent steel sentries, alongside the passenger.

The Six of Swords is one of the most compelling cards in the Tarot deck—one with many layers of deeply moving symbolism.

Traditionally, the card usually meant an upcoming journey or travel by water.

Symbolically, the boat represents you, as you float along the river of life. You are the passenger—the spirit—in the physical vessel of your body. The six swords that have been thrust into the bottom of the boat represent the wounds and injuries you have experienced in your past relationships. You can't ignore their existence. They have become a part of you. In fact, if you even tried to pull them out, your boat would be left full of holes, and you would sink. Naturally, those swords make it more difficult for you to navigate. They impede your view. Happily, you have help—a guardian angel or a spirit guide—in the form of the ferryman who gently steers and guides your boat along.

The river in the illustration might be the River Styx, the mythological river that separated the land of the living from the land of the dead. It symbolizes a transition from one life to another, from a troubled existence to a more peaceful reality.

When you see the Six of Swords in a romance reading, however, you are voyaging from one phase in life to another. The water behind you, which symbolizes your past, is choppy and rough. The water ahead is smooth. It looks as though there will be smooth sailing ahead.

Six is generally considered to represent the human being, because God created man on the sixth day. Six also symbolizes the sixth sense, psychic ability, as well as the six directions of space (left, right, forward, backward, up, and down).

Traditionally, the Six of Swords is known as the card of earned success. Astrologically, it corresponds to the second ten degrees of Aquarius, where Mercury, the messenger of the gods, is able to grasp abstract concepts and relate them to specific symbols.

The Seven of Swords: Thief of Hearts

The proverbial thief in the night, the figure in the Seven of Swords has stolen into his enemy's camp to make off with their weapons. As his opponents slumber, none the wiser, he slips away with five of their swords. He wasn't able to take everything; he simply couldn't manage to hold it. But if his hapless adversaries keep sleeping soundly enough, he might be back for a second attempt.

The stealthy burglar in the Seven of Swords probably had been watching his adversaries for some time, concealed in shadow or cloaked in darkness. He studied their movements and learned their habits. He may even have slipped into their camp as a double agent, where he lived in their midst, unrecognized as a traitor who would betray his comrades for his own profit and gain.

For now, their loss is minimal. The five swords he is carrying away might have been captured from other combatants and stored away as spoils of war. When they realize their loss, they will probably be humiliated; he stole their swords right out from under their noses. If he comes back for the rest of their swords, however, they will be more than embarrassed—they will be unable to defend themselves against further attack.

When you get the Seven of Swords in a romance reading, someone may be about to steal your heart.

Whether that's good or bad is up to you. You might be beguiled by the dapper Don Juan. You might be in the mood for a little adventure—a quick game of cloak and dagger. You might even leave your camp unguarded, just to see how far he'll go.

Just remember, however, that the dashing "bad boy" in the card can be guileless and cunning. He will go to great lengths to get what he wants. At the same time, he certainly doesn't want you to give your heart to him. There's no thrill in that. His goal is to steal your heart away.

In a romance reading, the Seven of Swords could also indicate that you are sleepwalking through a relationship and that you don't even know that you are vulnerable because your defenses are down.

Traditionally, the Seven of Swords is known as the card of unstable effort. Astrologically, it is associated with the third ten degrees of Aquarius, where the goddess of the moon sets high standards for those who want to express their feelings in a relationship.

The Eight of Swords: Damsel in Distress

Kidnapped, bound, and held against her will, a slender young noblewoman has been blindfolded and tied to a tree. Eight swords encircle her, each one driven firmly into the earth. She is not struggling against her bonds; she stands still, with her head bent.

In the old silent movie series, the *Perils of Pauline*, a young heiress was routinely abducted and entrapped by a money-hungry villain. Just as routinely, she was subsequently rescued by a dashing hero.

In the Eight of Swords, we see a young woman who is oddly reminiscent of that damsel in distress. While she hasn't been tied to a railroad track, she has been blindfolded and bound, encircled by swords that are reminiscent of prison bars.

Her capturer, however, has left the job unfinished. She doesn't need to wait for rescue, because her legs are unbound. She simply needs to start moving, to wiggle her way free, and to find her own escape. In fact, she really might be one version of Pauline. In those old silent movies, she didn't always wait for rescue. If her hero didn't make it to her side in time, she simply took matters into her own hands.

When you see the Eight of Swords in a romance reading, you have been starring in a drama of your own. You might simply be acting. You might be playing a game with your partner. You might even enjoy the thrill of allowing yourself to be captured. Either way, the show is about to end. It's time to cue your rescue, stage the grand finale, and close this installment of your life. Once the house lights come on, you can always move to a new theater or develop a sequel later.

Traditionally, the Eight of Swords is known as the card of shortened force. Astrologically, it corresponds to the first ten degrees of Gemini, where Jupiter, the god of luck and expansion, plays mind games and uses intellectual challenges to stay young.

The Nine of Swords: The Nightmare

Surrounded by inky blackness, a troubled woman in a white nightgown sits up in bed and holds her hands over her face. Her blanket is rumpled, as if she has been tossing and turning for hours. Nine ominous swords loom in the air above her bed.

It's always darkest just before dawn. At 3 A.M., when we are awakened by a nightmare or find ourselves battling insomnia, our worst fears can grow to monstrous proportions. They can even seem larger than life, like the nine swords that hang over the suffering woman in the card.

The Nine of Swords is a disturbing card. It suggests sadness, sorrow, and suffering. The anguished woman in the illustration is alone, unwilling or unable to call a friend or a partner to comfort her and keep her company.

If you look closely at the image, however, you will notice one important thing: the swords in the picture don't have any substance. There is no light reflecting off their surface and no shadows to indicate any depth. In other words, those swords aren't real. They are simply figments of her imagination.

When you see the Nine of Swords in a romance reading, you might find yourself fighting a few nightmares of your own.

If your romance is keeping you up at night—for the wrong reasons—you need to study your concerns by the bright light of day. If your problems are real, work on them during regular business hours. On the other hand, if your demons are simply a creation of your unconscious mind, air them out thoroughly and then tuck them back into bed, where they can simply drift off to sleep.

You can also try to use your dreams to solve problems.

Traditionally, the Nine of Swords is known as the card of despair and cruelty. Astrologically, it is associated with the second ten degrees of Gemini, where Mars, the god of energy and aggression, allows his mind to race.

The Ten of Swords: Crimes of Passion

A murder victim is lying flat on his back. In an obvious case of overkill, he has been stabbed ten times. The murder weapons, ten swords, are still embedded in his body. Ominous dark clouds swirl in the sky, but there seems to be a glimmer of light on the horizon.

The Ten of Swords is one of the most gruesome cards in the Tarot deck. One look at the victim, repeatedly impaled by a series of full-length swords, and there can be no mistaking that this is a crime of passion. No disinterested murderer would go to such lengths.

It's not a very romantic card—and it doesn't seem to bode well for a relationship, either. Most Tarot readers interpret it as a card of suffering, pain, disillusionment, and grief.

When you see the Ten of Swords in a romance reading, you might find yourself giving up the ghost of any dreams you had regarding a relationship. You might see, once and for all, that your plans are not coming to fruition in the way you had hoped. Live by the sword, die by the sword.

Alternatively, the Ten of Swords might suggest that you have been the victim of vicious personal attacks. Because Swords cards symbolize the power of words, it could indicate that others have spread gossip and malicious rumors about you—the slings and arrows of outrageous fortune. If that's the case, you already know it. Each unkind remark has left its mark on your soul.

There is a bright side, however. At least there is a glimmer of hope. The sun is either setting or rising along the horizon, which means a new day will dawn soon. The Ten of Swords is also the last card in the series of Swords cards, which means your struggle is over. Your situation can't get any worse. Look to other cards for ideas about what your next step should be.

Traditionally, the Ten of Swords is known as the card of ruin. Astrologically, it corresponds to the third ten degrees of Gemini, where the bright light of the Sun prompts its followers to think clearly and see the entire picture.

FANTE DI SPADE / KNAVE OF SWORDS
VALET D'EPEES / SOTA DE ESPADAS

BUBE DER SCHWERTER / ZWAARDEN SCHILDKNAAP

The Page of Swords: Man of Letters

A young, blonde man holds an upraised sword and gazes into the distance. He looks lost in thought, but he's leaning slightly forward on one leg, as if he's about to start running.

The bright young Page of Swords is the personification of air—the embodiment of the fast-moving energy that connects the suit of Swords to the world of intellect and communication. In other words, the Page of Swords is a graphic example of how air can take human form.

Actually, all of the Pages in the Tarot deck embody the elements they represent. Elementally speaking, the four Pages of the Tarot are all earthy, physical creatures. They simply combine the element of earth with the element of their suit. The Page of Wands personifies fire, the Page of Cups personifies water, the Page of Swords personifies air, and the Page of Pentacles personifies earth.

The Page of Swords, who personifies air, is probably the cleverest of the four.

Like all Pages, the Page of Swords is youthful, with childlike enthusiasm and an unbounded capacity to learn. He is a reader, a writer, and a talker. He is thoughtful and idealistic, and he communicates clearly. He is naturally drawn to teachers, scientists, and philosophers.

The Page of Swords is also perpetually observant and alert. He doesn't miss a thing. If he isn't officially in the loop, he'll conduct a little investigative research on his own to find out what everyone else in the castle is doing.

When you see the Page of Swords in a romance reading, he usually reflects a facet of your own personality. If you don't like or acknowledge the Page of Swords side of yourself, however, you might find yourself projecting all of his qualities onto someone else in your life—and you'll either love him or hate him. In either case, your relationship with the Page of Swords will be intellectually challenging and thought-provoking.

During the Renaissance, pages were the youngest members of the royal court. Pages would frequently serve as messengers; it was their job to take news from one person to another. And because they were young, pages were students learning their future roles through apprenticeships.

Because pages are students and messengers, his appearance in a romance reading might also be telling you that important lessons or messages are coming your way regarding the intellectual side of your love life.

Pages are purely elemental; they aren't associated with any astrological sign.

CAVALLO DI SPADE   KNIGHT OF SWORDS
CHEVALIER D'EPEES   CABALLO DE ESPADAS

RITTER DER SCHWERTER   ZWAARDEN RIDDER

The Knight of Swords: Fire and Lightning

A muscular knight brandishes a heavy sword over his head, as his galloping steed charges toward their destination. They are moving fast. The horse's hooves are kicking up a storm of rocks and dust, and the knight's cape is billowing out behind him.

Experienced riders will tell you that when they are on their horses, their minds and bodies work in perfect harmony. They no longer feel like two separate creatures. Their individual strengths and talents combine. The horse knows the rider's will from a gentle nudge or whispered command. The rider can sense how and where the horse will move and shifts his weight accordingly. Together, the two are greater than the sum of their parts. They have synergy, which makes each one stronger and smarter in partnership than they would be without the other.

The Knight of Swords is one of those riders who move in perfect union with their animals—and his mind moves as quickly as his mount.

Elementally speaking, the four Knights of the Tarot are all fiery. They simply combine the element of fire with the element of their own suit. In that regard, the Knight of Swords embodies the combustible combination of fire with air. He can literally ride like the wind.

The Knight of Swords is probably the knight who best matches most people's conception of a knight. He is a skillful, brave warrior. His armor is always polished, and his horse is always ready to ride. Occasionally, the Knight of Swords can be indecisive. Even more rarely, he can be deceitful. But the Knight of Swords didn't just memorize the code of chivalry—he helped write it. He is truly a knight's knight.

When you see the Knight of Swords in a romance reading, you may be in for a whirlwind love affair. Someone who will remind you closely of the Knight of Swords may storm into your life. With a clap of thunder and a flash of lightning, the atmosphere around you will be charged with passion and intensity. Just as quickly, however, the storm could break, the skies will clear, and you'll be looking for a place to dry off.

Traditionally, the appearance of the Knight of Swords in a Tarot reading has sometimes indicated a struggle with a rival.

Astrologically, the four Knights of the Tarot are also associated with the four mutable signs of the Zodiac. The Knight of Swords represents the mutable air sign of Gemini, which makes him versatile and quick-thinking.

REGINA DI SPADE / REINE D'EPEES — QUEEN OF SWORDS / REINA DE ESPADAS

KÖNIGIN DER SCHWERTER / ZWAARDEN KONINGIN

The Queen of Swords: A Cut Above

From the seat of her high-backed throne, carved with the emblem of a soaring bird, the Queen of Swords holds her sword upright in her right hand, and she raises her left hand as if she's about to pronounce a new royal edict.

The Tarot's four Queens are all examples of ideal women. Each one represents the fluid, emotional side of feminine nature by combining the element of water with the corresponding element of her suit. In that respect, the Queen of Swords embodies the steamy combination of water with the logic, intellect, and perception of the Swords cards.

Like all of the Tarot's Queens, the Queen of Swords is a mature woman, gracious and wise in the ways of the world. A regal, experienced leader, she is also one of the most compelling figures in the Tarot deck.

According to tradition, the Queen of Swords is well acquainted with sorrow and heartbreak. She is usually believed to be a widow or a divorcee, who has learned from her loss and developed an uncanny ability to draw accurate conclusions about other people and situations. She can be sharp-tongued as a result; critical of others; and possibly a bit elitist. Of course, she has probably earned that right. For the most part, she is simply confident, observant, and wise.

The Queen's personal tragedies don't keep her from enjoying the good things in life, either. According to some accounts, she is an excellent dancer who loves a good party.

Queens, of course, are rulers—but traditionally, their rulership is based on the feminine principles of safeguarding and nurturing their realms. When you see the Queen of Swords in a romance reading, she is probably there to safeguard and nurture you on an intellectual level. Look for the influence of an experienced, outspoken individual. She might be someone you know, or she might be a reflection of your own personality. You might recognize her by her quick wit and uncanny ability to make sense of any situation.

Astrologically, the four Queens of the Tarot are associated with the four cardinal signs of the Zodiac. The Queen of Swords represents the cardinal air sign of Libra, which makes her a gracious and charming leader.

The King of Swords: Man of Steel

The imposing King of Swords is leaning forward with a scowl on his face and a clenched fist resting on the arm of his throne. He is wearing a full suit of chain-mail armor, topped with a blue tunic and a red cape. He looks as though he's about to stand up and make a point with the heavy sword in his hand.

Like all of the Kings in the Tarot deck, the King of Swords is a seasoned, experienced man. He has successfully completed the mission he undertook as the former Knight of Swords. He was rewarded with the keys to the kingdom, and he now rules the entire realm, as well as its armies that defend and conquer in the name of the throne.

The King of Swords is a firm friend—or enemy. He is a powerful, authoritative commander, who makes decisions based on solid logic and intellectual prowess.

According to some Tarot readers, the appearance of the King of Swords could indicate involvement in a lawsuit or legal dispute. When you see the King of Swords in a romance reading, your relationship might lead to dealings with a lawyer, a legislator, or a physician.

Elementally, the four Kings of the Tarot are all airy intellectuals. They simply combine the element of air with the corresponding element of their own suit. In that regard, the King of Swords embodies the rarified combination of air with air.

Astrologically, the four Kings of the Tarot are also associated with the four fixed signs of the Zodiac. The King of Swords represents the fixed fire sign of Aquarius, which makes him a forward-thinking, socially conscious monarch.

The Ace of Pentacles: Let's Get Physical

In the air above a hedged garden, an otherworldly hand offers a gleaming, golden coin inscribed with the traditional symbol of our five senses united by Spirit. The star-shaped pentacle centered in a circle was also the symbol of the followers of Pythagoras, the ancient mathematician who believed in an orderly, unified cosmos.

The Ace of Pentacles is the first card in the suit of Pentacles, the suit that corresponds to the ancient element of earth. In that respect, the Ace of Pentacles is the embodiment of material and physical existence. It represents the essence of matter and reality. It promises a world of possibilities, ranging from new beginnings on the physical plane to an accumulation of spiritual treasures.

When you see the Ace of Pentacles in a romance reading, you can be assured that you will have the resources you need to pursue your dreams. You will be able to manifest your spiritual, emotional, and intellectual ideals. Occasionally, the Ace of Pentacles also portends physical pleasure, comfort, and luxury.

Ultimately, the Ace of Pentacles is a feminine symbol, similar in many ways to the unfertilized egg—or a developing fetus. In that respect, like all of the Aces, the Ace of Pentacles sometimes represents the potential for creation.

Traditionally, the Ace of Wands is known as the root of the power of earth. When you see the Ace of Wands in a reading, remember that you are dealing with practical, pragmatic issues. If you really want to see results, be sure to keep your ideas and your actions grounded and down to earth.

The Two of Pentacles: Balancing Act

A young man dexterously juggles two pentacles in a lazy figure-eight pattern. The shape is technically known as a lemniscate, and it is a symbol of infinity. Incidentally, you will find the same symbol in the Magician and Strength cards. The lemniscate suggests that there is no beginning and no end to the routine, because the juggling act is perpetual.

Traditionally, the Two of Pentacles is known as the card of harmonious change. In most Tarot readings, the presence of the Two of Pentacles often implies that you are juggling two or more major concerns, such as school and work, a family and a career, or marriage and children. It's a precarious balancing act, but it's one that you seem to be used to, and you make it look easy.

When you see the Two of Pentacles in a romance reading, you might be juggling your relationships in addition to all of your other responsibilities. The card can also take on an entirely new connotation, however. Its appearance may mean that you, or someone close to you, is considering a bit of two-timing. You might even be juggling two relationships.

Of course, your interpretation may be more literal than anything. It might simply mean that you need to be more conscientious about voicing your opinion in relationships. In other words, don't forget to add your two cents' worth.

All of the number two cards in the Tarot symbolize duality, partnerships, choices, and combinations. You may be facing a difficult choice. However, you are still in the early stages of forming your decision. For now, you may simply choose to keep dancing and keep the balancing act going—at least for the time being.

Traditionally, the Two of Pentacles is known as the card of harmonious change. Astrologically, it is associated with the first ten degrees of Capricorn, where Jupiter, the god of luck and expansion, pursues his worldly ambitions.

The Three of Pentacles: Form Follows Function

As a young sculptor puts the finishing touches on a life-size statue in the sanctuary, a bishop and a monk discuss the artist's progress. Three stained-glass windows, shaped like pentacles, seem to frame the sculpture in a halo of heavenly light.

The scene in the Three of Pentacles describes the process of giving substance and form to our spiritual ideas and beliefs. The sculptor, of course, is designing a work of art that will serve as a tangible reminder of God's grace and presence.

   The setting, a church, is an obvious allusion to the house of God. Less apparent, however, is the additional reminder that our physical bodies are also temples. That can be a hard concept for some people to accept. It can be difficult to acknowledge that we are all spiritual beings—in physical form. It even seems, at first glance, like a contradiction.

   To make the most of your life, however, you must integrate every aspect of your existence—body, mind, and spirit. Being a spiritual person doesn't mean you have to deny your physical self, or conform to some impossibly high ideals of how a spiritual or holy person should act. You can't pretend that you are a disembodied spirit, free from the everyday cares of the world—because that would exclude your spirit from enjoying the physical pleasures of the world, as well, which would actually limit your experience, your understanding, and your growth as a spiritual person. In fact, the word holy means "whole."

When you see the Three of Pentacles in a romance reading, it's a clear reminder that you can accept and enjoy your physical nature. It's also a reminder that physical attraction—and attractiveness—is an important component of a relationship. After all, it's human nature to be drawn to beautiful people, because most of us assume that physical beauty reflects inner beauty. That might not be as obvious when you're young, but it becomes more apparent with every passing year.

In that sense, the Three of Pentacles might be offering you some concrete advice. If your body is your temple, it might be time to make sure that your sanctuary still reflects the qualities you value and want to share with others. Look in the mirror. It might be time for a little sculpting, a bit of remodeling, and maybe even some stained glass.

Traditionally, the Three of Pentacles is known as the card of the material world. Astrologically, it is associated with the second ten degrees of Capricorn, where Mars, the god of energy and drive, feels compelled to make sure he looks good to others.

The Four of Pentacles: Alone Again

The body language of the miser in the Four of Pentacles couldn't be any clearer. He wants you to back off—and stay back—far, far away from the pentacle he's holding in his lap. He also has a pentacle balanced on his head, as well as two more pentacles under his feet. Don't even think about asking what he's keeping in that money bag next to him. It's none of your business.

The Four of Pentacles doesn't depict a man who's ready to share his life and love with anybody else. In fact, he is firmly, stubbornly planted and exceptionally self-protective. He has isolated himself from the rest of society—that much is clearly symbolized by the city in the background.

He knows where he has stored all of his spiritual, emotional, intellectual, and material resources. In fact, the traditional name for this card is "Lord of Earthly Power." He's got a firm hold on all of them, each symbolized by one of the four pentacles, and he's not letting go. He even holds one of them up like a shield in front of his heart.

When you see the Four of Pentacles in a romance reading, you can probably guess what it means. You are dealing with someone who is not ready, willing, or able to be a partner in a relationship. You might wish he were. You might beg, plead, and try to change him, but it won't work. Face facts. This man does not play well with others. He's not ready to share. He has barricaded himself in his room, and he is living in his own world. What's more, he probably won't change anytime soon. Your friend in the Four of Pentacles isn't going anywhere anytime soon.

In the real world, you might feel sorry for him—or hold him in contempt. When you see the Four of Pentacles in a Tarot reading, however, it's usually easier to cast aside your preconceptions and beliefs and simply read the story in the cards. You might even see yourself.

Traditionally, the Four of Pentacles is known as the card of earthly power. Astrologically, it is associated with the third ten degrees of Capricorn, where the Sun drives some people to focus all of their energy on the accumulation of wealth and power.

The Five of Pentacles: Poor in Spirit

Two bedraggled figures, dressed in rags, bent over against the cold, are trudging through falling snow. One of them hobbles on crutches. He is so bereft, he literally doesn't have a leg to stand on. They are making their way past a church, where a stained-glass window sheds some light on their path.

Don't worry. The Five of Pentacles doesn't mean you're about to lose everything you own. You aren't headed for the homeless shelter or the soup kitchen. But you might want to do a quick inventory of your most valuable possession—your soul. That's because Tarot images of sheer poverty, like this one, are metaphors for spiritual poverty.

Happily, the poverty-stricken pair in the Five of Pentacles is passing by the stained-glass window of a church. Everyone knows what that symbolizes: refuge, haven, and help from above. You can see by the glow from the window that the light is on inside, so that means the door is probably open. You might even be able to hear the heavenly sound of a church choir.

When you see the Five of Pentacles in a romance reading, it could indicate that your relationship has fallen on hard times. The church, however, represents the aid and comfort you can find from friends and social groups. You might want to start patching the holes in your partnership by accessing the support of a social or community group. You might need to go back to the church where you were married, revisit your spiritual beliefs, and reassess your direction.

If you aren't in a relationship, and you're hoping to connect with a soul mate, the Five of Pentacles has advice for you, too. Even though you are probably tired of being told to look for prospective partners at church, in this case it just might work. Interpreted more broadly, the Five of Pentacles might suggest that you could find romance in an organized social setting.

In either case, even though it might feel like you're trudging through the dark and the cold, there's a sanctuary for you just around the corner. The lights are on, the door is open, and you might even find coffee and doughnuts inside.

Traditionally, the Five of Pentacles is known as the card of material trouble. Astrologically, it is associated with the first ten degrees of Taurus, where Mercury, the god of communication, is a sympathetic and understanding listener.

The Six of Pentacles: Charity Begins at Home

A wealthy merchant with a balanced scale in his right hand uses his left hand to distribute alms—or pentacles—to two beggars, a man and a woman, who are kneeling at his feet. The man's wealth is apparent from his richly colored bright green tunic and red, fur-lined cape.

The Six of Pentacles is the card of giving, of charity, of benevolence and goodwill. The merchant pictured in the card is obviously successful in his work, and he seems to enjoy his ability to share his wealth. The scale he holds, reminiscent of the scales of Justice, illustrates the concept of social justice.

On a less obvious level, the Six of Pentacles also reminds us that money isn't the root of all evil—but the love of money can be. It also hints at the love-hate relationship that many people experience around money, as well as the discomfort some people feel when they are on the receiving end of a compliment, a favor, or a gift.

When you see the Six of Pentacles in a romance reading, it's actually a reminder that sometimes you'll be in a position to give, and sometimes you'll be in a position to receive—and that both give and take are important to the health of a relationship. Occasionally, the Six of Pentacles might suggest that someone may be trying to buy your love or that you might be begging for attention or affection. On a more optimistic note, however, the Six of Pentacles might also be describing how well you share your wisdom, knowledge, and spiritual enlightenment with others.

Ultimately, the Six of Pentacles is an allusion to the fact that when anything of value changes hands, money is simply a way to measure the energy that's being exchanged between two parties.

Traditionally, the Six of Pentacles is known as the card of material success. Astrologically, it is associated with the third ten degrees of Taurus, where the goddess of the Moon delights in material gifts and pleasures.

The Seven of Pentacles: Harvest Time

A young man stands next to a ripening crop of pentacle-shaped fruit. He has obviously been working, but he's currently standing still, his hands folded on the handle of his hoe. He might be resting, as he ponders the work that is still ahead of him. He might also be imagining the fruits of his labors, the final product of his harvest.

Farmers are notorious for seeing the worst possible future. Even when the sun is shining, the fields are flourishing, and the crops seem to be ripening on schedule, farmers will caution you that they still can't be certain of success. There could be too much rain, or too little. Hail could flatten the crop. Wind could uproot it. There could be an early freeze, or birds, or bugs, or blight. Any number of natural disasters could wipe out the crop in an instant. Farmers really don't rest until their harvest is in—and then they start worrying about next year.

When you see the Seven of Pentacles in a romance reading, it's time to get back outside and do all you can to assure the success of the relationships you have planted. You'll need to make sure that your soil can bear fruit. If your garden is dry and rocky, nothing more than weeds can take root. Good relationships need sun for energy and water for growth. You'll need to know when to weed, by ridding yourself of noxious personalities, and when to thin out the plants to make space in your life for quality, not quantity. But most of all, a garden of friendship needs time to bloom and grow.

Traditionally, the Seven of Pentacles is known as the card of success unfulfilled. Astrologically, it is associated with the third ten degrees of Taurus, where Saturn, the god of limitation and restriction, can make it difficult to appreciate success.

DENARI
DENIERS

8

PENTACLES
OROS

MÜNZEN

MUNTEN

The Eight of Pentacles: Strut Your Stuff

A woodworker, seated at his workbench, is carving a series of pentacles. A skilled crafts-man, it looks as though he is continually perfecting his skills and, at the same time, he's managing to produce marketable wares. He displays his work prominently, and he works in full view of customers and passerby.

The Eight of Pentacles is a card of craftsmanship, as well as the self-confidence that comes from being able to market your skills and provide for your own needs. The woodworker pictured in the card seems relaxed and satisfied with the quality of his work. He isn't afraid to demonstrate his skills, and he doesn't worry that anyone will steal his method or criticize his technique.

When you see the Eight of Pentacles in a romance reading, you aren't new to the art of love. What's more, you're not afraid to reveal your true self to others. You have been crafting relationships for some time now, and you know how to create a partnership that will stand the test of time. You understand that much of the work that goes into a relationship is not glamorous. In fact, most of the things you do for your friends and loved ones might even be fairly repetitive. Your greatest gift may be your perseverance, and your willingness to see a job through to its end. You are confident in your ability and relaxed enough to let others in on the techniques that work for you.

Traditionally, the Eight of Pentacles is known as the card of prudence. Astrologically, it is associated with the first ten degrees of Virgo, where the Sun shines on those who work diligently and with skill.

The Nine of Pentacles: A Garden of Earthly Delights

An elegant woman stands alone in a well-manicured garden with a falcon on her arm. She is alone, but she doesn't seem lonely. In fact, she looks as though she enjoys her solitude. She is in control of her surroundings.

Falcons are strong, wild birds. People who train them, falconers, must be equally strong and determined. The woman pictured in the Nine of Pentacles has obviously made a docile ally of the falcon on her arm.

When you see the Nine of Pentacles in a romance reading, it clearly suggests that you have tamed the wild side of your own personality. That same motif is repeated in the manicured, cultivated look of the garden in the card. You have managed to control nature, and your mind has superimposed its own design.

The Nine of Pentacles often symbolizes financial security, perhaps through an inheritance or wisely planned investments. When you see the Nine of Pentacles in a romance reading, that interpretation takes on an additional depth. It suggests that you enjoy security in all of your relationships—especially with yourself. In fact, you enjoy your own company as much as you enjoy the company of others. You aren't aloof. You are dignified, mature, and graceful, and maybe even more attractive as a result. Balance and serenity are important to you, and you have designed them to be an integral part of your life.

Traditionally, the Nine of Pentacles is known as the card of material gain. Astrologically, it is associated with the second ten degrees of Virgo, where Venus, the goddess of love and beauty, can cultivate her own garden of earthly delights.

The Ten of Pentacles: Grow Old with Me

In the courtyard of a medieval dwelling, three generations of a family are gathered together: a young couple, their small child, and a white-haired, bearded grandfather. Two attentive pet dogs are with them, as well, enjoying the company of their human relations. It's the picture of family unity and togetherness.

In the classic Celtic Cross spread, one position is reserved for a card known as your "house." By design, the card that lands in that position describes the people closest to you, who see you every day and know you well. In many respects, the Ten of Pentacles illustrates that "house" concept perfectly, simply by depicting several generations of a single family gathered under a single roof.

Whether you live in the same city or halfway around the world, your family knows you like no one else ever could. Many of your relatives have known you since the day you were born, and they have watched and commented on every phase of your development. Even if they weren't there in person, they've all seen snapshots of you as a chubby two-year-old in the bathtub. They remember the day you broke your arm on the playground, the day you dyed your hair purple in junior high, and the night of your first big dance. They have seen you succeed, and they have seen you fail. They have seen you at your best and at your worst.

In a romance reading, the Ten of Pentacles is a reminder that your family relationships were your first relationships, and they serve as a model for every subsequent relationship you forge for the rest of your life. If your family showered you with love and treated you with respect, it becomes easier for you to develop loving and respectful relationships with others. If your childhood was less than ideal, however, it may be more difficult for you to enter into friendships and love affairs with new people.

By their very nature, family relationships are lifelong. Most of us who enter into serious, committed relationships with others usually hope that our new partnerships will be equally long-lasting. That opens the door, however, to increasingly complicated relationships—not only with the new people we love, but also with their family members.

It is interesting to note that the card features a prominent brick wall and arched doorway. Their presence suggests that certain boundaries are essential, even among the most closely knit families. In the illustration, there is a healthy separation between the young family and their patriarch. In a romance reading, the Ten of Pentacles seems to imply that you are able to maintain appropriate boundaries, especially when it comes to managing the complexities of your interactions with both your own family and your in-laws.

Traditionally, the Ten of Pentacles is known as the card of wealth. Astrologically, it is associated with the third ten degrees of Virgo, where Mercury, messenger of the gods, is diligent about managing the lines of communication.

FANTE DI DENARI   KNAVE OF PENTACLES
VALET DE DENIERS   SOTA DE OROS

BUBE DER MÜNZEN   MUNTEN SCHILDKNAAP

The Page of Pentacles: The Tall, Dark Stranger

A young man stands with an oversized pentacle in his hand, as if he is displaying a work of art. He is standing in a green valley, wrapped in a green cloak.

The bright young Page of Pentacles is the personification of earth—the embodiment of the grounded energy that connects the suit of Pentacles to the world of matter and physical existence. In other words, the Page of Pentacles is a graphic example of how earth can take human form.

Actually, all of the Pages in the Tarot deck embody the elements they represent. Elementally speaking, the four Pages of the Tarot are all earthy, physical creatures. They simply combine the element of earth with the element of their suit. In other words, the Page of Wands personifies fire, the Page of Cups personifies water, the Page of Swords personifies air, and the Page of Pentacles personifies earth.

The Page of Pentacles is arguably the most mesmerizing of the four.

Like all Pages, the Page of Pentacles is youthful, with childlike enthusiasm and an unbounded capacity to learn. He is nurturing, generous, and kind. He is also studious, diligent, and perseverant. He may even be a child prodigy. Despite his high level of skill, however, he is usually extremely careful, even cautious, and he doesn't take many risks.

When you see the Page of Pentacles in a romance reading, he usually reflects a facet of your own personality. If you don't like or acknowledge the Page of Pentacles side of yourself, however, you might find yourself projecting all of his qualities onto someone else in your life—and you'll either love him or hate him. In either case, your relationship with the Page of Pentacles will be passionate, fiery, and hot.

During the Renaissance, pages were the youngest members of the royal court. Pages would frequently serve as messengers; it was their job to take news from one person to another. In addition, because they were young, pages were students learning their future roles through apprenticeships.

Because pages are students and messengers, the appearance of the Page of Pentacles in a romance reading might also be telling you that important lessons or messages are coming your way regarding the physical side of your existence, particularly money, physical resources, and the things that you treasure.

Pages are purely elemental; they are not associated with any astrological sign.

CAVALLO DI DENARI · KNIGHT OF PENTACLES
CHEVALIER DE DENIERS · CABALLO DE OROS

RITTER DER MÜNZEN · MÜNTEN RIDDER

The Knight of Pentacles: Slow but Steady

A knight in shining armor, seated on a sleek, black horse, pauses at the bank of a river while he seems to ponder the pentacle in his outstretched hand. Both he and his horse are at rest; neither one is moving. On the other side of the river, several fields have been cultivated and new crops are beginning to sprout.

The Knight of Pentacles doesn't fit most people's preconceptions of knights. He doesn't move very fast, he's not especially flirtatious, and when the rest of the knights ride off on adventures, he usually stays behind to take care of the kingdom's routine border patrols.

In fact, some people think the Knight of Pentacles is actually sort of dull. He is slow and careful. He pays an almost slavish attention to detail. He is remarkably patient and calm. His mission in life seems to be taking care of the ordinary details and everyday responsibilities that the other knights overlook.

In other words, the Knight of Pentacles could be the ideal mate. Once you have lived through a few dates with the macho Knight of Wands, the playboy antics of the Knight of Cups, or the wham-bam-thank-you-ma'am Knight of Swords, a relationship with the slow and steady Knight of Pentacles could come as a welcome relief.

Don't forget, either, that the Knight of Pentacles represents physical existence. He is far more attuned to physical needs and desires than the rest of his colleagues.

Elementally speaking, the four Knights of the Tarot are all fiery. They simply combine the element of fire with the element of their own suit. In that regard, the Knight of Pentacles embodies the rather uneventful combination of fire with earth.

Astrologically, the four Knights of the Tarot are also associated with the four mutable signs of the Zodiac. The Knight of Pentacles represents the mutable earth sign of Virgo, which makes him conscientious and conservative.

REGINA DI DENARI   QUEEN OF PENTACLES
REINE DE DENIERS   REINA DE OROS

KÖNIGIN DER MÜNZEN   MUNTEN KONINGIN

The Queen of Pentacles: A Woman of Substance

In a rich and verdant garden, the Queen of Pentacles gently cradles the emblem of her suit, almost as if she were holding an infant or a small child in her lap. The back of her throne is embossed with cherubs, but the rams' heads carved into its arms hint at her natural leadership ability. Flowers bloom all around, and the leafy green branches of an arbor shield her from the sun's rays.

The Tarot's four Queens are all examples of ideal women. Each one represents the watery, emotional side of feminine nature by combining the element of water with the corresponding element of her suit. In that respect, the Queen of Pentacles embodies the fertile combination of water with the earthy resources of the Pentacles cards.

Like all of the Tarot's Queens, the Queen of Pentacles is a mature woman, gracious and wise in the ways of the world. She is also quiet, kind, and unassuming. While she is practical, she can be extremely generous. She has a big heart, and she is liberal with her time, her emotions, and her resources.

Queens, of course, are rulers—but traditionally, their rulership is based on the feminine principles of safeguarding and nurturing their realms. When you see the Queen of Pentacles in a romance reading, she is probably there to safeguard and nurture you on a physical level. Look for the influence of a bright, outgoing, enthusiastic personality. She might be someone you know, or she might be a reflection of your own personality. Actually, you might recognize her by her flirtatious nature, which can sometimes lead to fickleness and periods of infidelity.

Astrologically, the four Queens of the Tarot are associated with the four cardinal signs of the Zodiac. The Queen of Pentacles represents the cardinal earth sign of Capricorn, which makes her a savvy businesswoman who can cultivate a wide range of resources for her people.

RE DI DENARI   KING OF PENTACLES
ROI DE DENIERS   REY DE OROS

KÖNIG DER MÜNZEN   MUNTEN KONING

The King of Pentacles: King of the World

From the walled courtyard of his villa, the King of Pentacles contemplates the kingdom that stretches out behind him. He holds a pentacle in his left hand, almost casually, and a scepter in his right. His throne is massive, and generally unadorned except for the bas relief heads of rams and bulls, the symbols of Aries' leadership and Taurus' stability.

Like all of the Kings in the Tarot deck, the King of Pentacles is a seasoned, experienced man. He has successfully completed the mission he undertook as the former Knight of Pentacles. He was rewarded with the keys to the kingdom, and he now rules the entire realm, as well as its armies that defend and conquer in the name of the throne.

The King of Pentacles is traditionally thought to be a friendly, married man. He is typically a successful businessperson who manages the affairs of his kingdom with mathematical precision. He is mathematical and practical, and he has a flair for ingenious solutions to complicated problems. It usually takes him a long time to get angry, but once roused, he can be furious. The rest of the time, he may seem emotionless, imperturbable, and insensitive.

When you see the King of Pentacles in a romance reading, you can expect to gain financially and materially from your relationships. You may also find yourself cultivating relationships that will be long-lasting and deep.

Elementally, the four Kings of the Tarot are all airy intellectuals. They simply combine the element of air with the corresponding element of their own suit. In that regard, the King of Pentacles embodies the heady combination of air with earth.

Astrologically, the four Kings of the Tarot are also associated with the four fixed signs of the Zodiac. The King of Pentacles represents the fixed earth sign of Taurus, which makes him a steady, reliable monarch.

Sample Reading: John

John, a 40-year-old executive, is worried about his marriage. His wife has been working late almost every night for the last month—and John isn't sure she's working alone.

Corrine: Shuffle this deck for me and, as you shuffle, describe what brought you here for a reading.

John: Well, I'm worried that my wife might be having an affair. I want to know if she's still faithful to me.

Corrine: What makes you think she might be having an affair?

John: Well, we had a baby girl eighteen months ago. For a long time after the baby was born, my wife and I were just adjusting to that, and our love life kind of hit the skids, if you know what I mean. Lately, it started to seem like everything was starting to get back to normal, but about a month ago my wife started working late almost every night of the week. She's hardly ever home. She leaves at six or seven in the morning, and she's gone until ten or eleven at night.

Corrine: What does your wife do for a living?

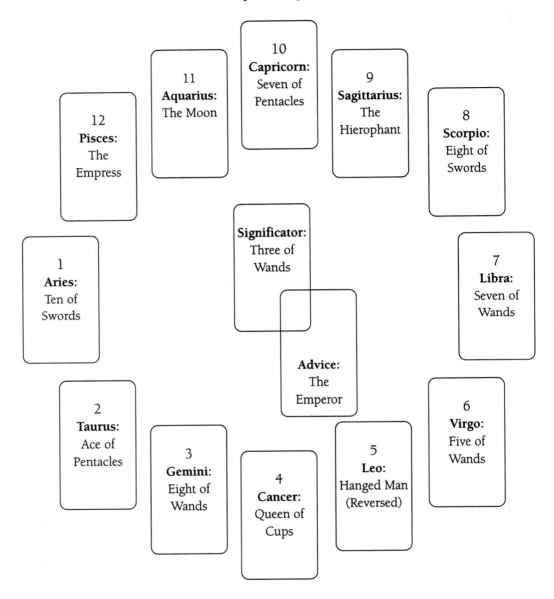

Zodiac Spread

John: She's a marketing executive. Her company is involved in a lot of projects right now, so she probably is at work, but I'm just not sure.

Corrine: Have you told her you're worried?

John: No, not really.

Corrine: Does she know you're getting a Tarot reading about it?

John: No. She doesn't know I'm here.

Corrine: Well, I'm hesitant to look into the cards to see just what she's up to, because she's not here and she can't give her side of the story. Ethically, I just wouldn't feel comfortable looking into her private life. But, I think we can look into your relationship with your wife. We can use an astrology-based spread, where every card will represent one room of your house. That way, on a symbolic level, we'll be able to see what's going on in your home life.

John: Okay.

Corrine: First, look through the deck and choose one card that reminds you of your relationship with your wife.

John: Can I look at the cards, or do you want me to just pull one?

Corrine: Look at the pictures.

John. All right … Okay, this looks like me.

Corrine: You've chosen the Three of Wands. Is that you, waiting for your wife?

John: Yes, and wondering where she is.

Corrine: All right, we'll put this card in the center of the spread, because it represents you. Now I'm going to shuffle the deck and lay out the twelve cards. Each one of them will represent a separate room of your house to symbolize what's going on in your home life. The first card, over here in the nine o'clock position, is the "Aries" card. On a horoscope chart, Aries represents the first thing people notice about you. It's like the front door of your house. The card that comes up in this position is the Ten of Swords.

John: That looks really bad. Am I going to be stabbed to death on my front steps?

Corrine: No, but in your mind, you certainly feel as though your marriage is under attack whenever your wife leaves the house.

John: Yeah, that's for sure.

Corrine: A horoscope chart flows counterclockwise, so the next card goes here, in the "Taurus" position. Taurus symbolizes a love of beauty and comfort. Most people usually make their living room the most beautiful, comfortable place in the house, so here we're looking at how you decorate and furnish your living room—metaphorically speaking. The card that comes up in this position is the Ace of Pentacles. It looks to me as though you and your wife are willing to spend money in order to make a beautiful home.

John: That's one reason she's working. We do want to provide a comfortable life for our children.

Corrine: Sure. That makes sense. The next card we'll look at is in the "Gemini" position, which symbolizes communication. This represents the communication system in your house—your phone and e-mail connection to the outside world. Oh, it's the Eight of Wands. This is *the* phone and e-mail card of the Tarot deck. You must do a lot of communicating by phone and e-mail.

John: That's true. My wife and I talk on the phone at least twice a day, and we send each other a lot of e-mail, too.

Corrine: Okay. Next, we'll take a look at the card in the "Cancer" position. Cancer symbolizes homemaking and nurturing and motherhood—the activities that usually center around the kitchen of your house. I think you've got a really nice card in this spread. It's the Queen of Pentacles, which symbolizes your wife, nurturing the family on a physical level. She's obviously a very loving person, especially toward your daughter.

John: Absolutely.

Corrine: This next card is in the Leo position, which usually describes how you parent, if you're a father, and how you relax, and how you have fun. It describes all the things you do in Dad's room of the house—the den. Now this is really, really interesting. This card shows you as the Hanged Man—but look. This card is the only card in the whole spread that's reversed. The end result is that you're not hanging upside-down like the Hanged Man. You're right side up. It might be telling you that you need a new perspective on your relationship. You might need to be looking at things from a different angle.

John: Interesting. What are all those lines coming out of the guy's head?

Corrine: That's you, getting enlightened.

John: Funny! Well, I guess that's what I'm here for.

Corrine: Okay, the next card is in the "Virgo" position, which symbolizes how you work and help other people. In this spread, I guess you could compare it to the way you take care of all of the housekeeping. You and your wife aren't doing so well here. You've got the Five of Wands, and you can tell by the card that everyone is trying to help, but you're just getting in each other's way. When you and your wife are together, you're not communicating your intentions very clearly. This is one area of your relationship where you definitely need to clean house, so to speak, and work better as a team.

John: Yes, I guess so.

Corrine: This next card might be the most important card in the spread, since we're looking at the issue of your relationship with your wife. It's in the "Libra" position, and Libra is the card that relates to marriage and partnership. Since it's directly across from your front door in this spread, it could symbolize the back door of your house. For some reason, the Seven of Wands has landed here. Why do you think that is?

John: That's me, fighting back all kinds of men with sticks. They all want to attack my marriage.

Corrine: Is that what you really think? You can't even see what's coming at you in that picture.

John: That's what it feels like.

Corrine: Well, you never know. You obviously feel as though outside forces are trying to break into both doors of your house and undermine your marriage. Let's see if it makes more sense after we look at the rest of the cards. The next card falls in the "Scorpio" position. Scorpios are usually fascinated by deep, very private issues, like sex and death. Those are the sorts of things most people deal with in their bedrooms. In this case, you've got the Eight of Swords. You're blindfolded, and you're tied up, and you're surrounded by eight swords in the ground. When I see this card, something tells me that you and your wife tend to avoid discussing your private life together. It's like you've turned a blind eye to the whole subject, and now you're trapped.

John: I haven't talked to her about any of this.

Corrine: Well, you might want to, now that you've seen this card, especially. You're not tied up so tightly that you can't free yourself.

John: Okay.

Corrine: On to bigger and brighter things. The next position is the "Sagittarius" position, which symbolizes your studies, your thoughts, and your philosophical explorations. Since we're comparing every card to a room in your home, this card would probably symbolize the types of books you keep in your library or on bookshelves in your house. It's the Hierophant, which shows you are a deeply philosophical thinker, and you're not afraid to explore the history and traditions of other cultures to help you make sense of your own life.

John: Yes. And we have a lot of books.

Corrine: The next card is the Seven of Pentacles in the "Capricorn" position. Capricorn is usually associated with career, and the career room of your house would be your home office. It looks, in the card, as though you are waiting for harvest—and this card applies to both you and your wife. You've planted the seeds, and the fields are almost ripe, but you're still waiting to really reap the rewards.

John: True enough.

Corrine: "Aquarius" is next, which symbolizes the way you plan for the future and rally around social causes. If this position were a part of your house, it would be your back deck, where you can sit out at night and look up at the stars and dream about tomorrow. The card that landed here is the Moon, which is a lovely, romantic card that symbolizes hopes and dreams and reflection. It couldn't be a nicer fit. That crab crawling out of the water onto dry land also symbolizes your evolution as a couple and as a family.

John: Well, good.

Corrine: Finally, we'll look at the twelfth position in the spread, which represents "Pisces." Pisces is the sign of intuition and unconscious knowledge buried deep below the surface. If you're comparing it to a room in your house, I'd say it was the basement. Now look at the card. It's the Empress. Well, I think, deep down, even in your subconscious mind, you know that your wife is an Empress. I have to tell you, when I look at this card, I think your wife really is just at work. Especially when I see all the other really positive cards here that relate to work, like the Ace of Pentacles trying to furnish a comfortable house, the Queen of Pentacles nurturing on a physical level, and the Seven of Pentacles waiting for harvest. I really don't see any other men in the spread, except for the ones you're afraid are trying to stab you on your front step or break in through your back door. And to tell you the truth, I think you're imagining them. There's nobody else in your marriage but you and your wife.

John: I think you're right.

Corrine: Let's throw down one more card, just to give you a final word of advice. I'll lay it right here in the center, on top of the Three of Wands we started with. Look, it's the Emperor.

John: It's the Empress's husband.

Corrine: Exactly. The Empress is loving, and giving, and nurturing, and creative—but all that creativity can be chaotic. Your wife has been gone a lot, and that's led to a fair share of chaos in your home life. You can take steps to change that. I think this card is giving you permission to take back some control, to create order out of chaos, and to reinforce the structure and stability of your empire.

John: Yes. That makes perfect sense. I'm going to talk to my wife tonight. Actually, I think I'll take her out to dinner, and I'll make sure everything works out. I really didn't think there was another man involved, but I just wanted to see what the cards said before I jumped to any crazy conclusions.

Corrine: You are an Emperor.

John: Yes, I am.

Sample Reading: Beth

Beth, a thirty-year-old businesswoman, is the divorced mother of a four-year-old son. Recently, she has been finding herself drawn to a thirty-nine-year-old divorcé with two small children. She wants to know how she should pursue a relationship with him. She's especially concerned about the impact a romance might have on their children.

Corrine: We'll start by looking at the center card in this spread, the significator. This is the card that signifies, or represents, you. Because the Three of Cups is your significator, it shows that you are basically a social person. You enjoy your time out with friends—but you don't necessarily find yourself out much with a romantic partner. You seem to be spending most of your time with girlfriends, like the three women dancing in the card.

Beth: Actually, I usually go out with my sister and her fiancé. It's fun, but lately I feel like such a tagalong. They'll call me up and say, "We're going out for dinner. Let's go." I can't believe they want me on all of their dates. I actually introduced them to each other because we were friends, but I'm ready for a change.

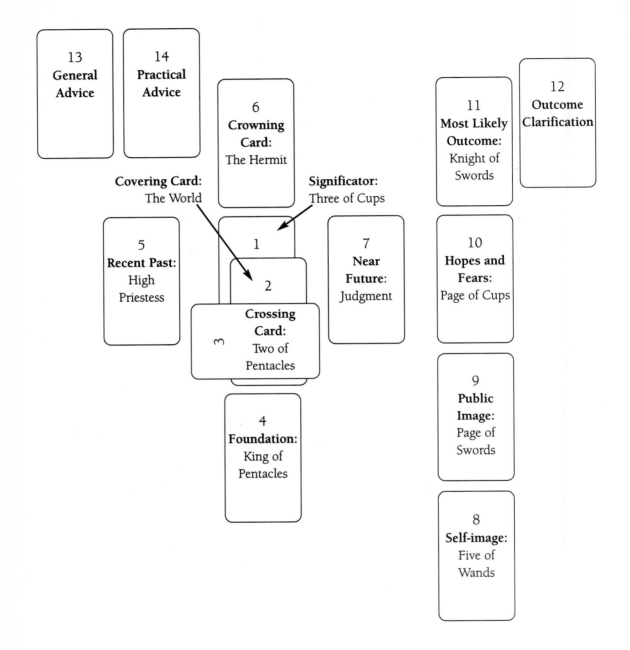

Illustration: Celtic Cross

Corrine: Well, your social life is changing. Your covering card, the World, shows that you're coming to the end of this cycle in your life. The World is a card of completion and preparation for new beginnings. It's a powerful card. It's the last one in the portion of the deck called the Major Arcana, which means "big secrets."

The next card, the crossing card, will show you what kinds of energy you're dealing with as you conclude this cycle in your life. It's the Two of Pentacles—the Juggler. Usually, when this card comes up in a reading, it means that people are juggling two major concerns in their life, like work and home. In this case, I think you might be trying to juggle the rest of your life as you begin a new relationship.

Beth: That's true.

Corrine: Your foundation card, here at the bottom of the spread, will show us how you manage to keep all of those balls in the air. It's the King of Pentacles. That tells me that you're used to taking an active role in managing your time and your resources, because Kings are actively involved in managing their realms, and the suit of Pentacles represents physical existence.

Beth: Yes, I'm usually in control. I run a business.

Corrine: Let's look at your recent past, the last six months to a year. This card is really interesting in light of your question about a new relationship. It's the High Priestess, who is usually associated with intuition, psychic ability, and the cycles of the moon. You can see here the crescent moon at her feet and the three phases of the moon in her headpiece: waxing, full, and waning. In the last six months to a year, you've been developing and relying on your intuition.

Beth: That is so weird, because something really is going on with me. Three years ago, I would have said you were crazy to believe in this stuff. If I had walked into a room and seen Tarot cards, I would have turned around and walked right out. I wanted nothing to do with any of this. But something has changed, and I'm feeling like there's something more to my life than I ever realized before. I feel things, and I see signs everywhere I look, and all I know is that this is much bigger than me. So now I'm just trying to learn as much as I can. It's my life.

Corrine: Well, that makes sense, especially when you look at your crowning card in this spread, the Hermit. When most people look at the Hermit, they think, "Oh, here's someone who is isolated and doesn't want to be with people." But it doesn't mean that you're running away. I think this card shows that you've learned a lot from your own experiences, and you still need some time to work through it in your own mind. But in the meantime, you're willing to share what you know with people who seek you out. But you're not the kind of person who is going to go looking for followers.

Beth: That's right.

Corrine: The next card in the spread—the Judgment card—represents the near future, the next six months to a year. It's really interesting that the past, present, and future cards in your reading are all such powerful forces. You've got the High Priestess, the World, and now, Judgment. You're not dealing with little concerns here.

The Judgment card is the card of resurrection and forgiveness. The angel Gabriel is blowing his horn, and an entire family is rising up from their graves. It's especially interesting in light of the fact that you're dealing with a divorcé, so there is kind of a third party involved in your relationship.

Beth: I was good friends with his wife before they divorced, and she is such a great person. I don't think she would interfere. Actually, I really believe that in their case, with their divorce, they want everyone involved to be happy.

Even so, I don't know if that's really an issue yet. We've talked about going out, and he's told me that he hasn't been on a date for almost twenty years, since he met his ex-wife. So in some ways, we're still talking about how we would even start a relationship.

Corrine: Okay. Well, let's look at the next two cards together, because they work in combination. One shows how you see yourself, while the second shows how others see you. In your case, the two cards don't mesh very well. You tend to see yourself like this Five of Wands, struggling to coordinate your efforts, but feeling a little disorganized. Others see you as being much more pulled together than you feel. They see you more like this Page of Swords, very pulled together and clearheaded, with a real ability to communicate clearly. When they look at you, they see that you have a point to make.

Sometimes when people see that there's a disparity between the two cards, they realize that they're not communicating how they really think and feel to the people around them. What do you think of the difference between these two images?

Beth: Well, I do feel more like the Five of Wands … but I'm glad others see me as the Page of Swords. That's not a bad image. I'll take it.

Corrine: This next card, the Page of Cups, represents both your hopes and your fears. Those two ideas are two sides of the same coin. Sometimes we hope that something will happen in our lives, but at the same time we fear it, because if it happens it will change everything else we've got going on.

Even so, I think this is really a romantic card, and it definitely applies to your situation. Here's a young man, offering you a gift in a golden cup. But it's not a very well-developed image. Pages are young; they're like children. Like you've said, I think it shows that you're still in the early stages of developing this idea of a relationship.

Finally, we look at the card that represents the most likely outcome of your current path. Now this is a surprise. It's the Knight of Swords. This isn't the same person shown in your hopes and fears cards. It's someone new. The Knight of Swords comes into your life quickly and unexpectedly. He'll have a fling with you, and then he'll be gone.

Beth: Oh, I hate hearing that. I've never gone out with anyone just for fun. I've had friends who've gone out with guys they didn't really feel serious about, and I've thought, "Why would they do that? What's the point of being with someone you wouldn't want to be with forever?"

Corrine: So you've never gone out with anyone, just for a date or two?

Beth: No, never. I wasn't really all that serious about the last guy I dated, but we went out for nine months.

Corrine: Let me throw another card on top of this Knight, just for clarification. Okay, it's Justice, the card of balance. I was really surprised when that Knight showed up, but I think the message is pretty clear. You need more balance in your dating life.

Beth: That's for sure. I take everything way too seriously.

Corrine: Well, let's pull another card to look for some advice. What do you need to do to find more balance in your life?

It's the Sun! The cards are reminding you that you need to feel radiant and optimistic, and, like this child on the horse, you need to be playful. Literally, you need to lighten up.

Beth: Everyone always tells me that. But how? I'm dealing with serious issues.

Corrine: Well, for one thing, maybe the cards are trying to tell you that you can stop thinking of a new relationship as a serious issue—you can stop worrying about the effect that it would have on your kids. Don't even think of "dating" in the traditional sense. Just get together and play with all three kids. Don't make a big deal out of it.

Beth: That might work.

Corrine: Okay, we'll pull a final card that will give you specific, practical advice that you can actually use today. Choose any card from the deck.

Beth: All right. Here. It's the Queen of Wands. What does that mean?

Corrine: I'm not sure. The picture shows a woman sitting in a sunflower field, kind of like the child in the Sun card. She's holding a wand, and there's a black cat at her feet. What does this image look like to you? What do you think it means?

Beth: I think it means I need to wear a low-cut shirt and show some cleavage, like the woman in the picture.

Corrine: That's a great idea. That's something you can do right away, and it will make you feel playful. Really, it's all well and good to get high-minded advice from a Tarot reading that says, "Don't take yourself so seriously," but I think that taking a step like changing into some playful clothes would be a step in the right direction.

Beth: Okay, I will. But I want to know if I'm going to have a relationship with this man. Can't you look at one more card and tell me what's going to happen?

Corrine: What, do you want to see a wedding in the cards? I can try. We'll just look at the next card in the deck . . . sorry, it's the Four of Swords, the card of rest and recuperation. You're still in a phase where the possibility of any relationship with this man is still in limbo. You'll just have to wait and see what develops.

Beth: All right. But in the meantime, I'm definitely going to get some new clothes.

Sample Reading: Julie and Bob

Julie, thirty-seven, and Bob, forty-five, met at the architectural firm where they work. Two years later, they were married. Now, nine months after their wedding, they are expecting a baby and wondering what the cards have to say about their relationship.

Corrine: Julie, this card in the first position represents your present situation, and it's the Tower. That's the card of sudden and unexpected change, the bolt from the blue that will shake your foundations and drastically alter the way you see the world. When is the baby due?

Julie: In four months.

Corrine: So maybe this change won't be all that unexpected, but your perspective will definitely be altered.

Bob, this card shows your present. It's the Chariot, and it pictures a man who's in the driver's seat, reigning in opposing forces and steering a straight course, mostly through the sheer power of will and intellect.

Julie: Well, Bob does like to drive.

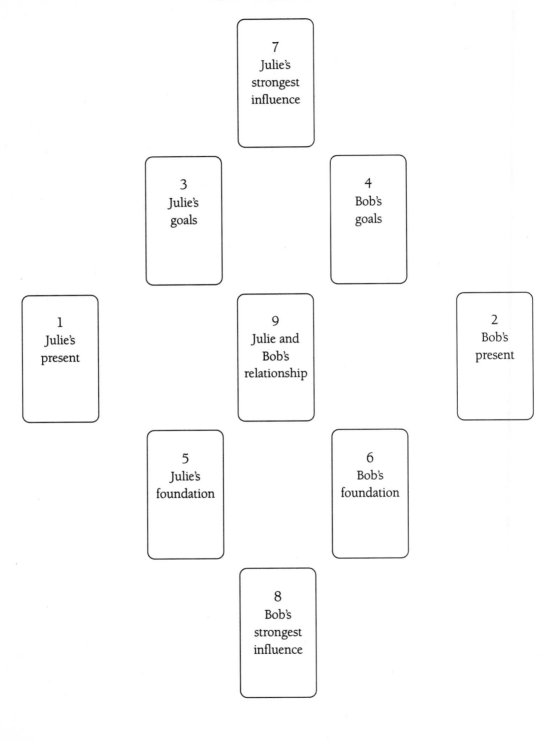

Corrine: Julie, this card shows your foundation—and lucky you, it's the Lovers. I would have hoped this card would show up somewhere in today's reading, since it's focusing on your relationship.

Over here, Bob, is your foundation card. It's the King of Swords. That's a powerful, authoritative man. It could be you at work. Aren't you one of the managers at your firm?

Bob: Well, yes, I'm a project coordinator.

Corrine: Julie, this card shows your goals. It's the Four of Cups. That shows someone who's being offered a new project, but he's just not ready to tackle a new challenge quite yet.

Julie: Good thing I've got a few months to get ready.

Corrine: And Bob, here is the card that pictures your goals. It's the Nine of Cups. That's the card of satisfaction and fulfillment, the man who has everything he's ever wanted in life.

Bob: Sounds good to me.

Corrine: Julie, this card represents your strongest influence right now. It's the Seven of Cups, and it shows a woman with her head in the clouds, dreaming, fantasizing, and building castles in the air.

Julie: Naturally. I'm pregnant, you know.

Corrine: Here's the strongest influence on Bob. It's the Three of Cups. It generally means you're involved in a lot of social events.

Bob: I'm involved with a charitable foundation, and we're doing a lot of fund-raising events.

Corrine: Well, that makes sense, then.

Finally, this card in the center of the spread summarizes your relationship. It's the Ace of Wands, which means new beginnings of a spiritual and creative nature—and, oddly enough, it often indicates the birth of a child.

This reading doesn't reveal any surprises, does it? I think it just paints a nice portrait of your marriage, and it should offer you some encouragement as you continue to strengthen your partnership and wait for a new addition to your family.

Appendix D

A Guide to Tarot Terms and Symbols

A

Abbey: refuge; holy place; symbol of the divine within one's self

Above: the Higher Self

Above/Below: heaven and earth

Abyss: depth; the origin and ending of the world; the underworld; the unconscious

Acorn: potential

Adam and Eve: the original couple

Adam Kadmon: the original man

Air: one of the four elements; active; masculine; corresponds to the Minor Arcana suit of Swords and the intellect

Air Signs: the "thinkers" of the Zodiac: Gemini, Libra, and Aquarius

Alchemy: Greek and Arab attempts to make gold; symbolic of salvation. The four stages of the alchemical process include (1) prime matter, symbolic of origins and guilt; (2) the first transmutation, symbolic of early efforts at transformation; (3) purification, symbolic of passion; and (4) gold, symbolic of spiritual attainment.

Allegory: a descriptive story that includes symbolic or hidden meaning, used for imparting ideas and principals

Alpha and Omega: first and last letters of the Greek alphabet; beginnings and endings

Altar: focus for worship, sacrifice, and spirituality; refuge and sanctuary

Amulet: a charm carried to ward off evil

Anchor: Christian symbol of salvation and hope

Angels: invisible forces. Four archangels appear in Tarot: Raphael, angel of air (the Lovers); Michael, angel of fire (Temperance); Gabriel, angel of water (Judgment); and Uriel, angel of earth (the Devil).

Animals: divine forces; human characteristics

Ankh: ancient Egyptian cross of life, with the perfect balance of masculine (Osiris) and feminine (Isis)

Antlers: the divine masculine; the father god

Anubis: ancient Egyptian jackal-headed god of wisdom; represents the evolution of consciousness

Anvil: earthly matter

Ape: Thoth, Egyptian god of wisdom

Apple: health; healing

Arcana: plural of the Latin *Arcanum*

Archer: offers direction; symbol of the astrological sign Sagittarius

Archetypes: innate ideas or patterns in the psyche expressed as symbols and images. Carl Jung's description of archetypes include the *anima*, the feminine aspect of a man's personality; the *animus*, the masculine aspect of a woman's personality; the *mother*, which typifies a nurturing, emotional parent; the *father*, a physical, protective parent; the *trickster* or rebel; and the *shadow*, the hidden, antisocial dark side of human nature, as well as the *hero*, the *maiden*, and the *wise old man*.

Armor: defense; protection

Ashes: spiritual purification

Ass: humility; patience; courage

Astrological Correspondences:

    Aries: The Emperor

    Taurus: The Hierophant

    Gemini: The Lovers

    Cancer: The Chariot

    Leo: Strength

    Virgo: The Hermit

    Libra: Justice

    Scorpio: Death

    Sagittarius: Temperance

    Capricorn: The Devil

Aquarius: The Star

Pisces: The Moon

Aura: energy field

B

Backpack: tools; karma

Bandages: newborn's swaddling and corpse's shroud; wounds

Basket: womb

Bat: blindness; darkness; chaos. Leathery bat wings offer a striking contrast to pristine angel wings.

Bear: lunar animal; prime matter; unconscious; the Great Mother

Beard: masculinity; strength; wisdom; power

Bed: sexuality; intimacy; rest; illness; nurturing

Bee: creative activity; monarchy; social organization

Bell: joy; victory

Bird: the soul; good news; soaring spirit

Black: negative; passive; receptive

Blindfold: lack of information; sometimes relates to Justice

Blood: sacrifice; passion

Blue: associated with spirituality

Boar: magic and prophecy

Boat: cradle; womb; the body

Boaz and Jachin: The pillars of light and darkness, mercy and severity, strength and stability, or spirit and matter that held the veil in the Temple of Solomon, the first temple of Jerusalem. Boaz was King David's great-grandfather. Jachin was a high priest.

Book: education; the universe

Bow and Arrow: sunlight; pangs of love

Box: feminine; maternal; unconscious

Branch: *See* Garland

Bread: fertility; communion with others; staff of life; money

Breast: love; nurturing; mothering

Bridge: connection between worlds; transition from life to death and from the secular to the divine

Broom: cleansing power; unity of male and female

Buckle: self-defense; protection

Bud: new beginning

Bull: symbol of the astrological sign Taurus

Butterfly: transformation

C

Caduceus: a winged wand entwined by two serpents; symbol of Mercury, messenger of the gods. The wand represents power, the snakes represent wisdom, and the wings represent diligence. Also, the wand represents earth, the wings represent air, and the serpents represent fire and water.

Canal: passage; childbirth

Candle: faith in spiritual things; enlightenment; the light and spirit of the individual

Canyon: vast unconsciousness

Cartomancy: the art of divination with cards

Castle: physical and spiritual refuge; stronghold of good or evil; a place of guarded treasure; to be watchful; embattled; otherworldly

Cat: domesticity; liberty; vanity; witch's familiar

Cauldron: vessel of magical change

Cave: the feminine; the unconscious; an entrance to the underworld; initiation

Celtic Cross Spread: a popular Tarot spread designed in the shape of a cross, with additional cards laid alongside for additional information

Cernunnos: Celtic horned god

Chain: bondage; restriction; communication

Chakras: seven energy centers of the body

Chalice: human heart; holy grail

Chalice (covered): heaven and earth

Chariot: the human body

Chariot Card: The young charioteer is in command of his physical and emotional drives, symbolized by the two opposing forces that pull the chariot.

Charioteer: the self

Chasm: division between worlds

Child: innocence; the future

Church: refuge; holy place; symbol of the divine within one's self

Circle: completion; infinity; enclosure; the feminine; heaven; the sun; nothingness; the fifth element, Spirit

Clarifier: an additional card used to enhance or explain the primary cards in a spread

Cliff: division between worlds

Cloak: veil; separation; something hidden

Clocks: under the law of time; something that is possible but not yet firmly in the future

Clouds: mysterious; sacred

Cock: resurrection

Cold: solitude

Collective Unconscious: Carl G. Jung's term for the underground stream of psychic energy and shared archetypes that link all people to each other

Colors:

Black, like the color of night, symbolizes darkness and obscurity. Black may also represent the absolute darkness of midnight, which symbolizes death.

Blue, the color of sky and sea, frequently symbolizes depth and calm. The clear blue color of heaven might also represent spirituality and clarity of vision and thought.

Brown, the color of bare earth, may represent untapped or undeveloped potential.

Gold, like the precious metal, may symbolize richness, wealth, and royal majesty. Gold can also represent the sun.

Gray, like a cloudy, overcast day, usually represents depression, neutrality, or indifference.

Green, the color of nature and vegetation, represents fertility and growth.

Orange, the color of fire, can represent heat, passion, and burning desire.

Pink, a mix of passionate red and pure white, can represent a more innocent, romantic form of love.

Purple, the traditional color of royalty, symbolizes leadership and divinity.

Red, the color of blood and wine, symbolizes passion and will. Red is also the color of danger, alarm, ambition, and anger.

Silver, the traditional color of the moon, symbolizes the passive lunar energy of reflection and intuition.

Violet, the color of spirituality and religion, is used to express God's power and dominion.

White, the color of bleached cotton and driven snow, symbolizes spirituality and purity.

Yellow, the color of the sun, represents fiery heat and radiant energy.

Columns: duality; choice; civilization

Conflict: a troubling or opposing force in the querent's life.

Corn: fertility

Cornucopia: the union of male and female; horn of plenty

Court Cards: The Page (or Knave), Knight, Queen, and King of the four suits of the Minor Arcana

Crab: symbol of the astrological sign Cancer

Crane: justice; longevity

Crescent Moon: symbol of Isis, the ancient Egyptian queen of heaven; symbol of virgin goddesses; the newborn; the ship of light that carries the soul through the dark night into dawn; emblem of Islam

Crest: thought

Crocodile: duality; capable of living on land and in water

Cross: protection

Cross, Blue: spiritual leader

Cross, Celtic: popular Tarot layout; fertility; union of heaven and earth

Cross, Inverted: humility; tree of life

Cross, Red: health; healing; medicine

Cross, Rosy: fertility; spilled blood of Christ; seven stages of initiation

Cross, Solar: positive and negative; equal arms indicate union of male and female

Cross, Yellow: philosopher or philosophy

Crossed Keys: unlock knowledge and truth. The gold depicts solar energy; the silver depicts lunar energy; St. Peter, as the Hierophant, held the keys that made him the founder of Christ's church on earth.

Crossroads: choice

Crow: messenger

Crown: attainment and mastery

Crux Ansata: the Egyptian ankh; union of male and female; heaven and earth; eternity; immortality

Crystal: transmits and magnifies energy

Crystals, Gems, and Stones:

Agate symbolizes strength and protection.

Amber symbolizes cycles and longevity.

Amethyst enhances wisdom, tranquility, and sobriety.

Aquamarine offers protection and calm.

Bloodstone improves circulation.

Blue Lace Agate improves self-expression.

Citrine relieves emotional and physical congestion.

Crazy Lace Agate enhances self-esteem and courage.

Diamond, the hardest of all elements, symbolizes permanence and incorruptibility.

Emerald strengthens memory, increases intelligence, and preserves relationships.

Garnet stimulates creativity and love.

Geodes encourages freedom of spirit and independence.

Green Moss Agate is a gardener's talisman.

Hematite grounds and connects with the earth and helps vent suppressed anger.

Jade assures a long, healthy life and a peaceful death; it also strengthens relationships.

Jasper promotes clear thinking and restrains dangerous desires and whims.

Lapis Lazuli is a symbol of wisdom, power, and royalty, as well as the journey into darkness in search of the Higher Self.

Malachite absorbs energy and focuses inner vision.

Marble protects the home and attracts money.

Moonstone symbolizes the lunar cycle and femininity.

Obsidian is useful during grief and growth.

Onyx transforms negativity, strengthens the will, and helps us separate from unhealthy relationships.

Opal contains all the colors of the chakras; it aids expression and purifies the spirit.

Pearl symbolizes the hidden wealth of the soul.

Peridot can teach self-parenting; it stimulates physical healing and can calm us.

Petrified Wood represents longevity and evolution; it aids past-life recall and helps deflect negativity.

Pyrite brings money and luck and aids in grounding.

Quartz Crystal conducts and amplifies energy and thoughts.

Rose Quartz comforts and heals wounded hearts.

Ruby symbolizes strength, compassion, and life force; it aids immunity and arouses passion.

Sapphire is a stone of prophecy and wisdom.

Shell represents watery qualities of fluidity, movement, and change.

Smokey Quartz grounds and purifies the base chakra.

Tiger's Eye represents integrity and personal power; it promotes confidence, courage, and perception.

Topaz brings strength and energy to the body.

Turquoise, a guardian of the soul, represents a connection between heaven and earth.

Cube: earth; material world; four elements

Cups: the second suit; symbolizes emotional life

Curtain: separation of worlds

D

Daffodils: springtime

Dagger: phallus; masculinity

Dance: union of space and time; creation; metamorphosis

Dawn: new beginnings

Day/Daylight: clarity; reason

Death: end of an era; sacrifice; destruction; leads to rebirth

Death Card: Not the frightening specter that most of us expect, the card of Death is one of transition; it foretells the completion of one stage of life and the exciting beginning of a new phase.

Desert: asceticism; deprivation; transcendence; abstract thought

Devil: subconscious desires; materialism

Devil Card: With tongue firmly in cheek, the Devil of the Major Arcana shows us that a selfish devotion to material possessions and ill-conceived passions ties us down and keeps us from true happiness.

Dew: spiritual illumination; approaching dawn

Directions:
    East: air; associated with the suit of Swords
    South: fire; associated with the suit of Wands
    West: water; associated with the suit of Cups
    North: earth; associated with the suit of Pentacles

Disk: spherical bodies, especially the earth but also the sun and the moon; the heavens; the pentacle

Dog: faithful companion; loyalty; protector or guardian; conscience; tamed beast

Dolphin: salvation

Door: access; opportunity; new situation; a barrier that only initiates may unlock and pass through; transition

Dot: seed; beginning; origin; the number one

Dove: peace; harmony; innocence; devotion; spirit; soul; Holy Spirit

Dragon: adversary

Drum: the heart; the spoken word

Duality: balance; equilibrium; opposing forces; choices; attraction of opposites

E

Eagle: keen vision and comprehension; symbol of the astrological sign Scorpio; John the Baptist

Earth: concrete physical manifestation

Earthquake: sudden change for better or worse

Earth Signs: the "maintainers" of the Zodiac: Taurus, Virgo, Capricorn

Eclipse: drama

Egg: potential; the world

Eight: infinity; the lemniscate; caduceus; eternal spiral; regeneration

Elements: The four ancient elements (fire, water, air, and earth) are said to correspond to each of the Tarot's four suits: fire for Wands, water for Cups, air for Swords, and earth for Pentacles. Some Tarot readers assign a fifth element, spirit, to the Major Arcana cards.

Elephant: physical strength

Emperor Card: the archetypical father. The authoritative Emperor brings order out of chaos so that civilization can prosper.

Empress Card: the archetypical mother. The Empress nurtures and protects all of nature, including humankind.

Esoteric: secret; intended for and understood by only a chosen few

Eve: primordial woman; mother of all

Exoteric: public; suitable for the uninitiated

Eye of Horus: symbol of the watchful Egyptian lord of the skies

F

Falcon: untamed will

Feather: wind; flight; words

Feather, Red: victory

Fingers: Traditionally,

    Thumb: Venus

    Index: Jupiter

    Middle: Saturn

    Ring: Sun

    Little: Mercury

Fire: one of four ancient elements; represents spirit, will, inspiration, desire; purifying force

Fire Signs: the "initiators" of the Zodiac: Aries, Leo, Sagittarius

Fish: creative inspiration; ideas; Jesus; symbol of the astrological sign Pisces

Five: five senses; five appendages; five vowels

Flag: victory

Flame: spirit; will

Fleur-de-lis: illumination; royalty; the triple majesty of God; the trinity of body, mind, and spirit

Flute: erotic or funereal anguish; masculine shape, feminine sound; associated with shepherds

Fool Card: Technically, the Fool is the Major Arcana's only unnumbered card. A wanderer, most Tarot experts agree that the Fool represents each of us—naive travelers through life, off on a grand adventure, and out to learn whatever experience the Tarot can teach us.

Fool's Journey: The procession of the Fool through the cards of the Major Arcana is often said to be an allegorical description of our journey through life, starting with the Fool and culminating with the World card.

Forces: people and circumstances that may help or hinder the querent; delineated as positive, negative, or hidden

Forest: the unconscious

Fortress: refuge; protection; safety

Fountain: life force; access to hidden secrets

Four: wholeness; stability; four suits of the Minor Arcana; four elements; four cardinal points; four seasons; four ages of humankind; four horsemen of the Apocalypse

Fox: slyness

Fruit: fertility; completion; temptation

G

Garden: control of nature; cultivation of the human soul

Gargoyles: captive cosmic forces

Garland: universal connections; links; fellowship; completion

Gazelle: the soul

Girdle: strength; connections

Globe: dominion

Globe, Winged: sublimation of matter through evolution

Glove: Traditionally, the right-hand glove is removed before a superior.

Glyph: a mark or a symbol (i.e., astrological glyphs)

Gnome: elemental creature of earth

Gnosis: spiritual knowledge

Goat: symbol of the astrological sign Capricorn

Gold: solar energy; material treasure

Golden Dawn: a mystical organization that popularized the Tarot and other occult studies at the turn of the last century. Members included A. E. Waite and Pamela Colman Smith, creators of the *Rider-Waite* Tarot.

Grapes: abundance; celebration

Grapevines: growth; coming harvest

Green: material; healing

Griffin: half eagle, half lion; guardian of the tree of life; vigilance; used to represent both the Messiah and the antichrist

H

Halo: Living people are portrayed with square or hexagon halos; dead saints are pictured with round halos; God is portrayed with a triangular halo.

Hammer: power, strength, force of might

Hand: open or closed in giving or restraint; raised in blessing or binding oath

Hanged Man Card: He sacrifices his comfort and passions for a time, like the Norse god Odin, knowing that better things will occur as a result.

Hare: love; fertility; the menstrual cycle; the moon

Harp: passage to the next world

Hat: thought

Heart: love

Hearth: the home; feminine receptacle for masculine fire; love; security

Heat: sexuality; maturity

Hermaphrodite: integration

Hermes Trismegistus: "Hermes the thrice great"; Greek name for Thoth

Hermetic: derived from Hermes Trismegistus and his lore; magical; alchemical

Hermit Card: Far removed from the hustle and bustle of everyday life, the Hermit reflects on spiritual concerns. He carries his light of wisdom as a beacon for others to follow.

Hexagram: six-pointed star; combination of material and spiritual

Hierophant: high priest

Hierophant Card: A symbol of traditional authority and influence, the hierophant is a spiritual link to humanity's higher powers.

High Priestess Card: Secretive and guarded, the High Priestess knows the secrets life holds, but shares them only with the wise.

Holy Grail: the mythological object pursued by King Arthur's knights; Christ's chalice at the last supper; receptacle for Christ's blood

Hood: spiritual secrets

Horn: an enemy's approach; the end of the world

Horse: controlled life force; solar animal

Hourglass: mortality; passage of time; cyclical nature of the universe; God's grace descending onto the earth

House: the human body. Floors of a house symbolize levels of consciousness, rooms symbolize private thoughts, and windows symbolize possible understanding and communication.

I

Ibis: ancient Egyptian bird, symbolic of thought and inspiration

IHVH: Hebrew initials of the holy name of God; also symbolic of the four Minor Arcana suits

Iris: Greek mythological personification of the rainbow connecting heaven and earth

J

Jester: a fool; the inverse counterpart of the king

Jewels: spiritual truths; status; power; riches

Judgment Card: All is revealed, as the Judgment card reminds us to forgive and be forgiven.

Jupiter: planet of luck and expansion

Justice Card: When blindfolded, the goddess of Justice is blind to superficial concerns. With her eyes unveiled, Justice sees all. In most renditions of the card, she holds a two-edged sword, a reminder that fairness cuts both ways.

K

Kabbalah (also spelled cabala, cabbala, kabala, kabbala, qabala): an ancient Jewish system used to explain the order and workings of the universe

Karma: cause and effect; the effect of past actions on the present and on future choices

Key: a new opening; change

Keys: the numbered Major Arcana cards; often referred to as keys to higher knowledge

King: active expression of the highest qualities of the suit

Knife: vengeance; instinct

Knight Cards: fast-moving people and events related to each suit

Knight on a Horse: mind over matter

Knot: infinity; bondage; luck

Kundalini: the path of energy as it moves through the chakras

L

Lake: the occult; mystery; contemplation; consciousness; revelation

Lamb: martyrdom; sacrifice; Jesus

Lamp/Lantern: intelligence; wisdom; the light and spirit of the individual

Laurel Wreath: victory, triumph; immortality

Layout: the spread, pattern, or design a reader selects to lay out the cards for a reading

Leaves: growth, life, and vitality

Left: negative; feminine; receptive

Lemniscate: figure 8; infinity

Lightning: a flash of illumination; a bolt from the blue; divine power; inspiration; intuition

Lily: transformation; afterlife

Lily, Water: symbol of the element of water

Lily, White: purity

Line, Horizontal: balance; stability

Line, Vertical: growth; phallic; masculine; active; connects heaven and earth; wand

Lingam: Eastern phallic-shaped symbol of masculine energy. *See* Yoni.

Lion: symbol of the astrological sign Leo; the sun; the ego; courage; untamed will; St. Mark

Lotus: spiritual awakening; in India, Brahma's dwelling place and the manifestation of his work

Lovers Card: While an appearance by this couple could encourage any hopeless romantic, the Lovers also signify a choice to be made between two equally strong desires.

Lyre: wisdom; moderation; prophecy. The seven strings connote the mystical properties of the number seven.

M

Magician Card: The Magician represents an individual in control of life's tools and techniques, like those on the table in front of him. Typically, they include a cup, a sword, a pentacle, and a wand—the four symbols of the Minor Arcana.

Magus: magician; wise man

Major Arcana: the Tarot's twenty-two "Greater Secrets"; often represent cosmic forces beyond our control

Mandela: geometric, circular design; representative of the divine

Mars: planet of energy, aggression, warlike emotions

Master Numbers: 11, 22, 33, 44; indicate the highest quality of the numbers themselves

Meadow: sanctuary; rest; rejuvenation

Mermaid: idealized, elusive form of female beauty; vanity; fickleness

Minor Arcana: the Tarot's fifty-six "Lesser Secrets"; often represent mundane events and forces within our control

Miter: the official headdress of the pope, bishops, abbots, and ancient Jewish high priests

Moon: reflects light; inspires thought; measures time and cycles of life; astrologically, the emotions and intuition; subconsciousness

Moon Card: Deeply rooted in the unconscious, the dreamlike Moon symbolizes secrets and mysteries that may not be understood—or even recognized.

Moon Phases: new; waxing; full; waning

Mountain: meeting of heaven and earth; ascent; struggle; obstacles

Mushrooms: decay and regeneration; home to fairies

Music: the pure manifestation of will

N

Necklace: unity; continuity; erotic links

Neptune: watery planet of illusion

Night: mystery; the unconscious; passive; feminine; anticipatory

Nimbus: halo or aura

Number Symbolism:

Zero precedes all of the other numbers. It symbolizes the period before existence or the state of nonbeing. Because it has a circular shape, zero also represents the cosmic egg, the wheel of the year, or the cycle of life. Like a ring, it has no beginning and no end.

One is the first number, so it represents the source of all existence. As a starting point, it represents a beginning, a thesis, or an original concept. It also symbolizes unity—the concept of oneness. When it is written with the Arabic numeral 1 or the Roman numeral I, it may be a phallic symbol. As a geometric figure, it is illustrated as a single point—a dot. Graphically, that point may represent either an egg or a sperm, symbolizing fertility.

Two symbolizes duality, partnerships, choices, and combinations. As a response to the number one, two can also symbolize an antithesis, counterpoint, or conflict. Two can sometimes symbolize an echo or a reflection. To Christians, the number two symbolizes the two natures of Christ, human and divine. Written as the Roman numeral II, it may be a representation of a gateway or of female genitalia. As a geometric figure, it is illustrated as a line that connects two points.

Three often represents creativity. It's a triad, the logical product of the combination of one and two or the child that is born from a mother and a father. Three represents a synthesis, the result of a thesis and an antithesis. Sometimes, the number three symbolizes the combination of body, mind, and spirit. It frequently symbolizes past, present, and future, as well as the course of human existence: maiden, mother, and crone, and birth, life, and death. Three also carries a religious connotation: many beliefs describe a holy trinity, such as Father, Son, and Holy Spirit, or the triple goddess of the New, Full, and Old Moon. Plato described the three sister fates—Lacheses, Clotho, and Atropos—who controlled each person's destiny. During the Middle Ages, there were three goddesslike Graces: Splendor,

Mirth, and Good Cheer, who were sometimes called Beauty, Gentleness, and Friendship. There are three theological virtues: faith, hope, and charity. Geometrically, three points constitute a plane. Many Tarot readers like to cut the deck three times before laying the cards out in a spread.

Four is the number of wholeness and stability. That's because, geometrically speaking, four points combine to form a solid. There are four dimensions: width, length, height, and time. There are four cardinal directions: north, south, east, and west. There are four seasons, four winds, and four periods of the day: dawn, day, evening, and night. There are four phases of the moon: waxing, full, waning, and dark. There are four ages of man: infancy, youth, adulthood, and old age. There are four corners in a room or a house. Christians have four evangelists—Matthew, Mark, Luke, and John—with four corresponding gospels, four horsemen of the Apocalypse, and four cardinal virtues: prudence, fortitude, temperance, and justice. There are four elements—fire, water, air, and earth—and four corresponding suits in the Minor Arcana.

Five. While the introduction of a fifth element upsets the stability of a perfect square, five often symbolizes the five senses, the five appendages (head, hands, and feet), five fingers, and five vowels. Some metaphysicians also consider five important because it symbolizes the "fifth element," or Spirit. The number five is frequently represented by a five-pointed star or pentacle.

Six is generally considered to represent the human being, because God created man on the sixth day. Six also symbolizes the sixth sense, psychic ability, as well as the six directions of space (left, right, forward, backward, up, and down).

Seven is an exceptionally mystical number. Classically, there were seven days of creation. There are seven gifts of the Holy Spirit: wisdom, understanding, counsel, fortitude, knowledge, piety, and fear. There are seven deadly sins: envy, sloth, gluttony, wrath, pride, lust, and greed. There are seven virtues: faith, hope, charity, fortitude, justice, temperance, and prudence. During the Middle Ages, there were seven liberal arts: the *trivium*, consisting of grammar, rhetoric, and logic, as well as *quadrivium*, made up of arithmetic, music, geometry, and astronomy. Alchemists had seven metals: gold, silver, iron, mercury, tin, copper, and lead. There are seven visible planets: the Sun, the Moon, Mars, Mercury, Jupiter, Venus, and Saturn. There are seven musical notes, and seven *chakras* or energy centers of the body. To fully randomize your Tarot deck before a reading, shuffle it seven times.

Eight symbolizes infinity, because it resembles the *lemniscate,* the symbol of infinity. The eight-sided octagon represents resurrection and rebirth, because Christ rose from the tomb after eight days. Eight is a symbol of baptism and spiritual rebirth; many baptisteries and baptismal fonts have eight sides. Eight also represents the eternal spiral of regeneration. There are eight musical notes in an octave.

Nine symbolizes conclusions. It hints at the nearness of the number ten, as well as the nine months of pregnancy.

Ten is the number of completion and perfection, probably based on the fact that human beings have ten fingers and toes. There are ten spheres on the mystical Kabbalistic Tree of Life and ten numbered cards in each suit of the Minor Arcana.

Eleven, written with Arabic numerals, is a graphic representation of pillars or a gateway.

Twelve represents the twelve signs of the Zodiac and the twelve months of the year. There were twelve gods on Mount Olympus: Jupiter, Neptune, Pluto, Vesta, Juno, Mars, Minerva, Vulcan, Apollo, Diana, Mercury, and Venus. There were also twelve tribes of Israel and twelve apostles.

Thirteen is usually thought to be an unlucky number, because there were thirteen diners at Jesus' last supper. In Tarot, the Death card is number thirteen.

Twenty-four is a significant number in Tarot symbolism, because there are twenty-four hours in a day.

Numerology: the language of numbers

Nymphs: spirits of running water, fountains, springs, and waterfalls; the immature feminine; temptation, multiplicity; may preside over some aspects of fertility, birth, and death

O

Octagon: spiritual regeneration; the intermediary between the square and the circle

Oracle: a tool for divination; anyone who practices divination

Orange: color of balance and seeking

Orb: dominion; the world; temporal power; when surmounted with a cross, a sign of spiritual authority

Ouroboros: The snake swallowing its tail is a symbol of totality, immortality, and infinity.

Outcome: The final card in any spread is often referred to as a "likely outcome." Because the Tarot offers us the chance to change the future as a result of a reading, however, that outcome is never set in stone.

Oval: female genitalia

Owl: spiritual wisdom

P

Page: messages, news; beginnings; young people related to the suit

Palm: masculine, active energy

Pansy: five petals; represents man and thought

Peacock: immortality

Pelican: self-sacrifice

Pentacle: materialism; values; treasures

Pentagram: an unending symbol of perfection and wholeness. Each point symbolizes one of the five appendages of the human body (head, arms, and legs), as well as the four ancient elements and the element of spirit.

Phallus: perpetuation of life, power, and propagation

Phoenix: mythical Egyptian bird that sets itself aflame and then is reborn from its own ashes; destruction and recreation; linked to both the sun and the moon

Pillars: duality; choice; civilization

Pine Tree: a sturdy character

Pip A numbered card of the Minor Arcana

Planets

    Sun: illumination, the self, the ego

    New Moon (1st Quarter): inspiration, beginnings

    Waxing Moon (2nd Quarter): growth, development

    Full Moon (3rd Quarter): maturity, completion

    Waning Moon (4th Quarter): reflections, planning

    Mercury: speed, communication

    Venus: love, attraction, spiritual treasure, fertility

    Mars: energy, aggression, self-defense, action

    Jupiter: luck, growth, expansion, enthusiasm

    Saturn: discipline, limits, boundaries, tradition

    Uranus: independence, rebellion, freedom

    Neptune: glamour, illusions, sensitivity

    Pluto: death, regeneration, unavoidable change

Plow: fertilization, cultivation

Pluto: endings, death, regeneration, change

Pomegranate: countless seeds symbolize fertility and diversity

Pregnancy: creativity

Primroses: fall season

Purple: color of spirituality

Pyramid: earth in its material aspects; suggests trinity of thought, action, and deed

Q

Queen: passive expression of the highest qualities of the suit

Querent: the person who receives a Tarot reading. The word querent is derived from "query," which means "inquiry" or "question."

Query: The question or focus of a Tarot reading

Quilt: synthesis; comfort; protection

R

Rabbit: fertility; spring

Rags: wounded spirit; holes in the soul

Rainbow: God's promise of protection

Ram: symbol of the astrological sign Aries

Reader: the person who reads the cards

Reins: intelligence; will

Reversals: cards that appear upside-down in a spread. They typically demand special consideration during a reading.

Ribbons: symbolic of immortality; victory; fulfillment

Right: active; positive; masculine

River: time; change

Rock: permanence; stability; solidity

Rope: lifeline; attachment; organization

Rose: love; appreciation

Rose, Red: passion

Rose, White: purity

Rota: Latin for wheel; anagram of Tarot

S

Salamander: elemental creature of fire

Saturn: planet of limitations, restrictions, time

Scales: justice; balance; symbol of the astrological sign Libra

Scarab: renewal; regeneration; endurance

Scorpion: symbol of the astrological sign Scorpio

Scrolls: hidden mysteries; divine law

Scythe: harvest; mutilation; death

Seal of Solomon: two triangles that form a six-pointed star; a symbol of spiritual potential and the connection between the conscious and unconscious

Seasons:

> **Spring:** Wands
>
> **Summer:** Cups
>
> **Fall:** Swords
>
> **Winter:** Pentacles

Sephira: one of ten spheres on the Kabbalistic Tree of Life. Each sphere represents one facet of God's being.

> 1. **Crown** (Kether): the Godhead; the Source
> 2. **Wisdom** (Chokmah): God the Father
> 3. **Understanding** (Binah): God the Mother
> 4. **Mercy** (Chesed): God the Merciful and Benevolent
> 5. **Severity** (Geburah): Almighty God; God the Forceful
> 6. **Beauty** (Tiphareth): God the Balancer and Healer
> 7. **Victory** (Netzach): God the Inspiration
> 8. **Splendor** (Hod): God the Intellectual

9. Foundation (Yesod): God the Etheric; earthly heaven

10. Kingdom (Malkuth): the physical world

Serpent: energy; wisdom; knowledge; temptation; forked tongue (deceit). A serpent biting his tail represents infinity and endless transformation.

Seven: seven heavens; seven planets; seven musical notes; seven chakras; seven gifts of the Holy Spirit; seven stages of initiation; seven days of creation; seven deadly sins

Shadow: alter ego; primitive instinct

Sheaf: unification; integration; strength

Shell: fertility; protection; defense

Ship: wealth; crossing. A rudder symbolizes steering ability and safe passage; sails symbolize the creative breath and oars represent creative thoughts and words and the source of action.

Shoes: base nature

Shuffle: to mix the Tarot cards, either poker style, hand over hand, or in a facedown slush pile on the table

Signature: binding agreement; contract

Significator: a card representing a querent, question, or situation. Other cards in the spread typically represent the *situation*, the *foundation* of the issue at hand, the *past*, the *present*, and the *future* of the situation, and the *most likely outcome* of the querent's current path.

Silver: lunar energy

Six: the human soul

Skeleton: death; putrification and decay

Skull: death's head; mortality

Sky: dome-shaped heaven

Smoke: combines air and fire; symbolizes the path of fire to heavenly salvation

Snow: sterility; cold; rigidity

Spark: creation of souls

Sphinx: a combination of four creatures—a human head, a bull's body, a lion's feet, and an eagle's wings—that represents all four elements and symbolizes the riddle of human existence

Spider: creativity; aggression; the Great Mother in her devouring aspect. A spider in the center of a web symbolizes the spiral structure of the universe.

Spinning: giving life

Spiral: the flow of energy through the universe

Spread: the layout, pattern, or design the reader uses to arrange the cards for a reading

Square: most stable of all forms; firm foundations; strength; stability

Staff: power; authority; support; instrument of punishment

Stag: wisdom

Stairs: a climb; an ascent

Star: hope; idealism; inspiration

Star Card: the card of faith and hope. The Star is a shining light in the darkness.

Tower Card: Should we build ourselves up too high, the Tower card warns that a bolt from the blue could shake us to our very foundations.

Tree: the mind

Tree of Knowledge of Good and Evil: bears five fruits; represents the five senses

Tree of Life: The roots are planted in heaven and the branches extend to earth. Its twelve fruits represent the twelve facets of personality, as well as the months of the year and the disciples of Christ.

Trees:

    Almond: early bloomer; sweetness; delicacy

    Apple: the world; totality; earthly desires

    Ash: sacred to the Norse god Odin (the Tarot's Hanged Man). The mythic World Tree Yggdrasil was an ash.

    Aspen: the autumnal equinox; old age; the tree of shield makers; associated with Hercules. Ancient Irish undertakers used rods of aspen wood to measure the dead for their caskets.

    Cypress: the tree of cemeteries, death, and resurrection

    Fig: associated with Dionysus, Juno, and fertility

    Hazel: useful for water dowsing and rainmaking

    Holly: symbolic of midwinter and the December solstice

    Juniper: protection against evil spirits, witches, and thieves

    Oak: strength and long life; Hercules's club; sacred to Jupiter; lightning rod

    Olive: peace and prosperity

    Palm: fertility; fruitfulness; victory; birth; the nesting place of the Phoenix

    Pine: immortality

    Poplar: sometimes symbolizes the Tree of Life, because the two sides of a leaf are different shades of green. Those two colors also relate to the moon and sun, water and fire, and positive and negative.

    Sandalwood: love; self-defense; divination

    Yew: death; used in bow making

Triangle: interest in metaphysics. *See* Three

Trickster: cultural variant of the Fool

Triple Goddess: maiden, mother, and crone; comparable to other triple deities such as Father, Son, and Holy Spirit

Trump Cards: the cards of the Major Arcana

Twins: symbol of the astrological sign Gemini

Two: duality; partnerships; choices; combinations; creative power; echo; reflection; conflict; occasionally a graphic female symbol

Typhon: the serpent; the five senses

U

Undine: elemental creature of water

Unicorn: chastity; purity; lunar; feminine

Uranus: planet of rebellion and the unexpected

V

Valley: fertility; cultivation; water

Veil: hidden emotions, actions, thoughts, and ideas

Venus: planet of love; morning and evening star

Virgin: symbol of the astrological sign Virgo

Virtues: The cardinal virtues of ancient Greece were philosophy, justice, prudence, fortitude, and temperance. Justice, Strength, and Temperance are represented in the Major Arcana.

W

Wand: channel for spirit and creative energy; creative power

Water Bearer: symbol of the astrological sign Aquarius

Water Lilies: eternal life

Water Signs: the "feelers" of the Zodiac: Cancer, Scorpio, Pisces

Wave: swelling emotional force and energy

Web: the snare of Satan

Wells: water and refreshment from the womb of Mother Earth; source of wish fulfillment

Wheat: abundance; growth; harvest

Wheel: cycle of cosmic expression; the year; time

Wheel of Fortune Card: Because nothing is certain but change itself, the Wheel of Fortune card reminds us all that what goes up must also come down.

White: positive; active

Wine: celebration; harvest; blood

Wolf: untamed; wild; uncivilized; underlying violence and fear

World Card: completion and success. The World is the last stop on The Fool's journey.

Wreath: victory

Y

Yggdrasil: the World Tree of Norse mythology

Yin-Yang: Chinese symbol of the balance between masculine and feminine; active and passive

Yod: Hebrew letter; the hand of God; divine intervention; gift; drop of light; descent of life force from spirit into material

Yoni: Eastern symbol of receptive, feminine energy. *See also* Lingam.

Z

Zero: nonbeing; the cosmic egg; the wheel of the year; the circle of life; completion

Zodiac: literally, "circle of animals"

Zodiac Signs:

Aries (the ram): March 21–April 20; the initiator; ruled by Mars

Taurus (the bull): April 21–May 20; the maintainer; ruled by Venus

Gemini (the twins): May 21–June 20; the questioner; ruled by Mercury

Cancer (the crab): June 21–July 22; the nurturer; ruled by the Moon

Leo (the lion): July 23–August 23; the loyalist; ruled by the Sun

Virgo (the virgin): August 24–September 22; the modifier; ruled by Mercury

Libra (the scales): September 23–October 23; the judge; ruled by Venus

Scorpio (the scorpion): October 24–November 21; the catalyst; ruled by Pluto

Sagittarius (the archer): November 22–December 21; the adventurer; ruled by Jupiter

Capricorn (the goat): December 22–January 20; the pragmatist; ruled by Saturn

Aquarius (the Water Bearer): January 21–February 18; the reformer; ruled by Uranus

Pisces (the fish): February 19–March 20; the visionary; ruled by Neptune

Recommended Resources

Berres, Janet. *Textbook of the Tarot* (International Tarot Society, 1990)

Bunning, Joan. *Learning the Tarot: A Tarot Book for Beginners* (Samuel Weiser, 1998)

Butler, Bill. *Dictionary of the Tarot* (Schocken Books, 1975)

Cicero, Chic, and Sandra Tabatha Cicero. *Experiencing the Kabbalah* (Llewellyn Publications, 1997)

Cirlot, J. E. *A Dictionary of Symbols* (Barnes & Noble, Inc., 1995)

Cowie, Norma. *Tarot for Successful Living* (Norma Cowie, 1979)

Decker, Ronald, Thierry dePaulis, and Michael Dummett. *A Wicked Pack of Cards: The Origins of the Occult Tarot* (St. Martin's Press, 1996)

Greene, Liz. *Mythic Astrology* (Simon & Schuster, Inc., 1994)

Greer, Mary K. *Tarot for Your Self* (Newcastle Publishing, 1984)

———. *The Complete Book of Tarot Reversals* (Llewellyn Publications, 2002)

Grey, Eden. *Mastering The Tarot* (Signet, 1973)

Hulse, David. *The Key of It All, Book Two: The Western Mysteries* (Llewellyn Publications, 1994)

Jung, Carl G. *Man and His Symbols* (Doubleday, 1964)

Kaplan, Stuart R. *The Encyclopedia of Tarot, Volume I.* (U.S. Games Systems, Inc., 1978)

Linn, Denise. *The Secret Language of Signs* (Ballantine Books, 1996)

MacGregor Trish. *The Everything Astrology Book* (Adams Media Corporation, 1999)

Masino, Marcia. *Easy Tarot Guide* (ACS Publications, 1987)

Payne-Towler, Christine. *The Underground Stream: Esoteric Tarot Revealed* (Noreah Press, 1999)

Pollack, Rachel. *Seventy-Eight Degrees of Wisdom* (Thorsons, 1997)

Riley, Jana. *Tarot Dictionary and Compendium* (Samuel Weiser, Inc. 1995)

Waite, Arthur Edward. *The Pictorial Key to the Tarot* (Barnes & Noble, Inc., 1995)

Wanless, James. *Voyager Tarot: Way of the Great Oracle* (Merrill-West Publishing, 1989)

Williams, Brian. *A Rennaisance Tarot* (U.S. Games Systems, Inc., 2003)

Internet Resources

Hurst, Michael J. *Michael's Tarot Notebook: Essays on a Late-Medieval Artifact.*
http://www.geocities.com/cartedatrionfi/

Little, Tom Tadfor. *The Hermitage: Tarot History.*
http://www.tarothermit.com/

Tarot Discussion List:
http://groups.yahoo.com/group/TarotL/

Free Magazine

Read unique articles by Llewellyn authors, recommendations by experts, and information on new releases. To receive a **free** copy of Llewellyn's consumer magazine, *New Worlds of Mind & Spirit,* simply call 1-877-NEW-WRLD or visit our website at www.llewellyn.com and click on *New Worlds.*

☾ LLEWELLYN ORDERING INFORMATION

Order Online:
Visit our website at www.llewellyn.com, select your books, and order them on our secure server.

Order by Phone:
- Call toll-free within the U.S. at 1-877-NEW-WRLD (1-877-639-9753). Call toll-free within Canada at 1-866-NEW-WRLD (1-866-639-9753)
- We accept VISA, MasterCard, and American Express

Order by Mail:
Send the full price of your order (MN residents add 7% sales tax) in U.S. funds, plus postage & handling to:

Llewellyn Worldwide
P.O. Box 64383, Dept. 0-7387-0548-9
St. Paul, MN 55164-0383, U.S.A.

Postage & Handling:

Standard (U.S., Mexico, & Canada). If your order is:
$49.99 and under, add $3.00
$50.00 and over, FREE STANDARD SHIPPING

AK, HI, PR: $15.00 for one book plus $1.00 for each additional book.

International Orders (airmail only):
$16.00 for one book plus $3.00 for each additional book

Orders are processed within 2 business days. Please allow for normal shipping time.
Postage and handling rates subject to change.

SPECIAL OFFER

Save 20% on the Romantic *Tarot Art Nouveau*

If you judged this book by its cover and liked what you saw, we invite you to save 20% on the romantic *Tarot Art Nouveau*, whose Lovers card image is featured on the cover of *Tall Dark Stranger*. Delicate curves, sweeping lines, and lush colors make this lovely deck perfect for all Tarot readings involving matters of the heart.

To order your *Tarot Art Nouveau* deck, please call 1-800-NEW WRLD and mention this ad to qualify for our special Tarot discount.

Tarot Art Nouveau
Antonella Castelli
0-7387-0008-8
$19.95 US • $29.95 Can.*
Boxed deck includes 78 full-color cards and instruction booklet